Walks & Easy Hikes
IN THE
Canadian Rockies

Graeme Pole

Mountain Vision Publishing
Hazelton, British Columbia, Canada

Researched and written by Graeme Pole.
Additional fieldwork and material by Marnie Pole
Editor: Marnie Pole
Design and maps: Scott Manktelow Design,
Canmore, Alberta
Photo scanning and processing: Graeme Pole
Printed and bound in Canada by Friesens, Altona,
Manitoba, on FSC paper using vegetable-based inks.

MIX
Paper from
responsible sources
FSC
www.fsc.org   FSC® C016245

Mountain Vision Publishing supports the reforesta-
tion work of Trees for the Future:
  🖵 www.treesftf.org

Library and Archives Canada Cataloguing in
Publication

Pole, Graeme, 1956-
    Walks and easy hikes in the Canadian Rockies /
Graeme Pole. -- 3rd ed.

"A Canadian Rockies companion guide".
Includes bibliographical references and index.
ISBN 978-0-9697249-5-7

    1. Trails--Rocky Mountains, Canadian (B.C.
and Alta.)--Guidebooks.
2. Hiking--Rocky Mountains, Canadian (B.C. and
Alta.)--Guidebooks.
3. Rocky Mountains, Canadian (B.C. and Alta.)--
Guidebooks. I. Title.

FC219.P65 2012   917.1104'5
C2011-908291-8

Distributed by Alpine Book Peddlers
140 - 105 Bow Meadows Crescent, Canmore,
Alberta, T1W 2W8
) 403-678-2280, 866-478-2280
) Fax: 403-978-2280, 866-978-2840
  🖵 www.alpinebookpeddlers.com
  ✉ info@alpinebookpeddlers.ca

Please support your local, independent bookseller.

Mountain Vision Publishing
Hazelton, British Columbia, Canada
  🖵 www.mountainvision.ca
  ✉ Graeme@mountainvision.ca

9 8 7 6 5 4 3 2

> *One should visit the Canadian Northland with
> eye and mind alert to the beauty of Nature's
> handicraft: the artistry in all of it; from the
> broad sculpturing of the crag and chasm to the
> delicate perfection of a tiny flower.*
>
> James Monroe Thorington, *The Glittering
> Mountains of Canada*, 1925

Look for these other Canadian Rockies Companion
Guides by Graeme Pole.

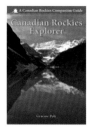

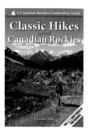

*Canadian Rockies
Explorer* is your
complete reference to
history, geology, plants,
wildlife, sights, and outings in the Rockies.

*Classic Hikes in the
Canadian Rockies*
describes the 63 best
day hikes and back-
packing trips in the
Rockies.

Front cover: *Saskatchewan Glacier from Parker
Ridge, Banff National Park*
Back cover:
Main image: *Peyto Lake from Bow Summit, Banff
National Park*
Lower images, l-r: *Moraine Lake, Bighorn sheep,
Red Rock Canyon, Moss campion, Prairie View*
Spine: *Takakkaw Falls, Yoho National Park*
Title page: *Moraine Lake, Banff National Park*
Contents: *Bow Lake from Bow Summit Lookout Site,
Banff National Park*

Contents

The Walks and Easy Hikes

The Walks and Easy Hikes

Acknowledgements

It's been 25 years since the first edition of *Walks and Easy Hikes* appeared. In that time and through three editions, the book has grown in breadth and in depth. Much of that development has come from the willing contributions made by the following: Harry Abbot, Peter Achuff, Wes Bradford, Mindy Brugman, Dave Cruden, Heather Dempsey, Duane Fizor, Ben Gadd, Cia Gadd, Mike Gibeau, Dave Gilbride, Rogier Gruys, Larry Halverson, Roger Hostins, Jenny Klafki, Edwin Knox, Andy MacKinnon, Locke Marshall, Diane McIvor, Mike McIvor, Roger McQueen, George Mercer, Joe Oberhoffner, Dave Palmer, Ian Pengelly, Jim Pojar, Catherine Reynolds, David Schindler, Cyndi Smith, Wayne Van Velzen, Robb Watt, Jesse Whittington, Joanne Williams, Terry Winkler, Ursula Winkler, and Kim Winter.

I owe a particular debt to Ben Gadd, whose *Handbook of the Canadian Rockies* and *Canadian Rockies Geology Road Tours*, in tandem set the gold standard for accuracy and detail about these mountains. Ben granted me blanket permission to cite facts and figures from his works.

Our three children have grown up in a hiking family. While they have added to the logistics of getting onto the trail, their keen eyes and ears have immeasurably added to our collective experience, and have enriched the content of this book.

At various times during the fieldwork we have been touched by the generosity of friends who have fed and sheltered us: Nadine Delorme and Mike Henderson, Ben and Cia Gadd, Diane and Mike McIvor, Alice Wagenaar and Edwin Knox, Nadine Fletcher and Joel Hagan, Peggy and Phil Muir, Ursula and Terry Winkler, and Doug and Samantha McConnery. I thank the late Eleanor Romp and my parents, Grace and Ernie Pole, for their support.

SPECIAL ACKNOWLEDGEMENT

Since we began "work" on the first edition of *Walks and Easy Hikes* in May 1991, Marnie Pole has logged thousands of kilometres on trail and has spent hundreds of hours proofing text and vetting photographs. While on the trail and at home Marnie has contributed countless ideas for the written and visual material, and has edited and honed the resulting text. As our family has grown, she has helped to keep us all on the trail. Having two minds focused on this project has more than doubled the richness and the quality of the book that you now hold in your hands. Thank you, Marnie.

NOTICE OF ASSUMPTION OF RISK

Trail walking and hiking in the Canadian Rockies can involve dangers. These include, but are not limited to: black bears and grizzly bears, aggressive wildlife, tick and insect bites, rough trails, slippery bridges, logs and rocks, suspension bridges, inclement weather, lightning, forest fires, falling trees, contaminated drinking water, avalanches, late-lying snow, rockfalls, mudslides and flash-floods. Perhaps the greatest danger is driving to and from trailheads. Summer traffic in the Rockies can be chaotic. Drive with caution and park safely.

I have walked every trail in this book at least once, (some of them dozens of times), and have endeavoured to render trail descriptions with accuracy and with safety in mind. However, trail conditions are not static, and the inclusion or exclusion of any information does not mean that you will find conditions as described. In particular, bridges and trail signs may or may not be present as described in the text.

Use caution on trails that cross roadways. Several of the outings cross railway tracks. Please note that modern day rail beds give very little indication of an approaching train. Stop, look, and listen before crossing railway tracks. Never race a train.

Critter Guide

These are the small mammals that you will see most often in the Rockies, along with two common birds of the forest, and one bird found above treeline.

The numbers indicate the outings where you are likely to see them. Although it may be tempting to feed these birds and animals, please refrain.

Least chipmunk

Where: meadows and boulderfields; treeline (13, 18, 19, 20, 21, 22, 23, 24, 27, 28, 33, 45, 52, 63, 64, 65, 76, 93, 118, 131)

Golden-mantled ground squirrel

Where: meadows and boulderfields; treeline (13, 18, 19, 20, 21, 22, 23, 24, 27, 28, 33, 45, 52, 63, 64, 65, 76, 93, 131, 136)

Columbian ground squirrel

Where: meadows at all elevations (10, 11, 13, 20, 23, 24, 25, 27, 28, 29, 38, 52, 58, 89, 121)

Red squirrel

Where: montane and subalpine forests (9, 12, 14, 15, 16, 17, 18, 19, 20, 21, 22, 23, 24, 25, 27, 28, 29, 30, 32, 63, 64, 65, 67, 68, 93, 94, 97, 99, 108, 117, 121, 135, 150, 151)

Pika

Where: boulderfields and rockslides at higher elevations (13, 16, 21, 27, 28, 29, 26, 33, 63, 65, 105, 118, 120, 121, 131, 133)

Hoary marmot

Where: meadows and boulderfields at higher elevations (13, 18, 20, 23, 24, 25, 52, 63, 65, 68, 76, 105, 117, 120, 121, 133)

Gray jay

Where: subalpine forest (1, 14, 16, 17, 18, 19, 20, 21, 22, 23, 24, 27, 28, 33, 45, 52, 63, 64, 65, 117, 119, 140, 141, 150, 151)

Clark's nutcracker

Where: subalpine forest (16, 17, 18, 19, 20, 21, 22, 23, 24, 27, 28, 33, 45, 52, 63, 64, 65, 117, 119, 140, 141, 150, 151)

White-tailed ptarmigan

Where: meadows above treeline (29, 32, 33, 52, 68, 105, 121)

Bow Summit Lookout Site

A Mountain Marvel

Welcome to the Canadian Rockies. These mountains are part of one of the world's great mountain regions – the Western Cordillera (core-dee-YAIR-ah) – which includes all of the mountains of western North America. The Rocky Mountains are the backbone of this region and of the continent, extending from New Mexico to Alaska. The Canadian Rockies proper are the subset range of mountains stretching from Marias Pass in Glacier National Park, Montana in the south, to near the Liard River in northern British Columbia (B.C.). In the southern part of the range, which is the focus of this book, the Rockies are oriented southeast to northwest along the continental divide. This height of land is the boundary between the provinces of Alberta and B.C., and separates rivers that flow to the Atlantic Ocean or the Arctic Ocean, from rivers that flow to the Pacific Ocean.

The Canadian Rockies appear different from other mountain ranges. The reasons for their distinctive appearance are not unique – they are sedimentary mountains in a northern climate, shaped by recent and present-day glaciation. However, the arrangement of these details has created a mountain biome whose features *are* unique. The details are also remarkably consistent throughout the range, from north to south, from east to west.

During mountain creation, the peaks were thrust skyward, when huge slabs of rock piled up, moving from southwest to northeast. You see this best in the front ranges of Banff, Jasper, and Kananaskis Country – where parallel ranges of steeply dipping, gray limestone peaks stand like waves made of stone. Along the continental divide in Banff and Jasper, the thrust sheets were not tipped as steeply. The rock formations lie more typically in horizontal layers, which have been eroded to create castle-like peaks.

Hiking and walking puts you boots-to-rubble with this geology, and usually, you are following a path carved by a glacier. Moving ice has chunked away at these mountains. Again and again as you hike, you will encounter variations on the glacial blueprint: you approach along a broad, U-shaped valley; you climb steeply to a waterfall-graced, hanging valley; then hike through meadows and boulderfields to the destination lake or pass at its head, perhaps with a relict glacier in view. Because most of the glaciation has taken place relatively recently in geologic terms (within the past 30,000 years), the mountains are still raw, with sharp edges and many abrupt points of transition – the wow! places.

The geology also affects what grows where and what lives where. As you become familiar with these mountains, you will find yourself sensing the transitions in the forest and in the ground cover that will take place at the top of a headwall, over the crest of a ridge, or where the trail draws alongside a glacier. You will begin to learn where to look for certain wildlife and plant species. You will become hooked, as so many other walkers and hikers have been, into the boundless fascination of the many intricacies of this mountain marvel.

How Difficult is "Easy"?

If you are a casual walker or hiker who is new to the mountains, *Walks and Easy Hikes* is especially for you. Experienced mountain walkers and hikers, travelling in reasonable weather, should find no difficulty with any of these outings. Everyone can use the ratings provided to help choose outings suitable to their abilities and to the conditions of the day. Please remember that poor or marginal weather can add considerably to the difficulty of any outing, regardless of your hiking experience. To make your outing more enjoyable and safer, at a minimum, always carry snacks, water, rain gear, and an extra layer of warm clothing.

All trails begin at established trailheads, parking areas or viewpoints. Please park safely and use caution in parking areas. The distance given for an outing is one-way (trailhead to destination), except for loop outings (circuits), in which case the distance is round-trip.

What to Wear and Carry

The hiking season in the Rockies generally lasts from late May to early October at lower elevations, and from late June to mid-September, higher up. Some of these outings – particularly those in the front ranges – may be viable in winter for those suitably prepared. Please enquire about trail conditions at a park information centre if you will be hiking early or late in the season, or in the off-season.

You can wear street shoes for some of the shorter walks, but for most outings sturdy runners or lightweight hiking boots are better choices. On wet days, rubber boots can be handy. If you are blister prone, experiment with different thicknesses of socks, or a combination of a thin inner sock and a thicker outer sock.

Mountain weather changes often and, sometimes, quickly. Some of the outings make their way in and alongside canyons, where cold, damp air prevails. If embarking on one of the longer outings,

Grizzly bear

carry a minimum of a rain jacket and a sweater as extra clothing. On hikes to higher elevations, take a warm hat and gloves as well. Rainfall in the Rockies is usually very cold. A full rainsuit, warm hat and gloves will be required on rainy days. An umbrella may suffice when showers are intermittent. Your rain jacket can also serve as a windbreaker.

The effects of sunlight are more intense in the mountains. Skin burns more rapidly because of the thinner atmosphere. Wind can also produce skin burns, and contributes to dehydration. Apply a good sunscreen on sunny days, and wear sunglasses and a light coloured sun hat. Drink lots of water. Avoid beverages that contain caffeine and alcohol, as these contribute to dehydration.

Carry your clothing, camera, binoculars, water bottle, snacks, sunscreen, insect repellent, and first-aid kit in a small day pack. Because these trails are popular, you should not drink any water from trailside streams or lakes. Bring your drinking water with you from your hotel, home or campground.

If you have a medical condition, you should take a cautious approach to hiking in the mountains, especially if you have recently arrived from near sea level. Go slowly. Turn around if you feel unwell. Keep essential medications with you at all times.

Basic Bear Safety

Bears are synonymous with the Canadian Rockies. They are the stuff of fear and fascination. Everyone wants to see one – that is, until they bump into one on a trail. Perhaps 150-200 grizzlies range through these parks. Even fewer black bears occupy the same area.

Most bears are wary of people. With its keener senses, a bear will usually detect you and leave before you become aware of it. As a result, on the trail, most times that you are close to a bear, you will not know it. You are more likely to see a bear while you are driving to a trailhead.

RATINGS

- **Viewpoint** outings are at roadside and involve very little distance or elevation change.
- **Easy** outings involve little or no elevation change on artificial or relatively smooth walking surfaces, and are less than 2.5 km long.
- **Moderate** outings have noticeable elevation change on natural walking surfaces that include roots and rocks, and are between 2.5 km and 5 km long.
- **Harder** outings have considerable elevation change and/or rough walking surfaces. Most of these outings are more than 5 km long. Those that are shorter are graded "harder" because they are steep. A few of these trails visit remote settings.

Avoiding Close Encounters

Nothing can guarantee that you will not encounter a bear on a trail. By heeding the following do's and don'ts, you will minimize the chances of being in the wrong place at the wrong time.

Do:

- Learn how to identify the two species of bears in the Rockies.
- Carry bear spray and know when and how to use it.
- Enquire at a park information centre regarding recent bear activity on your chosen outings. Choose to hike elsewhere if bear activity is reported.
- Travel with a partner or two. Stay close together.
- Make noise while hiking. Use your voice, especially when travelling alongside streams, through tall shrubs, crossing avalanche slopes, and during rest stops.
- Observe avalanche slopes and berry patches keenly before you cross them – use binoculars. Be cautious on trails lined with buffaloberry bushes in fruit.
- Pay attention to bear sign on the trail. Look for scats, tracks, and scrapes in muddy areas. Note the direction of travel. Might they be the tracks of a sow and cubs? Make more noise if the sign is fresh.
- Stop every once in a while when hiking through good bear habitat. Look and listen.
- Leave the area immediately if you discover an animal carcass.
- If you see a bear before it sees you, give it a wide berth.
- Pack out all your garbage.
- Report any bear sighting or encounter at a park information centre for the safety of those who follow.

Do not:

- Enter an area that is closed due to bear activity.
- Leave your pack unattended.
- Stop in areas where there is fresh bear sign.
- Take fresh meat, fish or seafood into the backcountry.
- Catch and retain fish.
- Expect that a bear will hear you coming.
- Hike at night.

Possible Causes of a Bear Attack

- You are between a sow and her cubs or have presented a perceived threat to the cubs.
- You have encroached on a buried kill or are passing through an area that offers a secure food source – a lush berry patch, a field of glacier lilies, a marmot colony.
- You surprise a bear on the trail.
- A heavy snowfall in late summer or early autumn has driven bears to lower elevations where they are in greater competition for food, and are less tolerant of people.
- You have encountered a predatory bear.

BLACK OR GRIZZLY?

	Black	Grizzly
Colour	Typically black, but can be any shade of brown	Typically brown with silver highlights to fur
Muzzle	Long and conical	Short, face is "dish-shaped," nose is upturned
Shoulder hump	None	Prominent
Ears	Pointed	Rounded
Claws	Short	Long

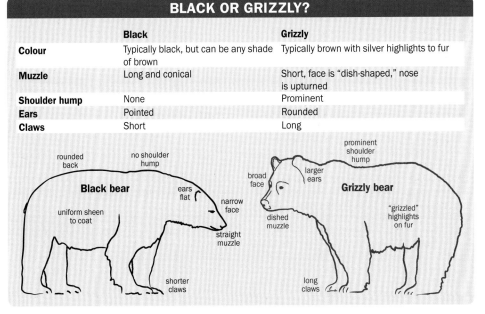

Black bear: rounded back, no shoulder hump, uniform sheen to coat, ears flat, narrow face, straight muzzle, shorter claws.

Grizzly bear: prominent shoulder hump, broad face, larger ears, dished muzzle, "grizzled" highlights on fur, long claws.

Kinney Lake trail

What to Do in a Bear Encounter

Consider yourself fortunate on three counts if you see a bear from a good distance. First, you are paying attention. Second, you have seen a bear. Third, you have a chance to leave before things develop into an encounter. Continue on the trail if you will not come any closer to the bear. Don't turn your back on the bear until you are well clear of the area. If continuing on the trail means that you will approach the bear, choose another route or turn back.

If the bear has seen you and is far enough away that you feel you can safely leave, do so by "quartering" away, either to the left or to the right of the trail, giving the bear a wide berth. Do not run and do not turn your back on the bear. When you first see a bear, assume that it is a sow with cubs until you know otherwise. If you see a small bear, assume that it is a cub until you know otherwise. Start looking for its mom and its siblings.

In a close encounter on the trail, a bear will probably be as startled at seeing you, as you are at seeing it. If a stand-off develops: stay calm, form into a group keeping children behind you, stand your ground, talk quietly to the bear, take out your bear spray, and keep your pack on. Do not run. Do not climb a tree. Look for cubs. Ideally, you want the sow to be between you and her cubs. You also want the wind to be blowing from you to the bear, so that it can smell you.

Drop your pack and climb a tree only as a last resort. If the bear has not made contact, climbing a tree is unnecessary and may provoke the bear to follow you. A black bear can climb up to 30 m. A grizzly bear can easily climb to 10 m, sometimes higher – and can do this much more quickly than you. If the bear climbs toward you, climb as high as you can. Kneel or squat on the uppermost sturdy branch. Do not leave your legs dangling.

For more information on bear safety, please talk to staff at a park information centre.

A Trail Etiquette

We each walk in the mountains for different reasons. Some of us do so for exercise, others to see the view. Others are motivated by particular interests in plants, birds, animals or geology. Whatever our motivation, we should strive to share the trails. We should also tread lightly. The following trail etiquette respects the

TRAIL FEATURES

🐦	Birding	〰️	Lake
∪	Canyon	🌀	River
🌲	Forest	🧍	Mega-view
🔍	Geology	💧	Waterfall
❄️	Glaciers	🌸	Wildflowers
🥾	History	🦌	Wildlife

DINING OUT?

🪑 **If you plan** on having breakfast, lunch or dinner in the outdoors before or after your outing, the picnic icon will guide you to trailheads that have tables and, in some cases, shelters.

rights of others to an enjoyable hiking experience, and strives to protect the natural environment.

- Say "hello" when you meet other trail users, and "thank you" if they step aside to let you by. Pass each other without stepping off the trail.
- Avoid shortcutting on switchbacks. Walk through wet or snowy areas. In other words: please stay on the trail. Walking off-trail results in the trampling of surrounding vegetation, and can create erosion problems. Twenty pairs of feet walking on pristine ground can create a permanent trail. At high elevations, it may take decades for damaged vegetation to recover.
- Report trail problems: chronic wet or muddy areas, broken steps or guardrails, downed trees, slumps, washed-out bridges, etc. The staff at park information centres will record and act on this information.
- Do not feed, entice or harass wildlife. Keep at least 30 m away from large animals. Report significant wildlife sightings to a park information centre.
- Do not remove, deface or disturb any natural or historical object – flower, tree, rock, fossil, dropped antler, etc. It is an offence to do so under the *Canada National Parks Act*.
- Be aware of trails shared with cyclists and equestrians. Cyclists should dismount to pass you. When you meet a horse party, make verbal contact with the lead rider, and quietly step to the downhill side of the trail. Do not speak or

TICKED OFF

Wood ticks resemble tiny, flattened spiders. Areas frequented by bighorn sheep, elk, and deer are havens for these parasites, especially between early April and late June. The tick life cycle has four stages, three of which require the tick to ingest a blood meal. It is the adult stage that preys upon larger mammals.

Adult ticks climb grasses and low shrubs to await their prey. Once lodged in the fur or clothing of a potential victim, the tick seeks out fleshy areas to inflict its bite and draw its meal of blood. When it bites, the tick injects an anti-coagulant to accelerate bleeding. The mouth parts penetrate the skin and the tick's body balloons with the fluid of its host.

The dangers to humans from tick bites are Rocky Mountain spotted fever – characterized by a headache and fever that develop 3-10 days after the tick bite; and tick paralysis – a reaction to tick induced toxins that can impair functions of the central nervous system. It develops 5-6 days after the tick bite.

What can you do to protect yourself? Wear long pants and long sleeves. Apply insect repellent to socks and pant cuffs. Tuck your pant cuffs into your socks. Tuck your shirt into your pants. Wear light coloured clothing so that you can spot ticks easily. Avoid grassy meadows during May and June. After any outing in tick terrain, search your clothing, equipment, skin, and hair thoroughly. Have a friend check your scalp, neck, and back, and the places where the elastic straps of underwear press against your skin. Ideally, you are trying to find a tick before it bites. If you find a tick after it has bitten, or if you detect a red circle around a bite, see a physician promptly. Change your clothes and boots, and empty your pack outside after your hike. Go through all your gear to ensure that you don't inadvertently transport a tick or three into your vehicle or dwelling.

LARCH FINDER

The Lyall's larch (see p. 47) is a deciduous conifer that sheds its foliage in late summer and early autumn, turning treeline in the southern Rockies into a ribbon of gold. The following outings take you to a larch treeline, or provide views of larches. The transformed leaves of aspens, poplars, and birches colour valley bottoms and mountainsides at other locations at the same time of year.

Goats and Glaciers Viewpoint

move until the last horse in the party is well past you.

- Leave your dog at home.
- Take all your litter back to the trailhead with you. Pick up and pack out any litter that you find. Recycle paper, plastic, glass, and cans. Deposit the remainder in the receptacles provided.
- Cigarette butts and spent matches are among the most common types of litter. If you smoke, pack out your cigarette butts. Be attentive when the forest fire hazard is high.
- Most of the major trails have outhouses at the trailhead. Please use them.
- Do not enter a trail or area marked with a closed sign.
- On trails where interpretive brochures are provided, return the brochures if you do not wish to keep them.
- Black bears and grizzly bears are present throughout the Rockies. Be bear aware and hike accordingly.
- Respect the rights of others to solitude. Hike in small groups. Use ear-gear for music devices. Limit cell-phone use to emergency calls only.
- Only three of these outings take you to a backcountry campground. If you would like to camp in the backcountry, visit a park information centre or refer to *Classic Hikes in the Canadian Rockies* to discover options.

COMPLEMENTARY OUTINGS

There are a handful of outings in this book that simply beg to be done together, usually because one provides an overview of the other, or because they explore the same area. Try these pairings and threesomes:

6. Bow River and Bow Falls and **8.** Hoodoos

16. Boom Lake and **109.** Fireweed

18. Plain of the Six Glaciers and **20.** Lake Agnes

21. Moraine Lake Rockpile and **23.** Lower Consolation Lake

27. Bow Summit, **28.** Timberline, and **29.** Bow Summit Lookout

31. Howse River Overlook and **49.** Howse Valley Viewpoint

32. Nigel Pass and **33.** Parker Ridge

37. Cascade Falls and **38.** Cascade Ponds

52. Wilcox Pass and **53.** Athabasca Glacier

59. Pyramid Island and **60.** Pyramid Overlook

63. Path of the Glacier and **65.** Cavell Meadows

80. Miette Hot Springs Boardwalk and **81.** Sulphur Pass

121. Ptarmigan Cirque and **122.** Highwood Meadows

138. Red Rock Canyon and **139.** Blakiston Falls

140. Cameron Lake and **141.** Akamina Lake

150. Wall Lake and **151.** Forum Falls

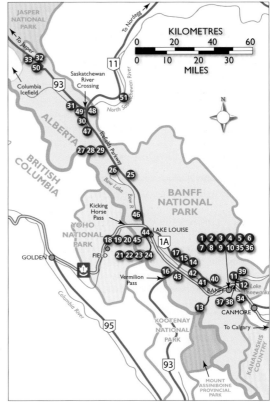

Bow River and Mt. Edith

Banff National Park

Established in November 1885, Banff is Canada's oldest and most celebrated national park. It includes 6641 km^2 of the front ranges and eastern main ranges, and features many of the trademark Rocky Mountain views. Banff town (129 km west of Calgary) and Lake Louise village (187 km west of Calgary) are the major centres. Access is by car or by passenger bus along Highway 1. You will find a full range of services, supplies, and accommodation at these places, and at Canmore 22 km east of Banff. You can purchase basic groceries and fuel at Castle Mountain Village and at Saskatchewan River Crossing. The park information centres are in Banff town on Banff Avenue and in Lake Louise village, adjacent to the mall.

Banff town and Lake Louise village are well suited to exploration on foot:

- This icon indicates trailheads that you can easily walk to from any place in town.
- This icon describes driving access to the same trailheads.
- In and around Banff town, you may use the Roam bus system to access many trailheads. Google "Banff Roam bus" to find a link to schedules, fares, and a mobile phone app.

1. Fenland

Fenland

The Fenland trail explores a shaded, white spruce forest along the banks of Forty Mile Creek – an area typical of the wetlands west of Banff town. These wetlands are being slowly transformed from open water to montane forest in a natural process called succession.

Much of the forest in the Bow Valley burned soon after the completion of the Canadian Pacific Railway in the late 1800s. The wetlands in this part of the valley protected this forest, so the white spruce here are ancient compared to most other species in tree stands nearby. These trees were big more than 125 years ago when Banff was being settled. You will see old stumps, evidence of logging from the town's early days.

The trail follows a meander of Forty Mile Creek, which loops around the fen. Look for a beaver lodge and for the aquatic pathways that these animals create through the lush vegetation. Trembling aspen and willows – two staples for beavers – grow nearby. Horsetails in the forest understory provide early season food for black bears. The trunks of some of the trembling aspen trees show dark scars created when bears have climbed to safety. Forty Mile Creek serves as a natural moat, making the fen an ideal place for elk calving in the spring. In the autumn, a

TRAIL THUMBNAIL

Trailheads

1. From Banff town, follow Lynx Street north. Across the railway tracks, Lynx Street becomes the Mt. Norquay Road. In 300 m, turn west (left) into the Forty Mile Creek picnic area.
2. From Highway 1, exit at the Mt. Norquay interchange. Follow the Mt. Norquay Road south toward town. Turn right in 150 m. Pick up the Bow River trail in town, and follow it north. Cross the railway tracks with caution. The trail leads into the woods and reaches the Fenland loop in about 100 m. Take the right-hand trail to reach the trailhead kiosk in about 225 m. See map, p. 18.

Rating: easy, 1.5 km loop. Wheelchair ♿ accessible with assistance.

Special considerations: Parks Canada often closes the Fenland trail during elk calving and elk rutting seasons. Use caution with regard to elk at all times when the trail is open. A brochure may be available at the trailhead or at the park information centre. Walk the loop clockwise if you would like to match the eight stops described in the brochure.

Best lighting: anytime

Nearby trail: ㉟

bull elk often collects a harem of females here. Keep at least 30 m away if you see an elk, and remember that the calves may be difficult to see.

For birders, this outing offers diverse habitats in a small area – flowing water, fen, dense coniferous forest, and patchy deciduous forest. The trunks of the spruce trees reveal abundant evidence of three-toed

WETLAND

"Wetland" is a generic term applied to any soggy part of a landscape. Canadian hydrologists are more specific, and have identified five classes. A *bog* has an accumulation of peat, a high water table, and no significant inflow or outflow. Bogs are distinctly northern features and may be ancient. They often formed in the depressions (known as kettles) left behind by melting ice blocks, and support acidic-loving vegetation. A *fen* is also underlain by peat, however its water and soil chemistries support the growth of sedges and wildflowers, and there is more water movement. Some wetland experts think that a fen is simply a few

centuries shy of stagnating into a bog. A *swamp* is associated with a stream, river or lake and has water flowing through it. Although it is almost perpetually flooded, a swamp supports the growth of trees and shrubs. This distinguishes it from a *marsh*, which supports only succulent vegetation. *Shallow open water* is the last wetland class. It includes ponds, oxbows, pools, and abandoned river channels. If you have all of this straight so far, you might despair at knowing that the experts have further subdivided the five classes of wetlands – yielding 70 sub-classifications – and they are still at work.

ELK (WAPITI)

Half again as large as an adult deer, a male elk is 1.5 m tall at the shoulder. The coat is light brown – darker on the neck and legs – with a shaggy fringe on the underside of the neck. In northern Europe, "elk" is the name used for the animal that Canadians call moose, thus many Canadians use "wapiti" (WAH-pih-tee) when referring to elk. This Shawnee name means "white rump". Elk prefer to eat grasses and tender vegetation. In autumn and winter they may peel the bark from aspen trees, which results in a black scarring of the lower tree trunk. As with other members of the deer family, elk ruminate – while resting they chew cud – food regurgitated from their multi-chambered stomachs.

Female elk (hinds) spend most of the year in the valley bottoms with the offspring and immature males, sometimes forming herds of 50 or more animals. The female gives birth to one or two calves in late May or early June. Mature males (stags) venture to higher elevations in late spring, spending the summer there alone or in small groups before returning to the valleys in late August or early September. The antlers of the males begin to grow in April. A fully developed antler rack on a healthy stag may reach 1.5 m in length and 1.8 m in width. The antlers fall off in February or March.

During mating in the autumn, stags and hinds bugle – making a strange combination of sounds that includes grunts and a resonant whistle. The courtship often takes place on the main streets of Banff and Jasper. Elk can be testy at this time, as they are when with young in late spring and early summer. Keep at least 30 m away. Elk have injured more people in the Rockies than all other wildlife species combined.

Wolves, cougars, and grizzly bears are the natural enemies of elk, but vehicles are the principal killers in the national parks. Nonetheless, elk are fairing well in Banff National Park, which is home to approximately 3200 of the animals, 900 of which live in the Bow Valley. An elk's lifespan is typically 12-15 years.

woodpeckers – red patches where the bark has been flaked off. Gray jays, Steller's jays, pileated woodpeckers, red-breasted nuthatches, golden-crowned kinglets, dippers, Canada geese, various flycatchers, Swainson's and varied thrushes, American redstarts, common yellowthroats, various warblers, and white-crowned sparrows will be among the other species you may see or hear.

2. Marsh Boardwalk

Cave and Basin wetland

TRAIL THUMBNAIL

Trailheads

Follow Banff Avenue to the south end of the Bow River bridge. Turn west (right) and follow Cave Avenue 1.6 km to the Cave and Basin National Historic Site. Walk to the north (right) of the pool building to reach the trailhead.

From the south end of the Bow River bridge, walk 1.6 km on the trail along the north side of Cave Avenue to the Cave and Basin National Historic Site. See map, p. 18.

Rating: easy, 500 m loop, boardwalk

Best lighting: anytime

Nearby trails: ❸ ❹ ❺

Of the roughly 70 known hot springs in Canada, 16 are near Banff town. The most celebrated of these are the Cave and Basin springs. Dispute over "ownership" of these springs led to the creation of

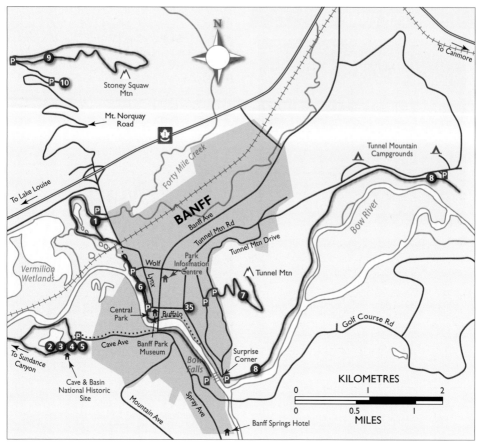

Banff National Park in 1885. The Banff hot springs have a combined outflow of more than 5 million litres per day, most of which drains into wetlands west of town. (One-fifth of this flow comes from the Cave Spring.) The hot water profoundly affects the local environment. The Marsh Boardwalk follows the edge of the Cave and Basin wetland, offering the opportunity to view plants and wildlife that are exotic to the Canadian Rockies. The area is great for birding. A viewing blind is provided.

The hot water that emerges at the Cave and Basin springs does not originate underground. It was originally surface water that filtered through cracks into the bedrock. The temperature underground typically increases 2°C for every 100 m of descent. Approximately 4 km below the surface, water reaches the boiling point and becomes pressurized. It returns to the surface along other crack systems. Near Banff town, the hot spring water surfaces along the Sulphur Mountain Thrust Fault.

In its journey, the heated water dissolves minerals from the bedrock. A few minerals (uranium and radium) make the waters slightly radioactive. Some people think this is therapeutic. Sulphur dissolved in the water, and sulphates metabolized by algae in the water, combine to create a "rotten egg" smell. In mineral content, the hot springs at Banff are similar to the famous ones at Bath, England.

Most of the rock in this area is limestone and dolomite. So the Banff hot springs carry calcium carbonate, an element of lime, in solution. When gasses in the water are released at the spring outlets, this lime-rich solution precipitates as calcite to create a crumbly rock known as tufa (TOO-fah). The tufa deposits at the Cave and Basin are 7 m thick. The crumbling of this material has twice led to the closure of the swimming facility – the most recent closure likely being permanent.

The hot spring water prevents most of the wetland near the Cave and Basin from freezing in winter. Some migratory birds stay year-round: killdeer, snipe, American robin, and mallard duck. Six species of orchids bloom in spring on the banks above the wetland, where you may also see the non-poisonous, wandering garter snake. Coyotes frequent the wetland, as do elk in late spring.

Interpretive panels along the boardwalk describe the hot spring ecosystem and the human history of the area.

3. Marsh Loop

Trailhead
As for the Marsh Boardwalk (outing 2). Walk west past the Cave and Basin National Historic Site, following signs for Sundance Canyon and Healy Creek.

Rating: easy, 2.3 km loop. The first 900 m is paved. You share part of the trail with equestrians.

Best lighting: anytime

Nearby trails: 2 4 5

The **Marsh Loop** makes a circuit around the Cave and Basin wetland, providing views of the Bow River, and opportunities for birding. The paved trail descends from the Cave and Basin National Historic Site to the Bow River in 700 m. At this point, look for a wide, dirt trail that heads sharply east (right). Take this, and walk northeast along the Bow River with the wetland on your right. After 1 km, make an abrupt turn south (right) at the east end of the wetland. Follow the crest of a dike, from which you ascend to the Cave and Basin parking area.

Sundance Canyon

At pavement's end you will find a bike lock-up, washroom, and picnic area. The 2.1 km loop trail through the canyon is best hiked clockwise. On the ascent, you climb in and out of the creek bed, which is eroding into a bedrock fault. The descent takes you through shaded forest, with two views of the Bow Valley. As with many canyons in the Rockies, this one marks the mouth of a hanging valley. The canyon commemorates a ritual dance of Stoney First Peoples.

4. Sundance Canyon

Trailhead
As for the Marsh Boardwalk (outing 2). Walk west past the Cave and Basin National Historic Site, following signs for Sundance Canyon and Healy Creek.

Rating: harder, 10.7 km return. The first 4.3 km is paved and is wheelchair accessible with assistance.

Special considerations: You share part of the trail with cyclists and equestrians.

Best lighting: morning

Nearby trails: 2 3 5

Sundance Canyon is located 4.3 km along a paved path from the Cave and Basin National Historic Site. From the rolling trail en route to the canyon you obtain fine views of the Bow River and the dogtooth spire of Mt. Edith (2554 m) to the north. See photo, p. 15.

5. Discovery Trail

Trailhead
As for the Marsh Boardwalk (outing 2). The trail begins at the staircase immediately south of the Cave and Basin National Historic Site building.

Rating: easy, 400 m loop, boardwalk

Best lighting: anytime

Nearby trails: 2 3 4

The **Discovery Trail** ascends onto the hillside above the Cave and Basin complex. Interpretive panels tell the stories of the discovery of the Cave and Basin hot springs, and their subsequent development. The trail visits the upper entrance of the Cave Spring, and crumbly outcrops of tufa – rock deposited by the hot spring water. You may complete this walk with a visit to the Cave Pool, and additional interpretive displays, both accessed from within the Cave and Basin National Historic Site (fee charged). Contact the Banff information centre for times and fees.

SPECIES IN PERIL

It is poignant that the Cave and Basin National Historic Site, birthplace of Canada's national parks system, has been the setting for the survival struggle of two unique species: the Banff longnose dace and the Banff Springs Snail. The Banff longnose dace, one of only two fish species native to the Cave and Basin wetland, was a tiny (5 cm long) creature, found nowhere else on Earth. It may have evolved, by adaptation to the hot water, from the population of eastern longnose dace in the adjacent Bow River.

To reduce biting bugs and thus make the park more enjoyable for tourists, the Dominion Parks Branch introduced western mosquitofish into the Cave and Basin wetland in 1924. Aquarium buffs subsequently added their favourite species. Whereas the

Banff longnose dace reproduced only once a year, the introduced species reproduced year-round and preyed on unhatched dace eggs. It may also be that the Banff longnose dace hybridized with the adjacent population of eastern longnose dace. By the early 1970s the Banff longnose dace was considered threatened as it had not been observed for several years. In 1986, it was officially declared extinct, a victim, at least in part, of human interference in a unique and supposedly protected ecosystem.

Even tinier than a dace, the most endangered lifeform in the Rocky Mountain parks is now the Banff Springs Snail, a creature also found nowhere else on Earth. Discovered in 1926 but not studied until 70 years later, the snail originally inhabited nine hot springs on Sulphur Mountain, but had disappeared from four of them by 1996. The species' population fluctuates annually, and drastically so; from a low of 1500 in 1996 to a high of almost 34,000 in 2005.

The Banff Springs Snail reproduces in all seasons, and may be capable of reproducing without a mate. Any disturbance of the spring water – such as walking through it, removing or disturbing the floating microbial mat, or bathing and dipping hands – all of which introduce sediments, oils, soaps, deodorants or insect repellents – can upset the water chemistry, temperature, and currents, possibly harming the snails. The snails and their eggs are easily crushed. The greatest threat now is drying of the springs due to climate change. The undeveloped hot springs near town are permanently closed to public entry to protect the snails. Fencing and surveillance equipment have been installed.

6. Bow River and Bow Falls

Banff residents and visitors are fortunate that the Bow River flows through town. The walk along the riverbank to Bow Falls offers escape from the bustle nearby, and features fine views of the river. You can visit the Banff Park Museum (fee charged) in Central Park on your way to the falls.

The Bow River is the longest river in Banff National Park. From its headwaters at Bow Lake, 90 km to the north, it drains an area of 2210 km². After flowing through Banff and out of the mountains, the Bow River, 587 km from its sources, joins the Oldman River in southern Alberta to form the South Saskatchewan River. The Bow River's name probably comes from the Cree words *manachaban sipi* – "the place from which bows are taken". First

TRAIL THUMBNAIL

Trailhead

Kiosk at the corner of Wolf Street and Bow Avenue in Banff town. See map, p. 18.

Rating: easy, 2.1.km. Wheelchair ♿ accessible in part.

Special consideration: The portion of the trail above and alongside Bow Falls is closed in winter. At this time, use River Avenue to reach the parking area below the falls.

Best lighting: morning and early afternoon

Nearby trails: ❶ ㉟

Bow Falls

Banff Park Museum

Peoples made hunting bows from saplings found on its banks.

Severe flooding of the Bow near Banff town has been reported 11 times since 1894, when high water washed out the railway line and stranded guests at the Banff Springs Hotel. The large coniferous trees along the riverbank and in Central Park are white spruce – the climax species in the succession of montane wetland to floodplain forest. Look for the wildflower, shooting star, on the riverbanks in June. American

BLACK-BILLED MAGPIE

On your way to Bow Falls you are likely to see black-billed magpies. The Latin genus and species name of this bird is *pica*, which means "black and white" – an accurate description of its attractive plumage. The long tail feathers are highlighted with iridescent green.

Magpies reside year-round in Banff. These large and vocal members of the crow family are not selective about what they eat; garbage is a favourite food. As with other members of the crow family, magpies will also eat the young and eggs from other birds' nests. The diet is 60 percent meat. In recent years, magpies have developed another food source – dead bugs on the fronts of vehicles. At the parking area in Banff's Central Park, you can watch magpies perched on automotive bumpers – their local bar and grill. The great horned owl is the magpie's principal predator. Magpies are known to mate for life. Their homes are a bulging assembly of sticks, often set in the crotch of a tree trunk.

trapper and prospector Joseph Healy wintered near here in 1874, in Banff's first non-native dwelling.

Constructed in 1903, the Banff Park Museum is now a National Historic Site, and is the oldest natural history museum in western Canada. Exhibits feature many of the mammals and birds that live in the park. The museum grounds were formerly the site of a zoo and aviary.

From the museum, ascend to Banff Avenue and turn south (right) to cross the Bow River bridge. Constructed in 1923, this span replaced a succession of bridges and ferries at this location. When the bridge was refurbished in 1990, the sculptures and much of the original "river stone" work were retained. Across the bridge, descend west (right). Turn east (right) onto the walkway that passes beneath the bridge, to continue along the riverbank.

The Bow River has not always followed this course through Banff. Before the Late Wisconsin Glaciation, the river may have flowed between Tunnel Mountain and Cascade Mountain, north of today's town. When the ice age glaciers receded, moraines blocked the river's course. A large lake formed west of the present town. Its waters eventually cut through the gap between Tunnel Mountain and Mt. Rundle at the present site of Bow Falls. The area west of Banff is still wetland – a legacy of the ancient lake.

Near trail's end you climb to a viewpoint above Bow Falls before descending to river level. Do not wade into the river. The 10 m-high falls are being eroded into Sulphur Mountain Formation siltstone, which dates to between 245-million and 207-million-years-old. The layers are tipped upwards, creating the rapids. If you are wondering if the falls have ever been successfully navigated in a boat, the answer is "yes". Several people have survived intentional and unintentional descents of the falls in kayaks and canoes.

Slightly downstream from the falls, the Spray River enters the Bow River at the site of the Banff Springs Hotel. To conclude your walk, you may ascend to the hotel to catch a Roam bus back to town, or return along the riverbank to your starting point.

7. Tunnel Mountain

Banff from Tunnel Mountain

Trailheads

1. Lower trailhead: At the parking area on the south side of St. Julien Road, 350 m south of Wolf Street
2. Upper trailhead: On Tunnel Mountain Drive, 400 m north of the Banff Centre. This road is closed in winter.

Walk east from town on Wolf Street or Caribou Street for 800 m to St. Julien Road. Turn south (right) to reach the lower trailhead. See map, p. 18.

Ratings
Lower trailhead: harder, 2.3 km
Upper trailhead: harder, 1.9 km

Special consideration: Watch for ice and snow on the route in the shoulder seasons.

Best lighting: anytime

Nearby trails: 6 8 35

With an elevation of 1692 m, Tunnel Mountain is the lowest feature to which the name "mountain" is applied in the Rockies. Although it is a steep climb, the well-beaten path to the summit hardly qualifies as mountaineering. From trail's end, you enjoy unrestricted views over the Bow Valley.

In 1882, Major A.B. Rogers, a surveyor for the Canadian Pacific Railway determined that Tunnel Mountain blocked the Bow Valley. He told his superior that a tunnel would be required for the rails to proceed. The boss was sceptical and ordered a follow-up investigation that found more than ample room for the railway in the valley between Tunnel Mountain and Cascade Mountain. The tunnel was never built, but the name remains.

The trail climbs steadily on the southwest slope of the mountain, crossing Tunnel Mountain Drive in 400 m. The forest here is an open one of lodgepole pine and Douglas-fir. Bearberry, twinflower, common juniper, harebell, and brown-eyed Susans colour the understory. Through the trees, you can see the Banff Springs Hotel. The Canadian Pacific Railway built the original structure in 1888. Most of the building we see today dates to 1928. The slopes behind the hotel rise to the ridge of Sulphur Mountain.

Tunnel Mountain was originally part of Mt. Rundle. Ice age glaciers eroded the gap between the two. Since then, the Bow River has whittled away at the breach. Tunnel Mountain's shape is characteristic of one of the more common mountain types in the front ranges of the Rockies – the dip-slope mountain. The steeply tilted slope that you have been climbing,

DOUGLAS-FIR

The steep, sun-exposed, southwest-facing slopes around Banff are ideal habitat for the Douglas-fir, the climax tree species of the montane life zone. This tree is not a true fir – its Latin genus name, *Pseudotsuga*, means "false hemlock". The thick, grooved, corky bark of the mature tree allows it to withstand moderate ground fires and infestation by many insects, although in places in the Rockies, entire stands are succumbing to beetles. Grass fires remove competing vegetation in older Douglas-fir stands, creating open parkland dotted with stately trees. Douglas-firs in such settings in the Rockies typically live 300 years; some live to be more than twice that age. The tree commemorates David Douglas, a Scottish botanist who collected in the Rockies in 1826 and 1827. At Surprise Corner on Tunnel Mountain Drive (see outing 8), Parks Canada has installed an excellent exhibit that features close-up views of this tree.

Tunnel Mountain

ends on a northeast-facing cliff. Parks Canada has installed fencing along that cliff edge. Stay back and please don't throw anything over the edge – climbers may be beneath, and there are trails near the cliff bottom.

In the view east from Tunnel Mountain's summit, the mountains of the Fairholme Range are prominent, extending along the east side of the Bow Valley, from Lake Minnewanka to Exshaw. Mt. Rundle (2949 m), to the south, was named for Methodist missionary, Robert T. Rundle. In 1844 and 1847 he preached to Stoney First Peoples near the present site of the Banff airstrip. To the north is Cascade Mountain (2998 m), highest near Banff. The Vermilion wetlands are to the west, beyond the rooftops of Banff town, with the peaks of the Massive Range on the skyline.

Given this view, you won't be surprised to learn that a fire lookout once occupied this spot. After King George VI visited in 1939, it became known as "Royal Lookout". It was one of seven in a system that covered Banff National Park.

Red-tailed hawk

8. Hoodoos

TRAIL THUMBNAIL

Trailheads

1. Follow Buffalo Street 1.2 km southeast from Banff Avenue to Surprise Corner. Walk downhill from the parking area and turn east (left).

Rating: harder, 4.7 km

2. On Tunnel Mountain Road, 6 km east of Banff.
See map, p. 18.

Rating: easy, 500 m. Wheelchair accessible with assistance

Special consideration: You share parts of the trail with cyclists.

Best lighting: afternoon and evening

Nearby trails: ❼ ㉟

The trail from Surprise Corner to the Hoodoos rambles through a mix of habitats typical of the Bow Valley – damp spruce forest, stands of lodgepole pine, meadows dotted with trembling aspen and Douglas-firs, and grassy river terraces. You begin at river level and, on a fair day, will be tempted to

Hoodoos

Limber pine

linger along this beautiful reach of the Bow. The river courses through coniferous forest, with beaches of gravel and cobble, and fine views of Tunnel Mountain (1692 m) and Mt. Rundle (2949 m). About 2.5 km from the trailhead, keep to the right as the trail begins to climb onto the hoodoo terrace. Look up; this is an excellent place to see red-tailed hawks (photo, p. 23) and osprey on the wing. The trail parallels Tunnel Mountain Road for 1.5 km to reach the trailhead for the paved path to the Hoodoos viewpoints. Views of Tunnel Mountain from here reveal why Stoney First Peoples called it "Sleeping Buffalo Mountain".

Although you can't see a glacier, the views from the Hoodoos terrace are all about ice: the massive U-shaped breach of the Bow Valley; the cirque-pocked flank of Mt. Rundle; the roche moutonée (see p. 87) form of Tunnel Mountain; the blue-green hues of the Bow River. Then there are the hoodoos themselves. Although there is no disagreement as to the source of the material in the pillars – it was eroded by ice age glaciers – geologists dispute how it came to be deposited here. The long-held theory is that it is a form of ground moraine, left behind as glaciers retreated. Large boulders protected some of the material from erosion, eventually becoming capstones for free-standing pillars. Because the hoodoo material is lime-rich, the gravel is naturally cemented together and remarkably resistant to weathering.

The upstart theory is that the hoodoo material came from debris flows as the ice age glaciers retreated. The debris flows surged into the Bow Valley from ice-dammed lakes in side valleys, as those ice dams gave way. If this were the case, these were not trifling events. In some places, the hoodoo material in the Bow Valley is 70 m thick.

The word "hoodoo" is used throughout western North America to describe natural columns of rock. Recent research into the origin of the word has debunked any solid connection between it and the word "voodoo". "Hoodoo" was a magic practice of

CHINOOK COUNTRY

The mountain front is a windy place. The Bow Valley funnels winds towards the foothills through a break in the mountain wall known as The Gap. The area is also affected by a warm, winter wind called a Chinook (shih-NOOK).

Chinook means "snow eater". The wind can raise local temperatures dramatically. The most precipitous rise recorded in Canada was 40°C in 20 minutes at Lethbridge. Calgary's record is 30°C in four hours. A Chinook results when warm air from a Pacific storm system breaks into the cold air of a high pressure mass situated over the foothills and plains. The drier air is heated as it sweeps groundward. A Chinook arch – a cloud that spans the length of the southern mountain front – often heralds the arrival of the wind. If a Chinook weather event terminates with the arrival of an Arctic front, an abrupt *drop* in temperature can take place. The U.S. all-time record for this occurred at Browning, Montana in January 1916, when the temperature fell from +7°C to -49°C in 24 hours. There is no corresponding Canadian record available.

In a typical winter there will be 30 Chinook days at the mountain front. Chinooks that last several days can warm the air as far away as Medicine Hat in south-eastern Alberta. During a Chinook the weather in the mountains is usually unsettled. Chinooks reduce snow accumulation at the mountain front and in the front ranges, and are a key element in the development of montane vegetation communities. Elk, bighorn sheep, and deer depend on grasslands here to survive the winter.

certain Black slaves, but was something entirely different from the practice of voodoo. Nonetheless, the word "hoodoo" took on a dark overtone in English and, in this particular instance, that overtone was reinforced by the local belief of Stoney and Siksika First Peoples, who thought that the Bow River hoodoos were giants turned to stone, or tepees that housed "bad gods". There are other hoodoo formations nearby in the Bow Valley. You can see them from Highway 1 between Banff and Canmore.

Douglas-fir, limber pine, and Rocky Mountain juniper grow near the final viewpoints. Limber pine has long, curved needles in bundles of five. Its trunk and branches are frequently contorted. The tree is locally common on cliff edges and other windy locations in the montane life zone, south of Saskatchewan River Crossing.

If you came from Surprise Corner, either retrace your route or catch a Roam bus (see p. 15) from the stop just inside the main entrance to Tunnel Mountain Campground. Ask the driver to let you off at Buffalo Street so that you can walk back to your vehicle (1.2 km).

Mt Rundle from Stoney Squaw

Douglas-fir and subalpine fir growing together, along with a few Engelmann spruce and lodgepole pines. *Usnea* and *Alectoria* lichens drape many of the fir trees, creating a fairy forest. Not far from the parking area, keep an eye out for the ultimate squirrel midden – a huge mound of discarded scales and cones, clearly the product of many generations of industrious rodents. Bird species that you may see and hear include Swainson's thrush, hermit thrush, and yellow-rumped warbler.

The trail undulates over a series of upturned rock edges. At about 1.3 km, you reach a junction. Go straight ahead and then descend left to carry on. Soon, views begin to open up to the south and east. The trail swings north to the high point and a break in the forest, with a great view east into the maw of the Bow Valley, and a point-blank view of Cascade Mountain (2998 m) to the north. I have watched a bald eagle from here, as it rode thermals over the valley. Use caution near the cliff edge. To make the loop outing, follow the trail as it swings around to the west. This narrow path contours the north slope of Stoney Squaw for 1.8 km back to the ski area, from where it is 600 m south (left) to the parking area.

9. Stoney Squaw

TRAIL THUMBNAIL

Trailhead
Follow Lynx Street north from Banff. Cross Highway 1 and follow the Mt. Norquay Road to the first parking area at the ski area, 6 km from town. See map, p. 18.

Rating: harder, 2.2 km one-way, or 4.6 km loop.

Best lighting: anytime

Nearby trail: ⑩

The Stoney Squaw trail climbs onto the 1884 m, forested summit of a modest mountain, to provide a grand prospect of the Bow Valley in the vicinity of Banff town. The mountain was named for the heroine of a Stoney legend, which tells of an injured man who lay at the mountain's base while his wife tended to him and hunted on the slopes above.

The forest on Stoney Squaw is unusual. It's a damp place for the front ranges of Banff, with an uncommon mix of tree species. Here you will find

SEDIMENTARY, MY DEAR WATSON

The awesome northeast rampart of Mt. Rundle (2949 m), rising 1560 m above the floor of the Bow Valley, features a classic sedimentary rock sequence of the southern Rockies. The basal tier of cliffs, more than 500 m high, is Palliser Formation limestone. The angled, shaly slopes above, 500 m high, are a sandwich of Exshaw Formation and Banff Formation shales. The capping cliff, 500 m high, is Livingstone Formation limestone, a member of the Rundle Group of formations. This alternation of resistant and recessive formations typifies the Rockies, providing these mountains with much of their visual and structural character. It also co-relates with ancient regimes of warmth (when limestone was created in marine environments), and ice age, when glaciers dumped loads of shale-making debris into ancient seas. The formations date from 366 million-years-ago to 326 million-years-ago.

10. The Green Spot

Trailhead
Follow Lynx Street north from Banff. Cross Highway 1 and follow the Mt. Norquay Road for 4.7 km to a small pull-off. Park on the right. See map, p. 18.

Rating: viewpoint

Best lighting: evening

Nearby trail: ⑨

The Green Spot, on the lower slopes of Mt. Norquay, is a prominent landmark in the view north from Banff. What created this opening in the forest? The best guess is that an intense forest fire burned here in the recent past, and that subsequent grazing by wildlife has kept the meadow open. Go green and walk out onto the slope for a fine view over Banff and the Bow Valley. Your companions are likely to be Columbian ground squirrels and, perhaps, bighorn sheep and elk. In May and June, check yourself afterwards for wood ticks.

11. Bankhead

Bankhead mine house ruin

The Bankhead loop explores the industrial area of a coal mining community that flourished in the early 1900s. You can see artifacts associated with the mine. Coal cinders are frequently underfoot.

Geologists working for the Canadian government discovered coal near Banff in 1883. Three years later, the Canadian Anthracite Coal Company began mining at a location in the Bow Valley on the Canadian Pacific Railway (CPR) line. The community that developed there became known as Anthracite. Not wanting to depend on an outside

Trailhead
Follow Banff Avenue 3 km east from town to Highway 1. Keep straight ahead on the Lake Minnewanka Road for 3.3 km. The trailhead is on the southeast (right). See map, p. 29.

Rating: easy, 1.1 km loop

Special consideration: The trail traverses an area that contains deposits of coal tar, a known carcinogen.

Best lighting: anytime

Nearby trails: ⑫ ㊲ ㊳ ㊴

supplier for its locomotive coal, the CPR obtained its own licence to mine coal elsewhere in 1903.

The CPR named the mine it established, Bankhead, after a Scottish town. It was initially intended only to serve the railway's needs. However, a coal shortage in 1906-07 created a huge, national demand. The CPR expanded operations rapidly and built a town adjacent to the state-of-the-art mine.

Mine production peaked in 1911; sources vary, reporting either 250,000 or 416,000 tonnes of coal. (One source says "up to 900 tonnes a day".) The town's population also reached maximum the same year. Officially recorded as 900 persons, some reports indicate that 2000 people lived at Bankhead. Most of the miners were immigrants: German, Italian, Swedish, Polish, and Chinese. The town featured a coal-burning power plant that also supplied electricity to Banff. Park managers in the early 1900s encouraged developments at Bankhead. The park superintendent praised the enterprise in 1911: "With its beautiful homes and its teeming industrial life, it has already become a popular stopping place for tourists."

Miners extracted Bankhead's coal in an unusual fashion. To access the seams, they tunnelled upward at a slight angle, then used dynamite to blast the coal loose. It then fell downward onto wooden bulkheads, which the miners opened to drop the coal into rail cars that gravity propelled back to the mine entrance. Workers excavated a total of 320 km of tunnels for mining, transportation, and ventilation on three levels of the mine.

You will see an example of a "dinky" – a narrow-gauge train. This particular train came from the Canmore mine, however, similar trains transported coal from the Bankhead mine to the tipple, where the coal was sorted. There were nine such locomotives at Bankhead. They were powered by compressed air

Mine locomotive

to prevent ignition of methane in the mine tunnels. Each locomotive pulled 30 boxcars, each of which held 2 tonnes of coal. In this fashion, 400 tonnes of coal was easily removed from the mine each day.

Bankhead's coal was desirable, high quality semi-anthracite. However, almost 50 percent of the coal was little more than dust by the time it tumbled down the pitching chutes into the mining cars and rumbled to the portal. To salvage this coal, the CPR imported pitch from Pennsylvania to manufacture briquettes. Despite the expense, the process proved successful. The briquette plant produced up to 500 tonnes of product each day.

As with most mining towns, Bankhead's history was one of boom and bust. A decade of labour troubles forced closure of the mine in 1922. Despite having produced more than 2,600,000 tonnes of coal, the mine never reopened. The miners moved on. Reflecting a less favourable outlook on mining in national parks, the Dominion Parks Branch attempted to erase Bankhead from the landscape. It was almost successful. Many of the town's buildings were moved to Banff, Lake Minnewanka, and Canmore. The Holy Trinity Church, built in 1908, was sawn in half and transported to Calgary. To see the church foundation and steps, follow the short trail northeast from the end of the turnaround loop in the parking area. The Bankhead railway station is now a hostel in Banff.

RIVALLING BANFF

During its heyday, Bankhead rivalled Banff as the most thriving community in the Rockies. Residents of Bankhead enjoyed many conveniences: rail service, a hotel, a school, two dairies, skating rinks, a law court, churches, tennis courts, and a library. Homes had running water, sewers, and electricity before these amenities came to Banff.

There were three Bankheads: upper, which was the residential area; lower, which was the industrial area; and "other", below the industrial area, where the Chinese labourers lived. The train station at Bankhead was a whistle stop. One night when the train carrying the CPR payroll passed through, a clerk threw the payroll bag in the general direction of the station. He missed. Concerned mine officials found the payroll the next day, in a snowbank 400 m from the station.

One thing that Bankhead lacked was a cemetery. Burials were made in Banff – much to the consternation of park officials, principally because Bankhead was "dry" and Banff town was not. Park officials did not take kindly to influxes from Bankhead at a burial, and the subsequent rowdiness. In 1907 the Bankhead mine manager agreed to build a cemetery at the mine. It must have been well planned because it was 1916 before the cemetery opened. However, no one wanted to be the first buried there, fearing that bad luck would befall their families. Eventually, the cemetery was used to inter a Chinese labourer, murdered in 1921 and thought to have no family. When word of the death reached China, his family requested that the remains be repatriated. This request was fulfilled in 1939, and, long after Bankhead was gone, its cemetery, used only once, was closed.

12. Johnson Lake

Johnson Lake

TRAIL THUMBNAIL

Trailhead
Follow Banff Avenue 3 km northeast from town to Highway 1. Keep straight ahead on the Lake Minnewanka Road. Turn east (right) in 1.2 km for Two Jack Lake and Johnson Lake. In 3.3 km turn south (right). Follow this road 2.3 km to Johnson Lake.

Rating: easy, 2.8 km loop

Special considerations: Elk frequent this trail. Use caution.

Best lighting: anytime

Nearby trails: 11 37 38 39

Johnson Lake is an artificial reservoir and, on hot days, is Banff's swimming hole. The loop trail around its shores features fine views of Cascade Mountain and Mt. Rundle (2949 m), and the opportunity to see elk, deer, muskrat, and waterfowl. Wolves and cougars are commonly observed in the area. Parks Canada closes the trail if there is an active wolf den nearby, or, as is often the case in the springtime, if carnivores are feeding on an elk carcass. In this description we circle the lake, clockwise.

Walk on a paved trail through the picnic area on the north (left-hand) shore of the lake. You may drop down to the viewing platform on the lakeshore, with its fine vista of Mt. Rundle (2949 m). Look for common mergansers and common loons. Casual walkers may turn back here.

Continuing along the north shore, cross the inlet stream on a bridge. Horsetails and spotted orchids grow in this damp area. From here to the east end of the lake, the trail alternates between forest stands of Douglas-fir, white spruce, and lodgepole pine, and savannah-like openings dotted with juniper, buffaloberry, and brown-eyed Susans. Red-winged blackbirds, dark-eyed juncos, and warbling vireos are common songbirds. Views southeast down the lake include Mt. Lougheed (3107 m), beyond Canmore.

While making the circuit, keep your eye out for two local treasures – a seat swing beneath an ancient Douglas-fir, and a rope swing for taking wild plunges into the lake. At the east end of the lake, the trail swings south to cross the earthen outlet dam. Cascade Mountain (2998 m), its flanks showing multiple folds, commands the view to the west. As you return along the lake's south shore, scan the shorelines for beaver bank burrows and muskrat push-ups. Near trail's end you follow a powerline right of way as the trail cuts through a doghair forest of lodgepole pine. Calypso orchids bloom here in June. If it's a hot day, you'll be joining a throng at the beach near the picnic area. You packed your swimming gear, right?

KEEPING ALL THE PIECES

Johnson Lake borders the Fairholme Environmentally Sensitive Area – the largest block of relatively undisturbed montane habitat in Banff National Park – an area where Parks Canada discourages human use. More than a century of managing protected areas has taught a hard lesson: setting aside a place, even a large place, does not protect it. The integrity of a protected area, no matter its size, will only endure if all of its natural processes, its habitats, and its species are preserved. The Fairholme area contains a mixture of habitats not found elsewhere in Banff, and is well-used by wildlife. A series of prescribed burns in the 1990s and 2000s has helped to restore some of the natural processes and to revitalize habitats. If we keep hands-off and feet-out, we will minimize the disturbances to species, and assist in the area's protection.

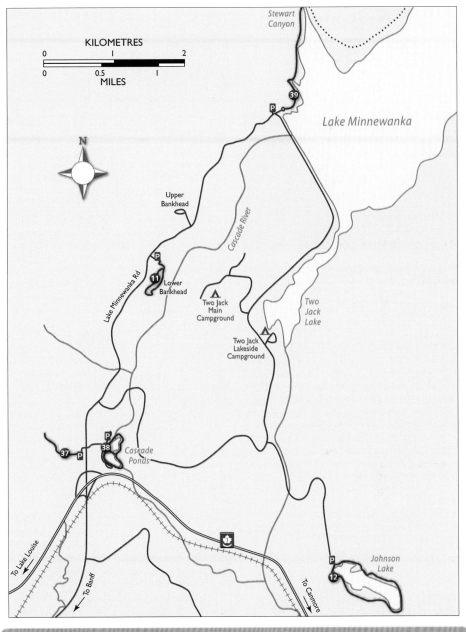

KILOMETRES
0   1   2
0   0.5   1
MILES

Stewart Canyon

Lake Minnewanka

Upper Bankhead

Cascade River

Lower Bankhead

Two Jack Main Campground

Two Jack Lake

Two Jack Lakeside Campground

Lake Minnewanka Rd

Cascade Ponds

To Lake Louise

To Banff

To Canmore

Johnson Lake

VENERABLE TREES

The Douglas-fir (see also p. 22 and p. 156) is the climax tree species of the montane forest in Banff National Park, typically achieving ages of 200-300 years. A Douglas-fir will burn with any other tree species in a large-scale forest fire, but when it grows in its prime niche in the Rockies – montane grasslands – it becomes relatively immune to destruction by fire. This is because grassland fires move quickly through their thin fuels, lingering only long enough to scorch the bark of mature Douglas-firs; not to set the trees ablaze. In such settings, individual Douglas-firs may reach tremendous ages. Just west of Johnson Lake, on a grassy terrace of the Bow River, dwells a Douglas-fir thought to be approximately 700 years old – the most ancient of its species in Alberta. When Parks Canada set prescribed burns in this area in 2003, it cut fireguards whose intent, in part, was to protect this tree and its ancient neighbours.

13. Sunshine Meadows

Standish Viewpoint

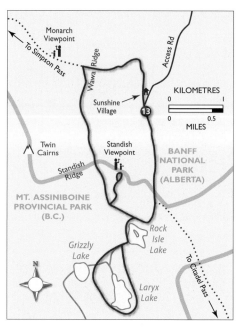

TRAIL THUMBNAIL

Trailhead
Contact White Mountain Adventures to book a seat (fee charged) on their Sunshine Meadows shuttle bus: www.sunshinemeadowsbanff.com, or phone 403-762-7889, 800-408-0005. Follow Highway 1, 8.3 km west from Banff to the Sunshine Interchange. Follow the Sunshine road 9 km to the parking area at its end, and the nearby ticket office. Allow 40 minutes from Banff. If you don't want to take the bus, you may walk the access road, 6.2 km to the trailhead, with an elevation gain of 503 m – not a walk or an easy hike.

Ratings
- Rock Isle loop only: harder, 8.5 km total
- Meadow Park loop, Standish Viewpoint: harder, 7.2 km
- Rock Isle loop, Standish Viewpoint, and Meadow Park loop: harder, 10.6 km
- Add Monarch Viewpoint: 12.6 km

Special consideration: Snow may cover trail sections well into July.

Best lighting: anytime

The Sunshine Meadows occupy a 14 km arc along the continental divide, at an average elevation of 2225 m. Together with the meadows at Simpson Pass, Healy Pass, and above Lost Horse Creek, they form a vast heath tundra. Mountain heather, woolly everlasting, fleabane, valerian, arctic willow, western anemone, and sedges are the characteristic plants. In addition, 340 other plants have been recorded. This represents more than one-third of the plant species of Banff and Jasper national parks. Some of the species are rare – both in Alberta and in Canada – and many are at either the extreme northern or southern limits of their ranges.

The average annual temperature on the meadows is -4°C. More than 7 m of snow falls each year. Snowbanks linger well into July. Vegetation is specially adapted, storing nutrients from summer's sunshine to release in a burst that promotes rapid growth the following year. With a growing season so short, it may take decades before some plants mature enough to carry blooms – 20 years is typical for moss campion. Snowmelt saturates the thin soils for much of the summer. Travel off-trail can cause long-lasting damage to the ground cover. Please keep to maintained trails.

The most common trees at Sunshine are Engelmann spruce, subalpine fir, whitebark pine, and Lyall's larch. (This is a great outing for larch-viewing in early September.) Many of the trees are in stunted, kruppelholz form. Their windward sides are sometimes devoid of branches. In the shelter of the tree islands, snowbanks linger, providing habitat for moisture loving wildflowers such as glacier lily and bracted lousewort. Columbian ground squirrels, hoary marmots, pikas, least chipmunks, and golden-mantled ground squirrels are common wildlife species that you may see.

You can link together two loops for an energetic day that takes in the best views on the meadows. Follow the crushed stone path south, through the sprawl of the ski area buildings. Fifteen metres past the avalanche station turn east (left) onto a gravelled

Rock Isle Lake

Mt. Assiniboine (3616 m) was the object of several mountaineering attempts in the 1890s. Its remote location and difficult approach thwarted all comers, but competition was keen. In 1901, Edward Whymper, of Matterhorn fame, visited the Rockies at the behest of the Canadian Pacific Railway, whose executives hoped that he would make Mt. Assiniboine's first ascent. However, Whymper was past his mountaineering prime and could not even be enticed to make the approach. James Outram (OOT-rum) and guides made the first ascent in September that year. They ascended the southwest face and descended the northeast arête. Although the climb is not considered to be difficult by contemporary standards, unpredictable weather, poor rock, and the presence of snow or ice make any attempt on Mt. Assiniboine a serious undertaking.

trail and ascend south through larch forest. Open vistas fill all directions. The towering horn of Mt. Assiniboine (3616 m) – 8th-highest in the Rockies, and the 2nd-highest peak south of the Columbia Icefield – beckons from the south. After 1.3 km, the trail crests the continental divide and crosses from Banff National Park, Alberta, into Mt. Assiniboine Provincial Park, B.C. The trail forks. Take the wider, right-hand trail.

Rock Isle Lake Loop

In 800 m you reach a junction. Turn south (left) if you want to hike the Rock Isle Lake loop. (Some of the B.C. Parks trail signs refer to the outing as The Garden Path.) You reach the Rock Isle Lake viewpoint in 500 m. Turn southwest (left) at the next junction in 200 m. The trail descends through a flower-filled larch forest. Turn southwest (right) at the next junction to pass along the east shore of Grizzly Lake. The trail curves south to a viewpoint that overlooks the upper Simpson Valley. After circling around Larix Lake, with impressive views west to The Monarch (2895 m), the trail climbs back to the loop junction north of Rock Isle Lake.

Twin Cairns-Meadow Park

From the Rock Isle Lake junction, head northwest on the Twin Cairns-Meadow Park trail. At the junction in 500 m, turn north (right) and climb steeply to the Standish Viewpoint for a grand view to the south. Backtrack to the junction and turn north (right) to climb through aptly named Meadow Park, crossing the continental divide back into Alberta. After 2 km, you reach the junction with the Simpson Pass trail. Turn east (right) to descend to Sunshine Village in 1.6 km. Or, if you have the energy and time, head west from the junction for 1 km to Monarch Viewpoint, with its fine vista of the continental divide to the west.

14. Johnston Canyon and the Ink Pots

Trailhead
East side of the Bow Valley Parkway (Highway 1A), 23.6 km west of Banff; 6.5 km east of Castle Junction. The trail departs the northeast corner of the parking area.

Ratings
- Lower Falls: easy, 1.1 km
- Upper Falls: moderate, 2.7 km
- Ink Pots: harder, 5.9 km

Special considerations: The Bow Valley Parkway east of Johnston Canyon is closed to vehicles from 8 p.m. to 8 a.m. daily, March 1 to June 25. The parking area and roadsides will be jammed on a fair summer day. Consider hiking early or late in the day. Use caution when there is ice or snow on the trail. You share the trail beyond the Upper Falls with equestrians.

Best lighting: anytime

Nearby trails: 15 42

Upper Falls

People have been visiting Johnston Canyon since the prospector it was named for staked a claim here in the 1880s. Because the features of interest are next to the trail, this is an excellent outing for poor weather days. You may see mule deer, red squirrels, porcupines, gray jays, dippers, and common ravens. Johnston Canyon is one of three known Alberta nesting sites for black swifts. Coyotes, wolves, grizzly bears, and elk frequent the Johnston Creek valley near the Ink Pots.

From the parking area, cross Johnston Creek and turn north (right). The trailhead is at an elevation that is normally part of the montane life zone. However, canyons chill the air within, creating environments more typical of higher elevations. The vegetation on shaded, north-facing slopes in lower Johnston Canyon is distinctly subalpine in character. On sun-exposed, south-facing slopes, lodgepole pines and a few Douglas-firs prevail – indicator trees of montane forest.

In Johnston Canyon, you walk through a sequence of sedimentary layers – rocks of the Rundle Group of formations. These were deposited between 350-million-years-ago and 300 million-years-ago. The lower canyon is cut into tough limestone and dolomite of the Livingstone Formation. The vicinity of the Upper Falls is eroded into fossil-rich limestone of the Mt. Head Formation. The more sinuous, upper canyon is cut into weaker shales and siltstones of the Etherington Formation. The Ink Pots lie within the siltstones, mudstones, and shales of the 245-208 million-year-old Sulphur Mountain Formation.

The trail in the lower canyon has been designed to accommodate the tremendous number of visitors. The most recent trail work, completed in 2002, includes a concrete slab catwalk suspended from the

THE HILLSDALE SLIDE

At the end of the Late Wisconsin Glaciation, 12,000 years ago, Johnston Creek flowed east of here along the base of Mt. Ishbel. The mountain's slopes had been undercut during the glaciation. After the ice retreated, layers of the mountain broke free and slid to the valley floor as the Hillsdale Slide. This landslide blocked Johnston Creek, forcing it to seek another course to the Bow River. The creek was captured by a fault in the bedrock, visible from a high bank in the upper canyon.

So goes one theory. Another holds that Johnston Canyon may be the course of an ancient underground stream. The cavern was exposed to daylight by erosion during the Late Wisconsin Glaciation.

Travertine

MIGRATING WATERFALLS

Johnston Canyon has a maximum depth of 30 m. It features seven waterfalls, each of which marks a place where a layer of dolomite bedrock has been uncovered by the flowing water. Dolomite is limestone that has been transformed. Water seeped into the limestone sediments before they lithified (became rock). Calcium in the limestone was replaced by magnesium. The magnesium-enriched rock – more properly described as a mineral – is harder than limestone. It naturally becomes the brinks of the waterfalls in this canyon. At the base of each waterfall, the incessant pounding of the water has created a plunge pool. The plunge pool eventually undercuts the brink, causing it to collapse. Thus the waterfall "migrates" slightly upstream, where the process is repeated.

INKY SPRINGS

The Ink Pots are the outlets of seven cold mineral springs. Fed by rainwater and snowmelt that has percolated into the surrounding bedrock, the spring water emerges at a constant temperature of 4.8°C. The combined volume of flow is 1800 litres per minute. The bases of the Ink Pots are covered in fine sediments that have the consistency of quicksand. Two of the springs run murky due to sediments disturbed by the rising water. Please keep to the designated paths to avoid trampling the surrounding vegetation.

canyon wall on steel supports. Although it might seem intrusive, you gain an appreciation of the effects of flowing water that would not be possible from the canyon rim.

You reach the Lower Falls at km 1.1. A bridge takes you across the creek where you walk through a natural tunnel to a balcony drenched by the spray of the falls. The shattered cliffs nearby have been coated with an artificial compound to minimize the chance of rockfall.

Lower Falls to Upper Falls

Many people turn back at the Lower Falls so the trail beyond is less crowded. The character of the canyon also changes. It is often wider and V-shaped, in contrast to the narrow, deep slot of the lower canyon. At km 2.7, you can descend a catwalk to the base of the 30 m high Upper Falls. The canyon wall opposite features a drape of travertine – crumbly limestone, precipitated from lime-rich water. Algae remove carbon dioxide from the water during photosynthesis, depositing a film of calcium carbonate as a waste product. This is the largest of the six travertine drapes in Johnston Canyon, and may be the largest in the Rockies. Twenty-five species of algae have been identified here.

Upper Falls to the Ink Pots

Back on the main trail, you climb to the crest of the Upper Falls and a viewpoint at the canyon's edge. Please keep within the guardrails. At least five people have died from falls into the canyon here. Less

Johnston Canyon

Silverton Falls

catastrophic slips and tumbles happen every year. The trail reverts to a natural surface just beyond. Twenty metres past the "end of interpretive trail" sign, a short spur trail leads west (left) to an abandoned canyon. Johnston Creek formerly flowed here as a waterfall. Downward erosion along the current stream course captured and redirected Johnston Creek, leaving this channel dry.

The trail angles away from the canyon, and the sound of rushing water soon fades. The forest becomes drier. At km 3.2, the trail joins the horse and skier route from Moose Meadows. Turn north (right) for the Ink Pots. The trail climbs and becomes narrower before it descends to the willow plain on Johnston Creek at the Ink Pots.

East of the Ink Pots, Mt. Ishbel (2908 m) is prominent. Its slabby layers and serrated ridges feature limestones of the Rundle Group of sedimentary formations. Mt. Ishbel epitomizes the sawtooth mountain form. It's no wonder that James Hector coined the name "Saw-back" for the surrounding mountains. You can see the hills and dales of the Hillsdale Slide to the south. To the north, grassy terraces on Castle Mountain (2850 m) provide excellent range for bighorn sheep and mountain goats.

TRAIL THUMBNAIL

Trailhead
On the Bow Valley Parkway at the Rockbound Lake trailhead, 29.5 km west of Banff, 200 m east of Castle Junction. You can access Castle Junction from Highway 1, 30 km west of Banff, 25.5 east of Lake Louise.

Rating: moderate, 850 m

Special consideration: The climb to the falls and the viewing area is unfenced. Use caution, especially with children.

Best lighting: late afternoon

Nearby trails: ⓮ ⓰ ⓱

15. Silverton Falls

Destinations on sidetrails are often overlooked. In this case, the Rockbound Lake trail lures hikers to its namesake destination, a worthy goal for capable hikers, 8.4 km away. But on this sidetrail, just a hop and a skip from the trailhead, you will find a pleasing series of cascades, the match of any this close to roadside in the Rockies.

Begin on the Rockbound Lake trail, climbing gently through lodgepole pine forest. The understory here will be flush with wildflowers and shrubs in late June and July. Look for arnica, yellow columbine, twinflower, white geranium, wild dandelion, one-flowered wintergreen, blue clematis, wild strawberry, yarrow, and buffaloberry. You will see some trees that have been killed by mountain pine beetle, and a few trembling aspens.

At the junction in 350 m, angle northeast (right). The trail to Silverton Falls at first cuts across a forested, alluvial landform, created where Silverton Creek dumps debris into the Bow Valley. Look for dwarf dogwood (bunchberry) and horsetails in this damp area. After about 250 m, where the trail draws alongside the creek, make a sharp turn to the northwest (left), and begin the switchback climb to the mouth of a hanging valley and the falls.

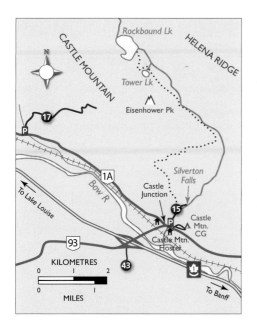

On the steep slope, the character of the forest understory changes. Gone is the dwarf dogwood, replaced by a dry regime of brown-eyed Susans, wolf willow, prickly juniper, wild rose, and common juniper. Where the trail angles northeast toward the creek you cross an exposed mud slope. You could fall here if you are not careful, especially when the footing will be slick during and after a rain.

Trail's end is on the north bank of Silverton Creek, at the principal drop of the half dozen cataracts. The creek has eroded into a weakness in the upturned rock layers. Note the plunge pool at the base of each cascade. On the opposite bank, you can see a cave, eroded by the pounding water when the principal cascade was slightly lower down on the creek. Wind-driven spray coats some of the rocks and vegetation near the falls, creating a damp micro-habitat. It may be slick underfoot. If you have children with you, perhaps have them sit down to enjoy the view so that you can enjoy it, too.

SILVER?... NO. CITY?... YES.

Silverton is short for Silver Town. If you had come to the Bow Valley in the 1880s looking for silver, you would have left, as many did, disappointed. In fact, you would have been duped. But you might have enjoyed your stay at a thriving locality, now only a meadow, called Silver City.

In the autumn of 1883, the Canadian Pacific Railway's "end-of-steel" reached this part of the Bow Valley. Construction halted in December with the rails just shy of the crest of Kicking Horse Pass. Three communities sprang up in the Bow Valley that year: Siding 29 near what is now Banff, Holt City at what would later become Lake Louise, and Silver City.

There is some silver in the Canadian Rockies but not in quantity to make mining worthwhile. Those who promoted Silver City sought to make their windfall by fleecing prospectors. Silver City went from boom to bust in less than two years, but at its peak in 1884,

it was larger than Calgary – 2000 people lived on the meadows with all the convenience you could, er, expect.

When it became clear that Silver City was a fraud, the prospectors moved on. Unfortunately, many of them followed the railway right-of-way west to Golden City (now Golden, B.C.), where the rumoured gold was also scarce. Locals dismantled one of Silver City's six hotels and floated it down the Bow River to Banff, where it was reopened for business. The only person who stayed at Silver City was Joe Smith, the community's third resident. Park wardens looked the other way as he hunted, trapped, and prospected in the area until 1937. Today, all that remains of Silver City are tree stumps. The meadows were the site of an internment camp during World War I. You may visit a memorial to the internees, on the Bow Valley Parkway, 4.5 km west of Castle Junction.

35

16. Boom Lake

Boom Lake

Trailhead
Boom Creek picnic area, north side of the Kootenay Parkway (Highway 93 South), 7.0 km west of Castle Junction; 97.7 km east of the junction with Highway 95.

Rating: harder, 5.1 km

Special consideration: Grizzly bears frequent the trail and the picnic area.

Best lighting: morning

Nearby trails: 14 17 105 109

Although the Boom Lake outing is an undemanding stroll through an ancient subalpine forest, its destination is the match of any lake in the Rockies. Its shores are a wonderful place to wile away the hours. If you time your hike for September you will be treated to displays of Lyall's larch surrounding the lake.

After crossing Boom Creek on a bridge, the broad trail – formerly a tote road to a mine – begins its gradual climb. Keep straight ahead at the Taylor Lake junction at km 2.3. The trail continues its rolling ascent for another 2 km before it descends gradually, becoming narrower, rocky, and rooted for the last

200 m. The trail emerges on the north shore of Boom Lake about 600 m west of the outlet. Rockslide debris makes travel difficult farther along the lakeshore.

Boom Lake is 2.7 km long, 30 m deep, and 366 m wide. With an area of roughly 100 ha, it is the 10th-largest lake in Banff National Park. It is remarkably clear given its proximity to glacial ice. Measurements have documented a reduction of silt

THE SUBALPINE FOREST

The Boom Lake trail is located a few kilometres east of the continental divide in an area of abundant precipitation. It traverses a classic subalpine forest of Engelmann spruce and subalpine fir. The spruce have scaly, reddish-brown bark; the firs have smooth, silvery bark. The spire-like form of the subalpine fir, with its downsloping branches, helps shed the heavy snow load. The association of these two tree species is so common and widespread in the mountains of western North America, that botanists nickname the resulting forests "ES-SF". Labrador tea, dwarf birch, feathermosses, clubmosses, and liverworts are prominent in the undergrowth.

Ancient subalpine forests provide ideal habitat for mice and voles, which are standard fare for great horned owls and for American martens. Moose use this forest for cover. You may see ruffed grouse and woodpeckers: three-toed, pileated, hairy, and Downy. Varied thrush, hermit thrush, and golden-crowned kinglet are common songbirds. The bark of some Engelmann spruce trees is reddish-purple where the brown outer scales have been removed by woodpeckers as they search for grubs and insects.

The damp and decay is in contrast to the lodgepole pine forest that you saw at the trailhead. The smaller pines seeded after the 1968 Vermilion Pass Burn. Spruce and fir will probably replace the pines

within 130 years. This process of transformation is called succession. Each forest type favours certain species of vegetation and wildlife. Nature uses fire to promote succession and revitalize stagnant forests. The mosaic of new and old, burned and unburned, creates the diversity of habitats required to maintain all species in the forest ecosystem.

The Boom Lake trail travels between the extremes of forest succession habitats in the Rockies. The forest at the trailhead is less than five decades old. Near Boom Lake you will see Engelmann spruce trees that measure 1 m in diameter at the base, and 40 m in height – indicating ages of perhaps 350-450 years.

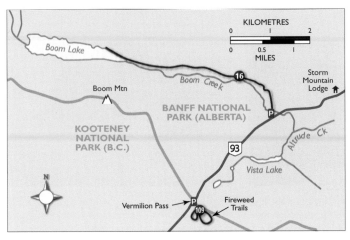

KILOMETRES

MILES

Boom Lake

Boom Creek

16

Storm Mountain Lodge

Boom Mtn

BANFF NATIONAL PARK (ALBERTA)

KOOTENEY NATIONAL PARK (B.C.)

93

Altrude Ck

Vista Lake

N

Vermilion Pass

109

P

Fireweed Trails

in the water – an indication that the glaciers that feed the lake are dwindling.

The lake is home to cutthroat trout. The log booms are natural formations created from avalanched trees swept into the lake. The trees then drifted toward the outlet and became lodged. The cold, damp, north-facing avalanche slopes on the south side of the lake support stands of Lyall's larch, a tree usually found 300 m higher.

The prominent ice-clad mountains northwest of the lake are Mt. Bident (3084 m) and Quadra Mountain (3173 m). The upper ramparts feature the "Middle Cambrian sandwich" – the lower cliffs are Cathedral Formation limestone, the terrace is Stephen Formation shale, the capping cliff is Eldon Formation limestone. The basin beneath is heaped with moraines, indicating the extent of glacial ice less than two centuries ago.

The rockslide boulders and the dark cliffs that ring the lake are Gog Formation quartzite (see p. 44). This rock was created from quartz-rich sediments deposited in prehistoric seas during the Early Cambrian. These rocks are home to colonies of pikas, tiny members of the rabbit family whose call is a shrill "EEEEP".

BRYOPHYTES

The damp forest along the Boom Lake trail is ideal habitat for bryophytes – a group of essentially rootless, non-vascular plants with poorly developed plumbing. For this reason, they must grow in wet places and they cannot grow very tall. Bryophytes – the name comes from the Greek words, *bryo*, which means "moss" and *phyton*, which means "plant" – grow from spores. They are among the overlooked miracles of the forest floor. Because you usually have to get nose-to-smelly-earth with these plants in order to make acquaintance, most people pay them little heed. But bryophytes are worth getting to know – even superficially – if only for the roll call of names, some perfunctory, some unusual, some as beautiful as the plants they describe: alpine apple-moss, stairstep moss, alpine star-moss, rock star-moss, silver worms, fire moss, grooved gnomecap moss, rolled-leaf pigtail moss, knight's plume, common dung-moss, and electrified cats-tail moss.

17. Castle Lookout

TRAIL THUMBNAIL

Trailhead
Parking area on the north side of the Bow Valley Parkway (Highway 1A), 4.9 km west of Castle Junction; 34.6 km west of Banff; 20.1 km east of Lake Louise. You can access the Bow Valley Parkway from Castle Junction on Highway 1. See map, p. 35.

Rating: harder, 3.8 km

Best lighting: anytime; afternoon and evening are especially good

Nearby trails: **15** **16** **105** **109**

If you wanted to build the Canadian Rockies from scratch you would need lots of sedimentary rock, you would have to pile the rock layers upward, and you would have to erode the raw mountains with

37

The Bow Valley from Castle Lookout

Castle Mountain

an ice age or ten. Although you spend much of this short outing in pine forest, the destination delivers a "Wow!" view – the massive, glacially-carved trough of the Bow Valley – which provides ample evidence of those key, mountain-building ingredients. With its southwest aspect, this trail is a great prospect for shoulder season hiking. If you go early in May or June, check for wood ticks during and after the trip.

The parking area buzzes with activity – it seems that many people, not intent on hiking, turn in here looking for... well, they're not quite sure what. They make a U-turn and soon depart. But some of that busy-ness carries on into the hike – you will hear noise from the roads and the railway throughout.

Evidence on many mountainsides in the Bow Valley testifies to a short-lived mining industry of the late 1800s. The hopefuls were in quest of gold, but lead, zinc, and copper were the only minerals present, and even those – especially given the remoteness – were not in quantity to make mining profitable. For just over half the distance to the lookout site, this trail is road-width. It may originally have been cleared that way by miners, but it was certainly maintained that way by park staff from the 1940s

to the 1970s, when the fire lookout was operational and park staff drove as far as they could to deliver supplies. You head north from the parking area for a short distance, before the trail swings to the east for the duration of the hike.

Much of the Bow Valley between Banff and Lake Louise burned in fires in 1881, 1895, and 1896. The near-homogenous lodgepole pine forest that surrounds this trail dates to one of those burns. As lodgepole forests go, this one is in decline. Forest fires should have occurred in the past century, and would have helped to maintain biodiversity. In the absence of fires, the pine forest of the Bow Valley now presents ideal habitat for mountain pine beetles. Scan the forest canopy for evidence: "red attack" trees, in which the beetles dwelled last year, and which have yet to lose their dead foliage; and "gray attack" trees, now standing dead.

If you are hiking in late June or early July, a special treat awaits in the understory – the blooms of blue clematis. They grow here with an abundance I have not seen elsewhere. Look also for calypso orchids and arnica. You will see a few Engelmann spruce and the occasional Douglas-fir at trailside.

ON THE EDGE

Whitebark pines thrive on the cliff edge at the lookout site. Whereas the mountain pine beetle holds the collective attention of many forest watchers in the Rockies, whitebark pines are being clobbered primarily by another affliction – this one introduced from Europe. White pine blister rust arrived in North America on a shipment of tree seedlings in 1906. It has taken a century for the rust to wreak its havoc to the crests of mountain ridges in western North America. In the Waterton-Glacier area, one researcher claims that the whitebark pine is "functionally extinct". Almost all of the trees there are infected; many are already dead. Seedlings succumb quickly. You will see dead whitebark pines near the lookout site, killed by the rust. In some areas, Parks Canada plans to use prescribed burns to help eliminate diseased trees in the hope that healthy seedlings can

regenerate. Botanists consider the whitebark pine a "keystone" species. Its disappearance would have profound impacts on Clark's nutcrackers and grizzly bears, which rely on whitebark pine seeds for food.

At about km 1.5 you pass the ruin of a cabin that may date to the mining era. About 700 m later, the trail narrows and soon breaks out onto the beginning of the cliffs and ledges that are emblematic of Castle Mountain. Wildflowers thrive in these openings. You switchback a few times, and cut up through a loose gully. The trail enters a stand of whitebark pines and descends slightly to the lookout site.

Built in the early 1940s by conscientious objectors, the Castle Mountain fire lookout was one of seven in Banff National Park. In the 1970s, Parks Canada began using helicopters for smoke patrols and the lookout was abandoned. It burned in 1983 after hikers inadvertently set fire to it. Everything but the concrete footings of the main building has since been removed. Take care at the cliff edge.

The views from the lookout site are grand and varied, in no small part due to the tremendous variety of the structural geology included. The Simpson Pass Thrust angles across the Bow Valley just south of here, dividing the front ranges, to the south and east, from the main ranges, to the west and north. Storm Mountain (3158 m), just west of the fault, is prominent in the view southwest. You can look farther west through Vermilion Pass (1680 m) to the peaks of the Rockwall in Kootenay National Park. Looking north in the Bow Valley, the massive hulk of Mt. Temple (3544 m) dominates. But my favourite view is southeast into the sweeping maw of the Bow Valley, with the Sawback Range of the front ranges on the east, and Pilot Mountain (2954 m) in the Massive Range on the skyline in the west. It's a big view. Just think: during the peak of the Late Wisconsin Glaciation, ice filled this valley to just about the elevation where you now stand. If you are visiting in late June or early July on a windy day, you may see clouds of yellow tree pollen near the valley bottom.

You can pick out two cliffs on Castle Mountain – the lower, closer one is Cathedral Formation limestone; the upper one, set farther back, is Eldon Formation limestone. Between them is a terrace of Stephen Formation shale, known as Goat Ledge. Mountain goats are less common than in the past. The only time I have seen goats here is through binoculars, from the highway. A climber's hut on the terrace serves as a base for a series of classic rock climbing routes on the upper cliff.

Blue clematis

18. The Plain of the Six Glaciers

Near the Plain of the Six Glaciers teahouse

TRAIL THUMBNAIL

Trailhead

From Lake Louise Village, follow Lake Louise Drive 5.5 km to the parking areas at the lake. Paved walkways lead to the lakeshore (distance included in rating). Walk along the lakeshore and keep to it at the junction just beyond the Chateau.

You can walk to the trailhead from Lake Louise Campground/village via the Tramline or Louise Creek trails. Inquire at the park information centre. See map, p. 40.

Ratings
- Teahouse: harder, 5.9 km
- Victoria Glacier viewpoint: harder, 7.5 km

Special considerations: Warning! Avalanche and rockfall danger! Portions of this trail are routed beneath cliffs and across avalanche slopes. Use caution, especially early and late in the hiking season.

Best lighting: anytime

Nearby trails: 19 20 45

Lake Louise is an icon known the world over. It's a Canadian birthright to make a visit; to be able, later, to send a mental postcard to yourself saying: "I've been there." Although every superlative has been worn out describing the lake and its setting, it can be a magical place on a still morning. If that's the experience that you desire, go early, before the birds and the first blush of the sun. Go much later and you may find

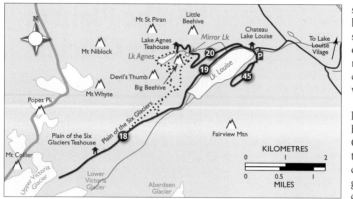

the parking areas and the trails teeming. But whatever you do and whenever you do it in the Rockies, go to the shore of Lake Louise.

The Plain of the Six Glaciers outing can be broken into four sections, each roughly equal in length: the lakeshore, the avalanche paths, the moraines, and the Victoria Glacier viewpoint. The lakeshore trail is carriage-width – widened in the early days of the Chateau so that patrons could visit the far end of the lake by horse and buggy. The width of the trail is an asset today, preventing a gridlock that might otherwise result. As you walk along the lake, you soon lose sight of Mt. Victoria (3464 m) – the centrepiece in the classic view – but gain better views of ice-capped Mt. Lefroy (3442 m) and Mt. Aberdeen (3152 m). The quartzite cliffs of Fairview Mountain (2744 m) fill the view to the south.

If you are hiking when the glacial melt season is on, note the milky green colour of the lake's surface – an effect enhanced by low-angled light in early morning and evening. Lake Louise is not a large lake, and it is fed almost entirely by glacial melt. If it weren't for the fact that it is 70 m deep, the lake's colour would typically verge on being gray – its waters choked with

sediment. The depth must help to disperse some of the sediment load, and shades of blue and green, caused by refraction of light by particles suspended in the lake water, are more typical.

At the far end of the lake, the trail passes beneath hundred-metre high cliffs of Gog Formation quartzite, that are popular with rock climbers. Look for the rock gardens at the base of the cliffs. The displays of red-stemmed saxifrage here are the best I have seen in the Rockies. Rounding the end of the lake, the trail draws alongside the delta at the lake's inlet. Look for the sediment plumes of rock flour spreading into the lake. You may see beavers here in the morning and early evening. This is the end of the Lake Louise Shoreline trail (outing 19). Those not wanting to carry on to the Plain of the Six Glaciers should turn back here.

You gain most of the elevation on this outing in two short climbs. The first of these takes you through subalpine forest and across the openings of several large avalanche paths on the lower slopes of Mt. Whyte. In the valley bottom to your left, look for a jumble of gray boulders – rockslide debris. Farther up the valley, the trail traverses a low cliff edge. Use care here if the rock is wet. Parks Canada has installed a handrail chain. If the exposure of the traverse is not to your liking, you can by-pass this section by dropping to the moraine on your left. Look for wild onion, shooting stars, star-flowered Solomon's seal, and false Solomon's seal nearby. Keep straight ahead at all trail junctions.

The "plain" is a 1 km-long, outwash area in the forefield of the Lower Victoria Glacier. From it, you

THE SNOW FOREST

The most common trees in this forest are Engelmann spruce and subalpine fir. The Engelmann spruce has scaly, reddish-brown bark, and spiky needles. It grows to be 20-30 m tall. The tree was named for George Engelmann, a German born doctor who moved to Missouri in the mid-1800s and became an adept botanist. The smooth, silvery bark of subalpine fir is often covered in resin blisters, which give this forest its sweet fragrance. The subalpine fir's shape is spire-like, to help shed the heavy snow load. Tree lichens drape the branches. A carpet of rootless plants called feathermosses thrives on the damp forest floor, along with the wildflowers, dwarf dogwood, and arnica.

The subalpine forest is sometimes called "the snow forest". More than 4 m of snow falls here each year. Common wildlife includes masked shrew, pack rat, least chipmunk, red squirrel, American marten, snowshoe hare, beaver, lynx, mule deer, wolverine, porcupine, great horned owl, spruce grouse, Clark's nutcracker and gray jay.

can see six glaciers: Lower Victoria, Upper Victoria, Aberdeen, Lefroy, Upper Lefroy, and Popes. (You can also see a seventh glacier, on the north peak of Mt. Victoria. It does not flow into this valley.) During the Late Wisconsin Glaciation, the combined flow of the six glaciers carved the valley that now contains Lake Louise. Since then, the ice has shrunk greatly in length and mass. Lower Victoria Glacier has receded almost 1.5 km in the last 180 years. By comparing the height of the moraines to the present level of the ice, you get a sense of how much ice mass has disappeared during that time.

You make the second climb on switchbacks just before the teahouse. Look for mountain goats and porcupines here, and for golden eagles overhead. The Plain of the Six Glaciers teahouse is at 2135 m. Constructed in 1924 by Swiss mountain guides employed by the Canadian Pacific Railway, the teahouse served as a hiker's destination and as a staging point for mountaineers. Today, lunch, refreshments and snacks are

GLACIER TYPES

Upper Victoria Glacier

Glacial ice forms in areas where more snow accumulates in winter than melts in summer. The shape of a glacier depends on its location and on features of the surrounding landscape. *Icefields* form on flat areas at high elevation. *Outlet valley glaciers* flow from icefields into valleys below. *Alpine valley glaciers* occupy high mountain valleys and are not fed by icefields. *Cirque glaciers* occupy and erode bowl-shaped depressions in mountainsides. A small cirque glacier is called a *pocket glacier*. *Catchment glaciers* form at high elevations where indentations in a mountainside trap windblown snow. If the indentation is deep, the glacier may be called a *niche glacier*. Where ice tumbles from a cliff edge and coalesces on the valley floor, the resulting body of ice is called a *regenerated glacier*.

Any of these glacier types can also be called a *hanging glacier* if the ice terminates on a cliff. A *rock glacier* is a lobe-shaped accumulation of rock that insulates permanent ice within. Except for icefields and outlet valley glaciers, you can see all these glacier types from the Plain of the Six Glaciers trail.

19. Lake Louise Shoreline

Lake Louise

Trailhead
As for the Plain of the Six Glaciers (outing 18).

Rating: easy, 2.6 km. Wheelchair ♿ accessible with assistance. The first 300 m is paved.

Best lighting: sunrise and morning

Nearby trails: ⑱ ⑳ ㊺

If you have only a short time to spend at Lake Louise, this is the outing for you. The trail follows the northwest shore to the inlet at the far end of the lake. (See p. 39-40 for a detailed description.) In 1882, pioneer guide and outfitter Tom Wilson made the first recorded visit to Lake Louise. He called it Emerald Lake. Two years later, the name was changed to Lake Louise to honour Louise Caroline Alberta, the fourth daughter of Queen Victoria, and wife of the Governor-General of Canada. The province of Alberta is also named for her.

Wilson's visit brought the lake to the attention of the Canadian Pacific Railway. In 1888, Wilson cut a trail to the lake. In 1890, the railway constructed the first chalet at the lake, and began to advertise its rustic shelter to clients who were well-heeled and willing to rough it a bit. From this building, which housed fewer than a dozen guests, the chalet underwent continual transformation. By the 1920s, it was known as the Chateau Lake Louise. *Chateau* (shah-TOE) is French for "mansion".

Lake Louise occupies a glacially carved valley adjacent to the continental divide. The lake is 2.4 km long, roughly 500 m wide, and 90 m deep. Its elevation is 1731 m – just over a mile above sea level. The surrounding mountains shade its waters for much of the year, and the lake's surface is frozen from November until June.

available in season. Overnight accommodation is no longer offered. If you are hiking early or late in the season and are counting on the teahouse being open, check at the Lake Louise information centre.

Victoria Glacier Viewpoint

The teahouse is the ultimate destination for many hikers. But if you have the stamina, consider extending this hike southwest for 1.6 km to the exposed crest of a lateral moraine that overlooks the Lower Victoria Glacier. Here, you are face to face with an ice age landscape. Massive limestone and quartzite cliffs glisten with glacial ice. Rockfalls and avalanches echo about. The moraine at trail's end is ice-cored. Use caution. Keep off the glacier.

In the view southwest, Abbot Pass (2920 m) separates Mt. Lefroy and Mt. Victoria. Abbot Pass Hut, built by Swiss guides in 1921-22, sits atop the pass. Although most of this building is made from stone quarried on-site, the guides packed more than two tonnes of supplies by horse across the glacier, and then winched and carried the freight the remaining distance to the pass. Named for Phillip Stanley Abbot, who died on Mt. Lefroy in 1896, the hut was the highest inhabitable building in Canada until the Neil Colgan Hut was constructed above Moraine Lake in 1982.

20. Lake Agnes

TRAIL THUMBNAIL

Trailhead

From Lake Louise Village, follow Lake Louise Drive 5.5 km to the parking areas at the lake. Paved walkways lead to the lakeshore (distance included in rating). Walk along the lakeshore to the junction just beyond the Chateau. The Lake Agnes trail veers uphill to the north (right).

You can walk to the trailhead from Lake Louise Campground/village via the Tramline or Louise Creek trails. Inquire at the park information centre. See map, p. 40.

Rating: harder, 4.0 km

Best lighting: anytime

Nearby trails: 🔟 🔟 🔟

Lake Agnes

The broad Lake Agnes trail climbs at a steady grade through subalpine forest for 1.6 km to a switchback that overlooks Lake Louise and the delta at its inlet. If the glacial melt season is on, you may see plumes of glacial sediment dispersing into the lake. The quartzite cliffs of Fairview Mountain (2744 m) rise across the lake. The trail narrows, turns sharply north and crosses a section of the wooden pipeline that provided drinking water from Lake Agnes to the Chateau during its early days. At the horse-hiker barrier, turn west (left) to reach Mirror Lake. The quartzite buttress of Big Beehive forms the backdrop for this pond, which is impounded by a moraine and has no visible surface outlet. The Canadian Pacific Railway (CPR) referred to Mirror Lake and nearby Lake Agnes as "the lakes in the clouds" in promotional material in the late 1800s.

Turn north (right) at the Mirror Lake junction, to switchback through larch trees on an avalanche slope on Mt. St. Piran. The mountain commemorates the English parish that was the birthplace of Willoughby Astley, the first manager of Chalet Lake Louise. In the 1890s, Astley supervised the cutting of many trails in the area, including this one. Turn west (left) at the first junction in 500 m. You reach the staircase climb to Lake Agnes 300 m later.

Walter Wilcox, an early visitor to Lake Agnes, called it "a wild tarn imprisoned by cheerless cliffs". True to Wilcox's description, the lake is a glacial tarn, 20.5 m deep. The wilderness character of the lake is now lost to the throngs of visitors, but the scene is impressive nonetheless. From south to north, Big

Beehive (2270 m), Devil's Thumb (2458 m), Mt. Whyte (2990 m), and Mt. Niblock (2976 m) form a tight cirque around the lake. Sir William Whyte was a vice-president of the CPR. John Niblock was a railway superintendent in the 1890s. The lake was their favourite fishing hole in the Rockies. Fishing is no longer allowed.

The Lake Agnes teahouse was one of a series constructed by the CPR to entice its hotel clients into the mountains. It built the first structure here in 1901. The present teahouse was privately reconstructed in 1981. It is typically open daily from mid-June to early October, serving lunch, refreshments, and baked goods. (Check at the Lake Louise information centre for details.) You can learn more about the history of the teahouses at an interpretive display on the south side of the lake's outlet. Look for striations – grooves etched by glacial ice – in the quartzite bedrock nearby.

The upper subalpine forest at Lake Agnes provides the seeds, berries, fungi, and insects eaten by Clark's nutcrackers, gray jays, golden-mantled ground squirrels, Columbian ground squirrels, least chipmunks, and red squirrels. (See p. 8.) Please do not feed these birds and animals. Your "kindness" may ultimately kill them. Reliant on handouts, the non-hibernating species may not cache enough food to tide them through the winter. Those that do hibernate may go to sleep run-down by junk food diets, never to reawaken.

WHO WAS AGNES?

Lake Agnes is named for Lady Susan Agnes Macdonald, wife of Canada's first prime minister, John A. Macdonald. Lady Agnes had been informed by the CPR that when she visited the lake in 1890, she would be the first woman to do so. Unfortunately, chalet manager Willoughby Astley, unaware of the arrangement, had guided another woman to the lake a few days earlier. By coincidence, the other woman's first name was Agnes. A member of the first lady's party defused the apparent consternation, pointing out that by giving the name "Agnes" to the lake, everyone would be kept happy.

21. Moraine Lake Rockpile

Moraine Lake

TRAIL THUMBNAIL

Trailhead
From Lake Louise Village, follow Lake Louise Drive 3 km to the Moraine Lake Road. Turn south (left). Follow this road 12 km to its end at Moraine Lake. The trailhead is at the southeast (left-hand) corner of the parking area. See map, p. 45.

Rating: easy, 450 m

Special considerations: Trails in the Moraine Lake area may be subject to a minimum group size. Enquire at the Lake Louise information centre.

Best lighting: morning

Nearby trails: **22** **23** **24**

The short walk to the crest of the Moraine Lake Rockpile yields a twenty-dollar view, and makes a fine place to contemplate two enduring controversies in the Rockies, one geological, the other historical.

Cross the bridge over the outlet of Moraine Lake. By late summer in most years, barely a trickle escapes. At the junction in 100 m, turn south (right) and follow the trail to the top of the knoll and the first point of controversy.

American explorer, Samuel Allen, first saw this lake from Mt. Temple, in 1893, and called in Heejee Lake. His colleague, Walter Wilcox, made the first visit to the lakeshore in 1899. Typical of his relationship with Allen, Wilcox gave the lake a different name. He called it Moraine Lake because he thought that the rockpile was a glacial moraine. Geologists now generally agree that the rockpile is rockslide debris from the peak called the Tower of Babel, although some think that the debris may have been transported on the surface of a glacier – which would make it a rockslide, a moraine, and a pile of erratics. So, perhaps Wilcox was wrong and right.

Meltwater from Wenkchemna Glacier feeds Moraine Lake. *Wenkchemna* (wenk-CHEM-nah) is a Stoney word that means "ten". And here is the second point of controversy. Samuel Allen named many of the peaks in the valley in 1894, reportedly using Stoney words for the numbers one to ten. For eighty years, the place was known as the Valley of the Ten Peaks. In 1979, the name Wenkchemna Peaks was officially applied to the mountains. But, ten peaks? I count sixteen that ring the valley. A few are unnamed, but even in Allen's time, at least one of those additional peaks was named – Mt. Temple.

Deltaform Mountain

Today, only peaks four, nine and ten – Tonsa, Neptuak and Wenkchemna – bear Allen's original names. Five of the peaks have been renamed for mountaineers (Fay, Little, Perren, Allen, Tuzo); one for its physical appearance (Deltaform); and another

ALL AGOG

The rockpile contains rocks of the Gog Group of formations. The quartzite member of this Group is a very hard, quartz-rich sandstone; the hardest rock in the central Rockies. It is composed of pebble-size, sand-size, and silt-size quartz particles eroded from the Canadian Shield, transported to the southwest by rivers, and deposited in ancient seas during the Early Cambrian, between 545 million-years-ago and 525 million-years-ago. The small spaces between the individual quartz grains are filled with tiny intergrown crystals of quartz that bind the sandstone together very tightly.

Green and black map lichens (*Rhizocarpon geographicum*, see p. 46) cover some exposures of Gog quartzite. Where protected from weathering, Gog quartzite is often white, pinkish or purplish; where exposed it can become stained brown and red with iron oxide. Fossil trilobites occur here and there in Gog rocks, but the fossilized burrowings of worms (*Planolites*, see photo) and of trilobites (*Rusphycos*) are much more common, as is iron pyrite ("fool's gold") – another source of colour. In some areas, deposits in the Gog Group are 4 km thick. In addition to quartzite boulders, the rockpile contains slabs of Gog siltstone, some of which are rippled, revealing the action of wavelets on a prehistoric shoreline.

PIKA CITY

Often heard but seldom seen, the shrill "eeep" of the tiny pika (PEE-kah or PIE-kah) will tell you that this member of the rabbit family is nearby. The pika lives among the blocks and rubble of boulderfields and rockslides. With a minuscule tail, big round ears, and a gray coat, it looks like a tennis ball with ears. Its folk name is "rock rabbit".

The pika inhabits a small home range. It scurries about during daytime, gathering grasses, lichens, leaves, and wildflowers; drying them on boulders then stashing the hay within the boulderfield. The pika does not hibernate. During the winter it uses rocky corridors under the snow to reach its food caches. It also eats partially digested pellets of its own dung. Yum.

A large boulderfield may be home to a colony of pikas, who take turns acting as lookouts. The pika's call warns its fellows of approaching danger. Eagles and hawks can pick-off a pika from above. More dangerous are martens and weasels that hunt the pika through its bouldery home. As the Earth's climate warms, pikas are encountering other stresses. Higher summer temperatures are cooking them in their rocky warrens; decreased winter snowpacks are causing them to freeze. As treeline shifts upwards, pikas that live at lower elevations and in warmer sites are dying off, unable to migrate quickly enough to where conditions are favourable.

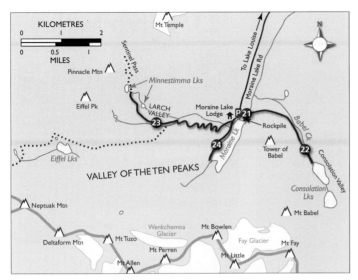

for a Canadian prime minister (Bowlen). Moraine Lake and the Wenkchemna Peaks were featured on the "verso" side of two engravings of the Canadian twenty dollar bill, in 1969 and 1979.

22. Lower Consolation Lake

TRAIL THUMBNAIL

Trailhead
From Lake Louise Village, follow Lake Louise Drive 3 km to the Moraine Lake Road. Turn south (left). Follow this road 12 km to its end at Moraine Lake. The trailhead, shared with Moraine Lake Rockpile, is at the southeast corner of the parking area.

Rating: moderate, 2.9 km

Special consideration: Trails in the Moraine Lake area may be subject to a minimum group size. Enquire at the Lake Louise information centre.

Best lighting: early morning, late afternoon

Nearby trails: 21 23 24

After his visit to Moraine Lake in 1899, Walter Wilcox made a side trip to the Consolation Lakes. To Wilcox, the environs of Moraine Lake had appeared sombre enough to merit the name Desolation Valley. In contrast, he perceived the valley into which this trail leads more favourably. Thus, the Consolation Valley and its lakes were named.

The trail initially contours around the base of the Moraine Lake Rockpile and passes through a quartzite boulderfield. Here, you walk on a natural rock causeway across the outlet of Moraine Lake. Keep straight ahead at the junction in 100 m. For the next two kilometres, the trail climbs gradually. As it swings southeast into the hanging valley that contains Consolation Lakes, the trail draws alongside Babel Creek. At km 1.6, the unmaintained route to Taylor Lake branches east (left). Keep straight ahead. Grouseberry carpets the forest floor. Look for spruce grouse and ruffed grouse.

For the last 500 m to the outlet of the lower lake, the trail borders a subalpine wet meadow, a frost hollow where cold air collects and stunts the vegetation. Elephant-head, fleabane, bracted lousewort, and vibrantly tinted paintbrush are among the flowers you may see in this opening in the forest.

The trail emerges near the shore of the lower lake to reveal a scene that Walter Wilcox described as, "One of the most beautiful pictures I have ever seen in the Rockies." At the far end of the valley, the glacier draped crags of Mt. Bident (3088 m) ("two teeth") and Quadra Mountain ("four summits") (3174 m), thrust skyward. Mt. Bell (2934 m) is to the east. The larch-covered slopes of Panorama Ridge (2872 m) flank the east side of the valley, while on the west rise the colossal cliffs of Mt. Babel (3103 m) and Mt. Fay (3234 m). In the foreground a jumble of lichen-covered, quartzite blocks dams the placid waters of Lower Consolation Lake. The view forward is a great one, but have a look over your shoulder at the massive bulk of Mt. Temple (3544 m) – sometimes it steals the show. The mountain, the 8th-highest in Alberta, was not named for a religious sentiment. Sir Richard Temple led a British scientific excursion to the Rockies in 1884.

The Consolation Lakes are tarns, occupying depressions gouged from the bedrock by glacial ice. The upper lake is slightly higher in elevation and concealed from view, a kilometre of rough and wet boulder hopping up the valley.

23. Larch Valley

Lower Consolation Lake

TRAIL THUMBNAIL

Trailhead
From Lake Louise Village, follow Lake Louise Drive 3 km to the Moraine Lake Road. Turn south (left). Follow this road 12 km to its end at Moraine Lake. The trail begins on the lakeshore in front of the lodge. See map, p. 45.

Rating: harder, 4.5 km

Special considerations: Trails in the Moraine Lake area may be subject to a minimum group size. Enquire at the Lake Louise information centre. If you plan to hike in larch season, go early or late in the day.

Best lighting: anytime

Nearby trails: ㉑ ㉒ ㉔

ROCK LICHENS: OLD TIMERS

A rock lichen is a rootless, leafless lifeform – a symbiotic relationship that contains fungus and algae. The fungus houses the algae, while the algae produces food for both. One byproduct of this relationship is humic acid, which accelerates the chemical breakdown of rock and the creation of soil. Rock lichens grow outward at an incredibly slow, consistent rate, so the diameter of a lichen patch can be used to estimate its age. It is thought that some rock lichen colonies in the Rockies may have begun life at the end of the Late Wisconsin Glaciation, 12,000 years ago. Two of the more common rock lichen species are the brilliant orange *Xanthoria elegans*, found on a variety of rock types; and the green and black, map lichen (*Rhizocarpon geographicum*, pictured), often found on quartzite boulders, such as in the Consolation Lakes valley.

From the trailhead kiosk in front of the lodge, follow the trail southwest for 35 m to a junction. The Sentinel Pass-Wenkchemna Pass trail branches north (right), and immediately begins its steep climb. In the next 2.5 km, the trail gains 352 m of elevation to the entrance to Larch Valley. You can see Moraine Lake through the trees. Listen for hermit thrushes, yellow-rumped warblers, and golden-crowned sparrows. The climb – which takes you to the crest of an ancient lateral moraine of the Wenkchemna Glacier – concludes with a series of ten switchbacks that lead to a trail junction and a well-placed bench. The trail to Larch Valley and Sentinel Pass branches north (right).

Larch Valley occupies a broad glacial cirque, centred on a bedrock fault south of Sentinel Pass. The trail winds through the lower valley and crosses a footbridge to a meadow. As early morning visitors

24. Moraine Lake Lakeshore

Trailhead
As for Larch Valley (outing 23). See map, p. 45.

Rating: easy, 1.2 km

Special consideration: Trails in the Moraine Lake area may be subject to a minimum group size. Enquire at the Lake Louise information centre.

Best lighting: morning

Nearby trails: ㉑ ㉒ ㉓

This outing follows the forested shore of Moraine Lake to its inlet, providing fine views of the Wenkchemna Peaks.

Minnestima Lake

will discover, the meadow is a frost hollow where cold air collects. Trees along the northern edge of the meadow display branches stunted by the cold. The meadow contains earth hummocks, caused by repeated freezing and thawing of the soil when it was underlaid by permafrost. To the southwest, you have a great view of Deltaform Mountain (3426 m; photo p. 44) – highest of the Wenkchemna Peaks, the 24th-highest mountain in Alberta, and the 39th-highest peak in B.C. American explorer, Walter

Wilcox, named the mountain for its resemblance to delta – Δ – the fourth letter of the Greek alphabet.

The trail swings north and climbs to treeline, passing some ancient larches and glades filled with western anemone. Following several bear encounters here in the early 2000s, Parks Canada pruned the trees at trailside to improve sight lines. Samuel Allen, a companion of Walter Wilcox, called the lakes in the tundra below Sentinel Pass, Minnestimma Lakes – Stoney for "sleeping waters". From the outlet of the upper lake, the trail heads east and begins the stiff climb along the lower flank of Mt. Temple to the switchbacks that lead into Sentinel Pass – a route for experienced hikers, described in *Classic Hikes in the Canadian Rockies.*

LYALL'S LARCH – GOLD IN THE HILLS

Larch Valley is named for the tree species, Lyall's (LIE-alls) larch – also called subalpine larch, and alpine larch. Of the three larch species in Canada, Lyall's is the least extensive in range. In the Rockies, you won't find it north of Clearwater Pass, 28 km north of Lake Louise. It grows only in the upper subalpine forest, frequently forming pure stands at treeline. The mature tree is 5m-10 m tall and has a ragged top, and brown bark highlighted with reddish-purple tones. Bright green needles grow from black, knobby twigs that are covered in dark woolly down. The wood burns easily, but because the tree usually grows in rocky terrain, forest fires rarely consume larches. Some trees in Larch Valley may be more than 400 years old.

The Lyall's larch is a deciduous conifer – it sheds its needles in late summer. Then the tree becomes dormant with the buds for next year's growth already formed. Before shedding, larch needles turn golden yellow, transforming the treeline forests of the southern Rockies into a wonderful sight. Visitors flock to Larch Valley during this time by the hundreds. In 2011, Parks Canada closed the Moraine Lake road several times in response to the gridlock. Eugene Bourgeau catalogued the tree. Its taxonomic name, *Larix lyalli*, commemorates David Lyall, a Scottish surgeon and naturalist who explored in the Arctic, Antarctic, New Zealand, and British North America in the mid-1800s.

25. Lake Helen

Helen Creek meadows

Crowfoot Glacier

TRAIL THUMBNAIL

Trailhead
At the parking area on the east side of the Icefields Parkway, 32.5 km north of Highway 1; opposite the Crowfoot Glacier viewpoint.

Rating: harder, 6.0 km or 6.9 km

Special considerations: The trail traverses prime grizzly bear habitat. You may share the route with equestrians.

Best lighting: anytime

Nearby trails: 26 27 28 29

Of the many "wildflower gardens" on trails in the Rockies, few match the meadows south of Lake Helen during the height of summer. You ascend steadily for the first 3 km as the trail contours around the south end of an outlying ridge of Cirque Peak. In 2000, Parks Canada set a prescribed burn above the trail to help regenerate whitebark pine. From treeline you have great views into the Bow Valley. Mt. Hector (3394 m) is the prominent glacier-clad peak, 14 km south.

Crowfoot Glacier is west, above the outlet of Bow Lake. Early travellers in the Bow Valley called it "Trident Glacier" because its terminus featured three separate lobes of ice, two of which draped the headwall toward Bow Lake. The present name likens the glacier's form to the foot of the American crow, which has three splayed toes. The extent of glacial recession makes the origin of the name less obvious today, as climate warming has trimmed two of the "toes". One lobe of ice fell off in the 1920s, in an avalanche reportedly (but not likely) heard at Lake Louise.

After a series of switchbacks, you make a hairpin turn north into the valley of Helen Creek. Cirque Peak (2993 m) is straight ahead. The castellated summits of Dolomite Peak (2950 m) tower over Helen Creek to the east. The true summit of Dolomite Peak is the fourth tower from the north. It was first climbed in 1930. Some of the other towers were first ascended by workers employed in the construction of the original Icefields Parkway, between 1931 and 1939.

The meadows nearby are a sea of colour in mid- to late-July, packed with an array of upper subalpine wildflowers: western anemone, bracted lousewort, paintbrush, fleabane, glacier lily, Sitka valerian,

LAKE HELEN OR HELEN LAKE?

Most locals, and those who make the trail signs, refer to Lake Helen as "Helen Lake". In the case of geographical features (other than rivers and passes) that were named in English to honour people, the generic part of the name is supposed to come first, followed by the specific. So... Lake Louise, Mt. Victoria, Mt. Stephen. When the feature is not named for a person, the arrangement is supposed to be the other way around: Glacier Lake, Castle Mountain, Saskatchewan Glacier. Scan your maps and you'll find many exceptions to the rule, but Lake Helen follows it. "Helen" was a daughter of H.P. Nicholls, who, in 1898, was a member of the first white party to cross Dolomite Pass. Nichols also named nearby lakes, one for his wife, Alice, and one for another daughter, Katherine.

Dolomite Peak

Hoary marmot

mountain heather, yellow columbine, and arnica. After the first frosts of August, the pungent stench of valerian fills the air – one of the harbingers of autumn in the Rockies.

The trail crosses the base of a quartzite rockslide – a good place to look for hoary marmots – and then descends into a ravine. Rock-hop the stream and continue north on a braided trail across the alpine tundra toward Lake Helen. Braids develop when hikers and horses avoid muddy sections of trail. As few as 20 pairs of feet travelling across untracked

tundra may create a permanent trail. Despite trail restoration efforts, thoughtless hikers and riders continue to beat new braids into the meadows here. Please – get your boots wet and muddy – keep to the most beaten path, thereby preventing the development of additional braids, and allowing the marginal braids to recover.

Lake Helen sits in a quartzite pocket. Golden eagles use the cliffs nearby as nesting grounds. The knoll just south of the lake provides inspiring views south to the Bow Valley. After leaving the lake, I often linger here before heading home – wringing every alpine moment from the day.

THE CROWFOOT DYKE

The Crowfoot Dyke is the most accessible exposure of igneous rock in the central Rockies. You can see it on the Icefields Parkway – a dull, green outcrop of diabase – 1.1 km south of the Lake Helen trailhead. A dyke is an intrusion of molten rock that flowed underground along cracks in existing sedimentary rock, and then consolidated. The Crowfoot Dyke formed between 570 million-years-ago and 730 million-years-ago. It extends 2.8 km east from the outlet of Bow Lake to the banks of Helen Creek, passing beneath this trail.

Over the Top

The footing can be loose and the way difficult to discern when snow-covered, but when the headwall beyond the lake is clear, you may want to push on for an even better view. Follow the east shore of the lake through the marmot grounds to a switchback ascent that climbs to the south ridge of Cirque Peak. You gain 137 m in just 900 m, but it's worth it – the trail summit reveals stunning views eastward onto the tundra of Dolomite Pass.

26. Bow Glacier Falls

Bow Glacier Falls

TRAIL THUMBNAIL

Trailhead
West side of the Icefields Parkway, 35.1 km north of Highway 1. Follow the Num-ti-Jah Lodge access road west for 400 m to the public parking area. Walk the gravel road west toward the lake (distance included in rating), curving northwest (right) in front of the lodge to the trailhead on the lakeshore. See map, p. 49.

Rating: harder, 4.0 km or 5.0 km

Best lighting: before early afternoon

Nearby trails: ㉕ ㉗ ㉘ ㉙

For more than a century, the shores of Bow Lake have been a favourite stopping place. No wonder. This outing is packed with variety – it offers a lakeshore stroll with fine views, an ascent alongside a canyon, a rough track across a moraine field, and a spray-filled vista of a thundering, 80-m high waterfall.

As you walk past the lodge, you may see barn swallows overhead; they nest in the various buildings. The rocky and rooted trail follows the north shore of Bow Lake, crossing the runouts of avalanche slopes and rockslides at the base of Mt. Jimmy Simpson (2966 m). Most of the rocks are quartzite of the Gog Group of formations (see p. 44). Look and listen for pikas. Flag trees dot the lakeshore. Bearing branches only on their leeward sides, they "flag" the prevailing wind from the Wapta Icefield. A superb array of wildflowers colours the trail margins. Look for the intricate blooms of shooting stars. When the lake level is high, you may get your feet wet on a few short sections.

You reach the delta on the west shore of the lake at km 2.4. A short section of trail here may be flooded, especially in late afternoon on a hot day. Skirt the wet area by keeping right, against the base of the cliffs. Elephant-head grows in the glacial silt at the water's edge. The trail carries on along the inlet stream. I have seen dippers and a solitary, solitary sandpiper here.

You climb over the first of three forested moraines and drop back to the floodplain. Cross a small tributary stream on a log bridge. The trail hugs the stream bank to skirt a second forested moraine 400 m later. If the water level is high, an alternate trail climbs over and descends the moraine. Keep

LIONS AND TIGERS AND... ZEBRAS?

The Middle Cambrian formations of the central Rockies contain a colourful assortment of rocks. The moraines on this hike are one of the better places to go on safari to appreciate them. Gray Eldon Formation limestone provides the surface onto which the Mixmaster of the Bow Glacier has dumped, among others: two-tone, tan-coloured Cathedral Formation dolomite (lion rock); black Cathedral limestone striped with apricot dolomite (tiger rock – photo); and gray Lyell Formation limestone striped with buff dolomite (zebra rock). Please remember: pick with your eyes and camera only.

Bow Glacier, 1897

Bow Glacier, 2002

to creekside for 200 m to where the trail reaches a third forested moraine. Skirt this along the creek or climb over it. Another 400 m stretch of floodplain, carpeted with mountain avens, intervenes before the trail delivers you to the mouth of Bow Canyon.

The climb alongside the canyon is withering but short. Use care if the trail is wet or snowy – especially on the way down. The canyon is about 20 m deep, and is carved into Eldon Formation limestone. Its central portion features a chockstone that spans the chasm. The trail levels near the upper end of the canyon, with a pleasing view ahead – past an ancient whitebark pine – to Bow Glacier Falls. Carry on for 50 m to the viewpoint on the crest of the Little Ice Age moraine of Bow Glacier.

Bow Glacier is one of four principal outlet glaciers of the 40 km^2 Wapta Icefield. The viewpoint marks the maximum of the glacier's most recent advance, which was about 1850. The terminal moraine of that advance is smeared against the knoll under your feet. Yellow columbine, pink wintergreen, white camas, daisy fleabane, and arrow-leaved groundsel grow at the viewpoint. Be careful not to trample them. If you've had enough, turn back here.

Moraine Viewpoint to Falls

The viewpoint provides the postcard shot of the falls, but for the full sensory experience, you'll want to carry on across the forefield for 1 km to immerse yourself in the spray. Head north (right) from the viewpoint a short distance, then descend sharply west (left) from the moraine crest to the forefield. A promising track heads toward the falls, but where a tributary stream comes down from Mt. Thompson (3089 m), piling rubble into the valley, the route becomes vague. Rock-hop and boulder-hop as required. You may get your boots wet, but the direction to your destination is obvious, and is well worth soggy feet. Pick your way carefully to avoid trampling the moisture-loving plants that grow here.

Any of the thousands of boulders at the base of the falls can serve as your ultimate stopping place. The closer you get to the stream, the wetter you will likely be, as spray from the falls coats the area – not such a bad thing on a hot day. But if it's cold, watch for ice on the rocks. Keep off snow patches. Lesser waterfalls cascade over the colourful, banded cliffs to the north. This amphitheatre was one of the honing grounds for waterfall ice climbers in the late 1970s, during the development of that pursuit.

DELTAS

Many streams and rivers in the Rockies are glacially fed. Where the angle of a stream bed is relatively steep, the water moves cobbles and gravels. Where the angle lessens, larger particles drop out of the flow, creating a rocky, fan-shaped landform. If this landform occurs on the side of a valley, it is called an alluvial fan. If it occurs on the shore of a lake, it is known as a delta. The name comes from the resemblance of the landform to delta – Δ – the fourth letter of the Greek alphabet.

Bow Lake features two deltas. The most obvious is on the northwest shore, where meltwater from Bow Glacier enters the lake. The constant deposition of silt and gravel, the shifting of the meltwater streams, and the cold air channelled along the water all combine to hinder the growth of vegetation.

Less obvious is the delta where the lodge sits. The stream that created this delta is now but a trickle and no longer transports glacial sediments. Vegetation has stabilized the underlying gravels. This delta was probably created thousands of years ago by a meltwater surge from a glacier near Bow Pass. The glacier has since disappeared.

27. Bow Summit

Peyto Lake

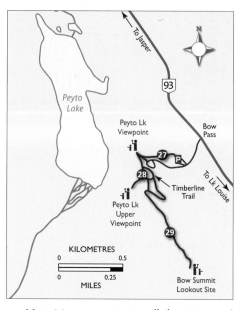

TRAIL THUMBNAIL

Trailhead
West side of the Icefields Parkway, 40.7 km north of Highway 1. Park in the first parking area on the north (right) side of the Bow Summit access road. Wheelchair ♿ access is available from the parking area at the end of the access road.

Rating: moderate, 600 m, paved

Best lighting: anytime

Nearby trails: ㉕ ㉖ ㉘ ㉙

With an elevation of 2,069 m, Bow Summit is the highest point in Canada crossed by a paved road that is open year-round. This dividing point between the Bow River and the Mistaya River offers three outings that explore a classic treeline environment.

The first thing that you will probably notice as you step out of your vehicle is that it's colder than it was at Lake Louise or Banff. Bow Summit's elevation alone will typically create a temperature a few degrees cooler than at Lake Louise. The 40 km² mass of the adjacent Wapta Icefield will cool the air more. So don't be surprised if the day has a wintry feel, even in mid-summer. Dress warmly, especially if it's windy. Carry an extra clothing layer.

Most visitors are content to walk the 600 m paved path to the lower Peyto Lake viewpoint, where a platform provides the most spectacular trailside view of a glacial lake in the Canadian Rockies. Almost 300 m below, Peyto Lake, 5th- largest in Banff National Park, stretches before you. The lake is 3 km long and 1 km wide, and is fed by meltwaters from Peyto Glacier, one of six outlet valley glaciers of the Wapta Icefield. It's a marvellous vista; so good it will often be elbow-to-elbow if you are visiting mid-day. However, if you linger you will eventually have the viewpoint to yourself for at least a minute or two. The throngs that arrive by bus do not stay long.

Peyto Lake, Glacier, and Peak commemorate Bill Peyto (PEE-toe), noted trail guide, and later park warden. An immigrant from England, Peyto arrived in the Rockies in the early 1890s. He readily adapted to the backwoods life, hunting, trapping, and staking

PEYTO LAKE: PARTICLE THEORY

Where the meltwater from Peyto Glacier enters the lake, the velocity of the water decreases and the rubble drops out, creating the delta that now encroaches on the lake. You may see sediment plumes. Most of these particles eventually settle, but the extremely fine particles (<0.01 mm), known as rock flour, remain suspended in the water and are responsible for the remarkable colour of the lake. This happens because the rock flour particles scatter, rather than absorb, the blue and green wavelengths of light. Geologist Ben Gadd speculates that the brilliance of the colours may be due to a shimmering caused by the billions of suspended crystalline particles.

28. Timberline Trail and Peyto Lake Upper Viewpoint

Trailhead
As for Bow Summit (outing 27).

Rating: moderate, 1.9 km return from lower parking area. Add Peyto Lake upper viewpoint: 350 m return.

Best lighting: anytime

Nearby trails: 25 26 27 29

Two paved trails head south from the Peyto Lake lower viewpoint (outing 27). The trail straight ahead is the beaten path to and from the bus drop-off, and may also be used for wheelchair access. The right-hand trail skirts the bus parking area and delivers you in 125 m to the Timberline Trail at a sign that says "Explore". (Do not descend the unpaved trail that branches west, 40 m from the viewing platform.) The Timberline Trail makes a 600 m loop. Take the right-hand trail at the "Explore" sign and hike counter-clockwise. Interpretive panels describe some of the species that live in treeline environments, and their coping mechanisms for abiding on the edge of perpetual winter. Please keep to established trails.

These slopes are buffeted by glacially cooled winds that deliver 6 m of snowfall annually, and cause repeated freezing and thawing of the ground. The treeline forest is comprised of Engelmann spruce, subalpine fir, and whitebark pine. On the lower slopes near the parking area, the trees are widely scattered and of normal stature. But on the upper slopes, stunted tree islands are all that can grow. Why? These upper slopes are more than twice as windy. Wind desiccates vegetation, making growth difficult and slow. The gnarled and twisted trees that result are known as *kruppelholz*, German for "crippled wood".

Subalpine fir has smooth, silvery bark. It is more tolerant of harsh conditions than is Engelmann spruce. Thus, firs are usually more numerous at treeline. They are able to take root either by seeding or by "skirting" – sending down shoots from their branches. These trees spend so much of the year covered in snow, they develop snow mould – a black growth that covers the lower branches.

The upright spruce have a more scaly,

reddish-brown bark, and grow from seeds that grow from the shelter provided by the mats subalpine fir. The spruce frequently display branches only on their eastern sides. In doing so they are said to "flag" the prevailing wind.

Despite waxy needles and thick sap, the new tree growth of each summer cannot withstand the cold winds of the following winter. Only branches that are insulated within the snowpack are spared this natural pruning. The firs have adapted to this harsh reality by growing horizontally, where their branches will remain protected by the snow. Dense, twisted mats result – classic "shintangle".

Snowdrifts accumulate in the lee of the tree islands. These drifts often take most of the summer to melt, providing a constant water supply for moisture-loving wildflowers in an area where only one quarter of the precipitation falls as rain.

Within the treeline forest are the flower-filled glades for which Bow Summit is renowned. One of the first wildflowers to bloom here is the glacier lily. Its nodding, yellow flower will often poke through receding snowbanks and ice crusts. The bulb is a favourite food of grizzly bears. Other common wildflowers are valerian, yellow columbine, paintbrush, bracted lousewort, fleabanes, arnica, black tipped groundsel, white globeflower, mountain heather (white, pink, and yellow), everlasting, and varieties of anemone (an-EMM-owe-nee); including western anemone (photo, above) and Drummond's anemone. Anemone means "wind flower".

At Bow Summit, the perennial wildflowers have but six weeks to resurrect themselves, flower, and seed. They do this with energy stored in their bulbs, often permitting growth at temperatures below freezing. Without such adaptation, a few shorter than average summers would kill them off. The wildflowers are usually at their peak in the third week of July.

After about 150 m, at an interpretive panel, an unmarked trail heads west (right) for 175 m, side-hilling and descending slightly to a quartzite bluff – the Peyto Lake upper viewpoint. As you might expect, it's a loftier view here than down below, and, without the bus traffic, much less busy.

Back on the Timberline Trail, you reach the apex of the loop about 300 m from the "Explore" sign. Swing north (left) to complete the loop. To carry on to Bow Summit Lookout site, angle south (right) onto the dirt track of the old fireroad.

29. Bow Summit Lookout Site

Mistaya Valley from lookout site

Bow Lake

Trailhead
As for Bow Summit (outing 27). See map, p. 52.

Rating: harder, 3.1 km from lower parking area. Add Peyto Lake upper viewpoint: 350 m return.

Best lighting: anytime

Nearby trails: ㉕ ㉖ ㉗ ㉘

From the apex of the Timberline Trail (outing 28), the fireroad makes a couple of long switchbacks before heading south through treeline, climbing steadily. After about 1.4 km, the road descends into a rocky basin where a stream drains a snowmelt pond. Rock-hop the stream and look for mountain marsh marigold. The paintbrush that grow here have a deep crimson hue. Hermit thrushes often sing their ethereal songs from the trees nearby. The sinuous climb resumes to where the road curves east around a rock-slide. Trail's end is on a meadowed knoll on this shoulder of Mt. Jimmy Simpson, at an elevation of 2315 m – the former site of the fire lookout.

The drive along the Icefields Parkway in the Mistaya Valley features the finest parade of roadside peaks in the Rockies. From the road, you see the peaks on the west side of the valley best. From this lookout site, you obtain detailed views of the peaks on the east side of the valley. Among these, in the middle-distance, is the chaos of summits that comprise Mt. Murchison (3337 m). Closer are Mt. Noyes (3085 m) and Mt. Weed (3080 m), each named for members of the Appalachian Mountain Club who climbed in this area in the late 1890s. To the east and southeast, you have fine views of Observation Peak (3174 m), Cirque Peak (2993 m), and Dolomite Peak (2950 m).

The lookout builders were not, of course, motivated solely by scenery. Although not quite in line of sight with the next closest lookout to the south – Little Beehive – Bow Summit was in line of sight with two lookouts to the north – Sarbach and Sunset. This alignment provided almost complete coverage of a 140 km length of the Bow, Mistaya, and upper North Saskatchewan Valleys. I have, on a particularly fine day, discerned from here the summit of Sunwapta Peak, just over 100 km to the north, in Jasper National Park.

By following beaten paths south for 175 m, you are rewarded with superb views of Bow Lake and Mt. Hector (3394 m), Bow Peak (2868 m), and Crowfoot Mountain (3050 m). If you plunk down, keep an eye on your lunch. You are in the middle of a marmot colony. Be vigilant for another reason. Grizzly bears frequent this area, in quest of marmot snacks.

mineral claims. Peyto began work as a trail guide in 1892 or 1893. He led several important mountaineering expeditions, including the ones that discovered Columbia Icefield in 1898, and that made the first ascent of Mt. Assiniboine in 1901. During explorer Walter Wilcox's 1896 expedition, which camped at Bow Lake, Peyto disappeared one evening to sleep in solitude near this viewpoint. Later, upon seeing the lake from here, Wilcox christened it "Peyto's Lake". The Mistaya (miss-TAY-yah) Valley fills the view north. *Mistaya* is reportedly Stoney for "grizzly bear".

Least chipmunks, golden-mantled ground squirrels, and a few pikas populate the viewpoint area. Columbian ground squirrels inhabit the meadows nearby. The chatter of red squirrels will greet you from the treetops. See p. 8 for photos of these animals.

30. Mistaya Canyon

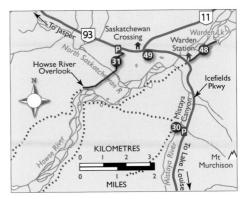

Mistaya Canyon

Trailhead
Parking area on the west side of the Icefields Parkway, 70.1 km north of Highway 1; 5.1 km south of the junction with Highway 11.

Rating: moderate, 450 m

Special consideration: The canyon is unfenced. Use caution. Stay on the bridge.

Best lighting: afternoon

Nearby trails: ③① ④⑧ ④⑨

As ice-age glaciers retreated at the end of the Late Wisconsin Glaciation, the mouth of the Mistaya (miss-TAY-yah) Valley was left hanging above the floor of the North Saskatchewan Valley. At first, the Mistaya River probably plunged into the North Saskatchewan River as a waterfall. Over a period of 12,000 years, the river, loaded with coarse glacial silt, has eroded a deep and narrow canyon into the Eldon Formation limestone of the step at the mouth of the valley.

The trail descends to a sturdy bridge, offering a safe place from which to appreciate the canyon and an unusual feature. Downstream, the canyon opening makes a series of short, symmetrical dogleg turns. The river has taken the line of least resistance to follow what geologists call a joint set – a system of parallel cracks in the bedrock. The rock terraces flanking the canyon feature wonderful potholes – circular depressions drilled into the rock by boulders caught within the stream flow for long periods of time. You may also see a natural arch. Stoney First Peoples reportedly crossed the canyon here on fallen trees, rather than attempting a dangerous ford of the river upstream or downstream. "Danger" is all relative, I suppose.

Natural arch

Upstream from the canyon, Mt. Sarbach (3155 m) is prominent. Mountaineer John Norman Collie named this fine peak for Peter Sarbach, the first Swiss guide to climb in Canada. He led Collie on the mountain's first ascent in 1897.

You would normally expect to find a damp forest near a canyon. However, the wall of mountains that borders the western flank of the Mistaya Valley creates a rain shadow in this area. The forest at trailside is dry, and is dominated by lodgepole pine, with an undergrowth of buffaloberry and juniper.

Mistaya is a Stoney word that reportedly means "grizzly bear". For a while, the river was known as Bear Creek. Explorer Mary Schäffer renamed it Mistaya River in 1907 in order to avoid duplication with the multitude of other Bear Creeks and Bear Rivers in the Rockies and elsewhere.

BLACK BEAR

Although Mistaya means "grizzly bear", you are more likely to see a black bear near Mistaya Canyon. Black bears were formerly assumed to be numerous in the Canadian Rockies. However, studies have indicated that there may be as few as 50-60 black bears in Banff National Park. Unlike the grizzly bear, which ranges through a variety of habitats from valley bottom to mountaintop, the black bear prefers valley bottoms in the montane life zone, which account for only 5 percent of the park's area.

The black bear eats berries, leaves, insects, and carrion – 75 percent of its diet is vegetarian. Males are solitary; the females usually spend two years caring for cubs. The black bear is dormant for most of each winter, denning in a natural shelter on lower mountainsides – typically a cave, an overhang or a fallen tree. The animal is a more adept tree climber than the grizzly bear, and will use this tactic to avoid danger. Although its coat is generally black, sometimes with a white patch on the chest, cinnamon-coloured bears occur in the Rockies, especially in Waterton Lakes National Park. There are also records of albino (white) bears.

Because their prime habitat is also our "prime habitat", black bears get into "trouble" with people more often than do grizzly bears. If a bear consumes unnatural food, it loses its innate wariness of people. This is the kind of bear that breaks into vehicles or raids picnic tables in campgrounds. Park staff will use aversive conditioning – rubber bullets, bear bangers, bear dogs – to attempt to dissuade these bears. If a bear persists, it may be live-trapped and relocated.

Unfortunately, habituated bears usually return to where the pickings are easier. Including vehicle strikes, between 1990 and 2009, 449 black bears died as a result of interactions with people in the mountain national parks. Eighty percent of these deaths were on highways and railways. Although they reproduce more frequently and abundantly than do grizzly bears, the replacement rate of black bears cannot keep pace with this kind of population drain.

What can you do to help? Stay in your vehicle if you see a bear. Do not stop. Take photographs with a telephoto lens. Do not approach or feed a bear. Do not leave food or packs unattended. Store your camping food in the locked trunk of your vehicle or in campground storage facilities.

31. Howse River Overlook

The Howse Valley

TRAIL THUMBNAIL

Trailhead
Glacier Lake trailhead, on the west side of the Icefields Parkway, 1.2 km north of the junction with Highway 11, 76.4 km north of Highway 1, 148.8 km south of Highway 16. See map, p. 55.

Rating: moderate, 2.5 km

Best lighting: morning and evening

Nearby trails: 30 48 49

While fur trader and map-maker David Thompson waited for snow to melt in the mountains in 1807, he spent two weeks camped in the lower part of the Howse Valley. Follow Thompson's footsteps along this trail to a piece of low elevation wilderness unlike any other in the Rockies.

The trailhead is in a dense lodgepole pine forest, the product of the Survey Peak Burn of July 1940. The fire consumed 40 km², and forced closure of the Icefields Parkway a few weeks after its official

Double bladderpod

opening. Buffaloberry and bearberry, whose fruits are favourite foods of bears, are common in the undergrowth near the trailhead. I often see ruffed grouse along the first kilometre of trail.

The trail descends a series of ancient river terraces to an I-beam bridge over the North Saskatchewan River at km 1.1. Here, the river's course has been captured by a bedrock fault, creating a small canyon. The North Saskatchewan River is 1216 km long. More than 80 percent of the water it carries to Hudson Bay (via Lake Winnipeg and the Nelson River), originates in glaciers. The 49 km section within Banff National Park was proclaimed a Canadian Heritage River in 1989. Just downstream from here was the location of the fabled "crossing" – where expeditions in the late 1800s and early 1900s confronted the fords of three rivers in succession: the Mistaya, the Howse, and the North Saskatchewan. The trail climbs away from the river and continues through pine forest to the edge of a terrace above the Howse River at km 2.3. Walk a few hundred metres east along the terrace to take in the view.

This terrace "feels" different than most at similar locations in the Rockies. Usually what's immediately underfoot on the bank of a glacial river is the rubble of moraine. Not here. This riverbank, and those across the valley, contain silt called loess (LURSS). *Loess* is a German word that means, not surprisingly, "loose". Scoured over millennia from the valley floor by the prevailing southwest wind, the loess has piled here into dune-like mounds where the river turns east. Calcium carbonate derived from the surrounding rocks helps cement the resulting mounds together. These loess deposits are the most extensive in Banff, and are colonized by wildflowers that prefer arid habitat, such as double bladderpod (*Physaria didymocarpa*). This showy member of the mustard family is also known by the folk name, twinpod, because its fruit divides into two sections while on the plant. It grows in circular patches or in clumps; its stems can be flat-lying but often turn upwards at the end. The lower Howse Valley is also noted for its kettle lakes. Seven appear on the topographic map.

To the southwest, Mt. Outram (OOT-rum) (3245 m) commemorates reverend and mountaineer James Outram, who made first ascents of many high peaks in the Rockies in 1901 and 1902. Tucked behind Mt. Outram is Mt. Forbes (3617 m), the 7th-highest mountain in the Rockies, the 4th-highest in Alberta, the 2nd-highest south of the Columbia Icefield, and the highest mountain entirely within Banff National Park. James Outram teamed up with the party of mountaineer J.N. Collie, to make the first ascent. James Hector of the Palliser Expedition named the mountain – not for the eminent geologist of his day – but for Edward Forbes, Hector's professor of natural history at the University of Edinburgh. To the south, the craggy summit of Mt. Sarbach (3155 m) rises above its northwest-trending scree ridge. Collie was in the first party to climb this peak, too.

THE HOWSE VALLEY: A ONCE AND FUTURE HIGHWAY?

As its heavily braided appearance suggests, most of the flow of the Howse River comes from glaciers. Meltwater from three icefields – Freshfield, Mons, and Lyell – that cover more than 100 km², combine to form the river. Named for Joseph Howse, a trader who crossed it in 1810, Howse Pass (1530 m), at the head of the valley, was part of the first fur trade route across the Rockies. Pioneered by traders La Gasse, Le Blanc, Jaco Finlay, and David Thompson, it saw use from 1800 until 1810 when Piikani First Peoples blocked it. The Howse Valley is a haven for many large mammals, including elk, mule deer, moose, black bears, grizzly bears, wolves, mountain goats, and coyotes.

Although the Banff National Park Management Plan precludes the construction of new roads, two communities east of the Rockies – Red Deer and Rocky Mountain House – continually advocate extending Highway 11 across Howse Pass. (It doesn't help that Parks Canada itself promoted the idea in 1971.) Such a highway would decrease transportation times and costs between some places in Alberta and B.C., but would destroy one of the last wilderness enclaves in the Rockies while diverting only eight percent of the traffic from Highway 1. An economic analysis of the proposed highway's effects has also shown a net economic loss for communities in central Alberta, because the road would divert traffic from the Highway 2 corridor. The idea of constructing a road over Howse Pass has very little support in B.C.

32. Nigel Pass

Nigel Pass

Brazeau Valley Overlook

TRAIL THUMBNAIL

Trailhead
Parking area on the east side of the Icefields Parkway at Nigel Creek, 111.8 km north of Highway 1; 113.4 km south of Highway 16; 12.7 km south of the Icefield Centre. If you are southbound, use caution making the awkward turn into the parking area.

Rating: harder, 7.2 km to Nigel Pass; 8.7 km to the Brazeau Valley Overlook

Special consideration: This trail visits a wilderness setting and is prime habitat for grizzly bears.

Best lighting: anytime

Nearby trails: 33 50 52 53

Alternating between deep forest and avalanche slopes, the hike to Nigel Pass provides a taste of the front range wilderness along the eastern margins of Banff and Jasper national parks. Travel bear-smart on this trail, which is the longest outing in this book.

Beyond the gate, head north along the "Wonder Road" – the original Icefields Parkway – for 2.1 km to the yard of a park patrol cabin. Veer north on a signed trail, crossing Hilda Creek and Nigel Creek to gain the hiker trail on the east bank of Nigel Creek at km 2.5.

This is "Camp Parker". Many trees nearby feature carvings – the handiwork of travellers along the Icefields Parkway in the 1940s. In the days before the road was paved, the 237 km journey from Lake Louise to Jasper was at least a two-day adventure. This grove of trees was near the halfway point, and was, for motorists, a camping place as popular as it had been for trail riders and First Peoples. Please don't add graffiti – many of the older carvings have been disfigured.

The horn shapes of Mt. Athabasca (3442 m) and its outlier, Hilda Peak (3058 m), form the backdrop to the west. To the northwest, the southern summit of Nigel Peak (3020 m) displays the U-shaped fold of the Mt. Wilson Syncline.

The trail swings north into the upper valley of Nigel Creek. Don't be deceived by your proximity to the Icefields Parkway. Grizzly bears frequent this area. I have hiked here perhaps a dozen times and have had three bear experiences – one of them intense. Keep your head up and make lots of noise while you cross the avalanche slopes. I have also seen mountain caribou and bighorn sheep on the trail.

The last kilometre of the climb is on a steep, eroded track that leads to a craggy limestone bluff that overlooks the Brazeau River. This point is 1 km to the east of, and slightly higher than Nigel Pass proper. Here, you are astride the boundary between Banff and Jasper, and between two geological provinces – the eastern main ranges to the west, and the front ranges to the east.

Parker Ridge, Mt. Saskatchewan (3342 m) and the rounded peaks adjacent to Saskatchewan Glacier are prominent in the view south. To the southeast, you can see Cataract Pass (2500 m) and the southerly source of the Brazeau River. Nigel Peak (3211 m) rises above massive limestone cliffs in the view west.

Brazeau Valley Overlook

If you would like to extend this outing another 1.5 km to a bluff that overlooks the Brazeau Valley, drop from the pass into Jasper National Park and cross the Brazeau River. Depending on the water level, this will be a rock-hop or a straightforward ford. We were once entertained here as a ptarmigan hen, fleeing our presence, coerced her chicks into crossing the river. Ptarmigan are ground-dwelling birds. However, as this hen and her brood demonstrated, they are capable of short bursts of flight when threatened.

The trail climbs away from the river, above its north bank, and for the next kilometre winds through rockslide debris dotted with hardy alpine flowers – moss campion, sawwort, cinquefoil, white mountain-avens, and yellow hedysarum. Just before it commences a steep descent, the trail crests a small windswept bluff that offers a panorama of the upper

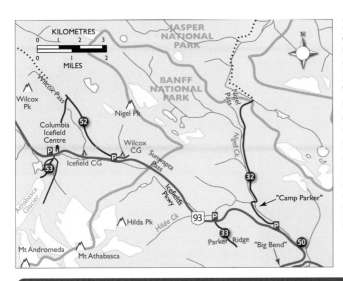

Brazeau Valley. This is a graphic dip-slope landscape – the steeply tilted southwest facing slopes of the front range peaks in view terminate on northeast facing cliffs. The colourful quartzite ridge to the north divides the drainages of Boulder Creek and Four Point Creek. Particularly pleasing are the meanders, verdant wet meadows, and waterfalls along the Brazeau River. Scan the meadows for mountain caribou and wolves. Day-hikers should turn back here and retrace the route, 8.7 km to the trailhead.

GRIZZLY BEAR

In the Rockies, the grizzly bear is not a marauding hunter, neither is it at the apex of the food chain. (The wolf is top dog.) Grizzly bear diet in the Rockies is 90 percent vegetarian. Much of the meat that it eats is carrion or carcasses strong-armed from other animals. There are far fewer grizzly bears in the Rocky Mountain parks than most people imagine – 150 to 200. Of these, 40 to 60 frequent Banff National Park. The grizzly bear is listed as a threatened species because of its dwindling numbers, low fertility rate, and habitat loss. An adult male grizzly in the Rockies requires a vast area – 2000-4000 km^2 is common – larger than Yoho and Kootenay national parks combined. Preservation of safe, connected habitat is key to preserving this species.

A grizzly bear spends almost every waking moment in quest for food to tide it through its winter dormancy. At the peak of its feeding in August, an adult grizzly may gorge for 18 hours each day, during which time it may consume 36 kg of food, representing 40,000 calories. (A large human adult male typically eats about 2500 calories a day.) The bear's aim is to lay on a 13 cm thick layer of fat – insulation and fuel for winter. Berries, roots, horsetail, herbs, and the occasional rodent comprise the bulk of grizzly diet in the Rockies. When the buffaloberry crop is on, an adult grizzly may eat 200,000 berries in a day. (Yes, someone has counted them – after processing.) The grizzly bear is a truly efficient seed distribution device.

The grizzly bear passes most of the winter in a den dug into a steep hillside on a north- or east-facing slope. It does this at high elevations where deep snow provides insulation. During denning, the grizzly's body temperature drops a few degrees and its respiration subsides to 2 to 4 breaths a minute. A natural plug of coarse food blocks its intestines – the bear neither defecates or urinates until spring. The dormancy begins in November and, although it may be broken on warmer days when the bear rises to look around, sleep lasts until April.

Breeding typically commences at age five to seven years. Female (sow) grizzly bears mate every two or three years. The litter in the Rockies is usually a single cub. This represents the lowest reproduction rate among large North American land mammals. Mortality rate for cubs is 10 to 40 percent in the first 18 months. Grizzly off-spring enjoy a lengthy apprenticeship with their mother – two summers, sometimes three, sometimes four – during which the cubs become familiar with the diverse food sources that comprise bear diet.

The only natural threat to a cub is the father (boar) who might try to kill it when it emerges from the den. If more than one cub is born, it is common for the siblings to remain together for a brief time after leaving the sow. Otherwise, grizzlies are solitary. Life expectancy is 20-30 years. The largest grizzly bear recorded in Banff National Park weighed 336 kg.

Most bears will be more concerned with avoiding you than you are with avoiding them. However, when a bear has learned to associate people with easily obtainable food, perceives a threat to its young or to a nearby food source, or is suddenly surprised on a trail, it may stand its ground and, in some cases, become aggressive. See pages 10-12 for what to do and what not to do in a bear encounter. Report sightings to Parks Canada.

33. Parker Ridge

Saskatchewan Glacier

Mt. Athabasca and Hilda Pk.

TRAIL THUMBNAIL

Trailhead
Parking area on the south side of the Icefields Parkway, 115.5 km north of Highway 1; 9 km south of the Columbia Icefield information centre; 109.6 km south of Highway 16. See map, p. 59.

Rating: harder, 2.4 km

Special consideration: Parks Canada keeps the trail closed until most of the winter snowpack is melted – early July in most years.

Best lighting: morning

Nearby trails: ㉜ ㊿ ㊾ ㊿

Parker Ridge packs ancient forest, alpine meadow, boulderfields, glacial views, and, often, extreme weather into an exhilarating, short outing. The ridge-crest can be a chilly place. Be prepared to bundle up.

The trailhead is located in a treeline forest where vegetation growth is hindered by high elevation, cold glacial air, near constant winds, poor soils, avalanches, and a northeast aspect. From the parking area, the trail crosses a subalpine meadow – a frost hollow, typical of areas adjacent to glaciers. Cold air from Hilda Glacier collects here, creating a local growing season so short, that mature trees cannot develop.

The horn mountain shapes of Mt. Athabasca (3442 m) and its outlier, Hilda Peak (3058 m), are prominent to the west. The summits of these mountains protruded above the kilometre thick ice sheets of the Late Wisconsin Glaciation. Since the retreat of the ice sheets, alpine glaciation has continued to whittle away at the upper mountainsides, creating the horns.

The climb begins across the meadow where the trail enters ancient forest. At one point you squeeze between two massive Engelmann spruce trees that are probably at least 400 years old. However, most of the vegetation here is in stunted, kruppelholz form. (*Kruppelholz* is a German term that means "crippled wood".) The gnarled, dense, evergreen mats with silvery bark are subalpine fir trees. Taller, Engelmann spruce grow from within the mats. Although they appear to be shrubs, these are mature trees, possibly hundreds of years old.

The treeless areas on the northeast slope of Parker Ridge are either avalanche swept rock, or tundra comprised of sedges, white mountain-avens, mountain heather, snow willow, arctic willow, moss campion, woolly everlasting, and purple saxifrage. Vegetation here is low in stature to reduce wind exposure, and to enable the plants to absorb heat

KEEPING ON TRACK

Parks Canada built the Parker Ridge trail in the 1960s with ease of access in mind. Gentle switchbacks carved the slope. Unfortunately, those impatient with the trail have shortcut the switchbacks, creating trenches that channel runoff. On your way to the ridgetop you will see dozens of signs that block the shortcut trails, encouraging you to keep on track. Parks Canada installed the signs when the trail was rehabilitated in a costly project in the 1980s. Seeds from plants on Parker Ridge were grown in greenhouses, and the resulting seedlings were transplanted back to the ridge to revegetate redundant trails. Three decades later, the trail requires another overhaul. Many of the trail posts now lean downhill – evidence of soil creep. Please help to protect this fragile landscape by keeping to the gravel path.

from the dark soils. Thick, waxy leaves help retain moisture. Fuzzy stems create natural insulation.

More than 6 m of snow falls annually at Parker Ridge. Because of the shaded, northeast aspect and cold temperatures resulting from the elevation and the proximity to the Columbia Icefield, this snow takes a long time to melt. A few of the drifts at trailside are perennial features. Needless to say, the slopes of Parker Ridge are popular with skiers in winter and spring. If you look north you may be able to pick out the summit of Mt. Alberta (3619 m), the 6th-highest peak in the Rockies; and the 3rd-highest peak in Alberta.

The Ridgecrest

A blast of icy wind may greet you where the trail gains the open ridgecrest. Follow the beaten path southeast (left) for 500 m for a full view of Saskatchewan Glacier. With a length of almost 7 km, this outlet valley glacier of the 215 km² Columbia Icefield is the longest in the Rockies. It descends 750 m in elevation from the icefield rim to terminate in a marginal lake, the principal headwaters of the North Saskatchewan River. The braided river flows through the rubble of the valley below, an area occupied by the glacier less than a century ago.

The surface of Saskatchewan Glacier features no icefalls and has relatively few large crevasses. Of interest is a medial moraine, a strip of lengthwise rubble on the glacier's surface. This type of moraine forms where two tributary glaciers merge. The terminus features an ice cave and a marginal lake. *Saskatchewan* is a Cree word that means "swift current". Mt. Saskatchewan (3342 m) is the high peak protruding above rounded summits, 8 km south of Parker Ridge.

Immediately south (left) of the head of the Saskatchewan Glacier is Castleguard Mountain (3083 m). South of this mountain is the entrance to Castleguard Cave, one of the larger cave systems in Canada, and the 3rd-deepest in Canada and the U.S.A. Cavers have explored more than 18 km of passages. Some of these follow ancient drainages beneath Columbia Icefield to terminate in dead-ends that are choked with glacial ice. If the day is clear, the view beyond Castleguard Mountain will include the lofty summit of Mt. Bryce (3507 m), the 13th-highest peak in the Rockies, and the 14th-highest peak in B.C.; 19 km distant.

If you look uphill (west) along the crest of Parker Ridge, you will notice how the outlying ridge is rounded in appearance, becoming much more rugged toward Mt. Athabasca. The rounded parts of the ridge were completely covered by moving ice during the Late Wisconsin Glaciation, while the jagged areas were probably not. If you choose to explore along the ridge to the cairn at the high point (2255 m), please stay on the beaten path. The ridgecrest features kruppelholz forms of whitebark pine, a common tree in windy locations. The limestone bedrock of the Southesk Formation contains coral-like fossils called *Syringopora*. Please do not remove the fossils.

Mountain goats, white-tailed ptarmigan, gray jays, Clark's nutcrackers, pikas, and ravens are among the frequently observed wildlife on Parker Ridge. If you are fortunate, a grizzly bear or wolverine may lumber over the crest, or a golden eagle may wheel overhead. I have seen a harrier skim by. The ridge was probably named for Herschel Parker, an American mountaineer who made several first ascents of mountains near Lake Louise at the turn of the 20th century.

THE GLACIER TRAIL

Mountaineering parties in the early 1900s, intent on ascending peaks at the southern edge of the Columbia Icefield, followed the Alexandra River southwest to a base camp in Castleguard Meadows. If they wanted to continue farther north, they were obliged to return along the Alexandra River to the North Saskatchewan River, before crossing Sunwapta Pass – a journey of approximately three days. This backtracking frustrated outfitter Jimmy Simpson and his clients, who felt that the supplies used descending the Alexandra could be better used exploring new ground. On the 1923 expedition of mountaineer James Monroe Thorington, Simpson took a one-day shortcut from Castleguard Meadows to Sunwapta Pass – he led the packtrain down the Saskatchewan Glacier and over Parker Ridge.

It was a day-long effort. The horses fussed, but less than expected. Simpson repeated the ploy on the Smithsonian Institution, Columbia Icefield expedition of 1924. For two decades thereafter, the crossing

of Saskatchewan Glacier with horses became standard fare. In the late 1920s, outfitter Jack Brewster incorporated a visit to Castleguard Meadows via Saskatchewan Glacier into his pack trips from Jasper to Lake Louise – an outing known appropriately as "The Glacier Trail".

34. Valleyview

The Bow Valley from Valleyview

TRAIL THUMBNAIL

Trailhead
On Highway 1, 8.4 km east of Banff. The viewpoint is available to eastbound motorists only. Cyclists may access it from the Legacy Trail.

Rating: easy, 100 m

Best lighting: morning and evening

As it enters the front ranges, the Bow Valley forms a massive breach in the mountains. At Valleyview picnic area, you can walk through the wildlife fence to a rough trail on a terrace above the Bow River, and savour the majestic array of limestone peaks on the west side of the valley. The blooms of prairie crocus and calypso orchids colour the terrace in early summer.

35. Banff Cemetery

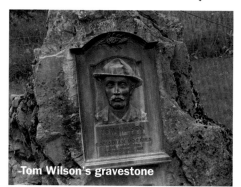

Tom Wilson's gravestone

TRAIL THUMBNAIL

Trailhead
From the corner of Banff Avenue and Buffalo Street in Banff, walk 300 m east along Buffalo Street. See map, p. 18.

Rating: easy, 500 m

Best lighting: anytime

Nearby trails:

Established in 1890, Banff's cemetery is the internment place for more than 2000 former residents. These include many who played major roles in the history of the Rockies: Tom Wilson, Bill Peyto, Jim Brewster, Byron Harmon, R.G. Brett, Mary Schäffer, and Peter and Catharine Whyte. Please be respectful during your visit. Close the animal gates behind you.

36. Sulphur Mountain Boardwalk

On Sanson Peak

TRAIL THUMBNAIL

Trailhead
At Banff Gondola, 3.5 km south of town on Mountain Avenue. Consider using a Roam bus. Google "Banff Gondola" for hours and fees, or phone 800-760-6934. Board the gondola (fee charged). The trail begins at the upper terminal.

Rating: easy, 600 m

Best lighting: anytime

The Sulphur Mountain Boardwalk provides panoramic views of the Bow Valley, Spray Valley, and Banff town. The boardwalk heads north along the crest of Sulphur Mountain to a weather observatory that was built in 1903. Norman Sanson, curator of the Banff Park Museum from 1896-1942, was a regular visitor to the observatory. In all, he made more than 1000 trips to this ridgetop to gather weather information, without the benefit of the gondola. The last of these trips, in July 1945 when Sanson was 83, was to observe a solar eclipse. The north peak (2256 m) of Sulphur Mountain is named Sanson Peak in his honour.

In the winter of 1956-57, the National Research Council constructed a Cosmic Ray Station near the observatory, as part of the International Geophysical Year. The station operated until 1978. The building was removed in 1981. Its location is now a National Historic Site. Interpretive panels along the boardwalk describe the natural history of the area and the operation of the Cosmic Ray Station. Bighorn sheep frequent the ridgecrest. Please do not feed them.

Cascade Falls

human use of this area but has not yet summoned the gumption to close the airstrip. As long as airplanes are still allowed to fly in and out of here, hiking should be OK. The trail passes through a wonderful stand of trembling aspen as it ascends to the base of Cascade Falls. A few Douglas-firs and white birches dot the forest. Listen for warbling vireos, Swainson's thrushes, and flycatchers.

From near the base of the falls, which are a favourite waterfall ice climbing destination in winter, you can look south for fine views of Mt. Rundle (2949 m) and the Bow Valley, and southwest for views of Tunnel Mountain (1692 m), Sulphur Mountain (2285 m), and the environs of Banff town. The falls are what prompted Stoney First Peoples to name the mountain above, *Minnehappa* – "the mountain where the water falls". In 1858, James Hector translated that phrase and applied the name, Cascade Mountain. Do not ascend the cliffs or ledges alongside the waterfall.

37. Cascade Falls

TRAIL THUMBNAIL

Trailhead
Follow Banff Avenue 3 km from Banff town to the Highway 1 interchange. Keep straight ahead (northeast) on the Lake Minnewanka Road for 300 m. Park on the west (left) side of the road, opposite the Cascade Ponds turnoff. See map, p. 29.

Rating: harder, 600 m

Special considerations: Warning! Rockfall danger is a significant hazard near Cascade Falls. Because of avalanche danger, do not hike this trail when the upper slopes of Cascade Mountain are snowbound. Check at the Banff information centre regarding avalanche conditions. Cougars and wolves frequent this area.

Best lighting: morning

Nearby trails: 11 12 38 39

The trail skirts a montane meadow that also happens to be the north end of the Banff airstrip. In the aim of maintaining a wildlife corridor on the north side of Highway 1, Parks Canada discourages

38. Cascade Ponds

TRAIL THUMBNAIL

Trailhead
Follow Banff Avenue 3 km from Banff town to the Highway 1 interchange. Keep straight ahead (northeast) on the Lake Minnewanka Road for 300 m. Turn east (right) into the entry to the Cascade Ponds picnic area. See map, p. 29.

Rating: easy, 1.2 km

Best lighting: morning and evening

Nearby trails: 11 12 37 39

Cascade Ponds

The trail to Stewart Canyon follows the north shore of Lake Minnewanka through a shaded pine forest, to a bridged canyon where the Cascade River enters the lake. The river flows along a bedrock fault, clearly visible in the view upstream. Geologists refer to it as a strike canyon (see p. 70). The canyon was named for George Stewart, the first superintendent of Banff National Park. The second-oldest, known archaeological site in Banff lies partly submerged in Lake Minnewanka near the mouth of the Cascade River. It dates to 10,400 years ago. You may see bald eagles and ospreys over the lake. The parking area is home to a flock of bold bighorn sheep. Please do not feed them.

Before Lake Minnewanka was dammed, the Cascade River flowed wild through this part of the Bow Valley. The river is now a trickle. It feeds the Cascade Ponds, which owe their existence to the impoundment and to gravel mining. Their industrial origins aside, the ponds offer a beautiful setting for views of Mt. Rundle (2949 m) and Cascade Mountain (2998 m). You can make a figure-eight loop around the principal pond, traversing one of its two gravel islands on bridges – this gives the illusion of two ponds where there is only one. (The lesser pond is slightly to the north, away from the trail, and not visited by many.) Common wildlife that you may see include elk, mule deer, white-tailed deer, Columbian ground squirrels, and black-billed magpies.

40. Cory Bluff

The Bow Valley from Cory Bluff

39. Stewart Canyon

TRAIL THUMBNAIL

Trailhead
Follow Banff Avenue 3 km from Banff town to the Highway 1 interchange. Keep straight ahead (northeast) on the Lake Minnewanka Road for 5.9 km to the Lake Minnewanka parking area. Park on the north (left) side of the road. Walk east from the parking area to the gate. The trail begins as a road through the picnic area (distance included in rating). See map, p. 29.

Rating: easy, 2.2 km. The first 700 m is paved and wheelchair ♿ accessible.

Best lighting: anytime

Nearby trails: ⑪ ⑫ �37 ㊳

TRAIL THUMBNAIL

Trailhead
Follow Highway 1 west from the Mt. Norquay (Banff) interchange for 5.6 km to the Bow Valley Parkway exit (Highway 1A). Follow the Bow Valley Parkway 500 m west and turn east (right) onto the Fireside picnic area access road. Follow this narrow road 600 m to its end.

Rating: harder, 1.8 km

Special considerations: The Bow Valley Parkway east of Johnston Canyon is closed to vehicles from 8 p.m. to 8 a.m. daily, March 1 to June 25. If you hike in May or June, check yourself and your gear for wood ticks afterwards.

Best lighting: morning

Nearby trail: ㊶ ㊷

Cross the footbridge over "Fireside Creek" and turn south (right) onto a broad trail. At the junction in 200 m, turn north (left). This part of the trail is in a forest typical of south-facing slopes in the montane life zone of the front ranges.

You reach the Cory Pass junction at km 1.1. Turn north (left), and get ready to engage low gear as you climb steeply for the next 700 m. The initial part of the grind is on a grassy, flower-filled slope, dotted with aspens and frequented by elk, deer, and bighorn sheep. Your destination is a meadowed knoll that offers superb views of the Bow Valley in the vicinity of Banff, from Mt. Bourgeau (2930 m) in the southwest, to Mt. Rundle (2980 m) in the southeast.

41. Muleshoe

TRAIL THUMBNAIL

Trailhead
Follow Highway 1 west from the Mt. Norquay (Banff) interchange for 5.6 km to the Bow Valley Parkway exit (Highway 1A). Follow the Bow Valley Parkway 5.5 km to the Muleshoe picnic area. Cross the road with caution to the trailhead.

Rating: harder, 1 km

Special considerations: The Bow Valley Parkway east of Johnston Canyon is closed to vehicles from 8 p.m. to 8 a.m. daily, March 1 to June 25. This hike is wood tick heaven in May and June. Check yourself and your gear thoroughly before you get back into your vehicle.

Best lighting: morning and evening

Nearby trails: 14 40 42

This rough trail grinds unrelentingly uphill, gaining 250 m – that's right; it's a 25 percent average grade. Your destination is a meadow on the lower slopes of Mt. Cory. On the way, you traverse forest that burned in a 1993 prescribed fire. On a fair day, the views of the Bow Valley will be fine, but early season hikers will probably choose this hike for its wildflower displays. The Muleshoe, adjacent to the picnic area, was formerly part of the Bow River but was made an oxbow lake when impounded by the railway grade. Note how the aspen trees near roadside are scarred where elk have eaten the bark during winter.

42. Pilot Pond

TRAIL THUMBNAIL

Trailhead
Accessible to eastbound travellers only on the Bow Valley Parkway (Highway 1A), 9.2 km east of Castle Junction. Park at a small pull-out. This is 2.7 km east of Johnston Canyon, for those returning from that outing. See map, p. 33.

Rating: 400 m, easy

Special consideration: The Bow Valley Parkway east of Johnston Canyon is closed to vehicles from 8 p.m. to 8 a.m. daily, March 1 to June 25.

Best lighting: morning and evening

Nearby trails: 14 40

It's a short walk downhill to Pilot Pond, which occupies a depression in the debris of the Hillsdale Slide. The surrounding forest features trembling aspen and balsam poplar. Banff locals know Pilot Pond as Lizard Lake because it was, and once again is, home to long-toed salamanders. Between 1926 and 1988, Banff National Park stocked the formerly fishless waters with rainbow trout and brook trout. The fish preyed upon the salamander larvae, with the result that the salamanders – uncommon in the Rockies – disappeared for a while. A few must have survived, because in the time since stocking ceased, the salamander population has recovered. The shores of the pond offer pleasing views of its namesake, Pilot Mountain (2954 m).

43. Copper Lake and Smith Lake

These two lakes each sit in depressions in the rubble left behind at the end of the Late Wisconsin Glaciation, 12,000 years ago. At Copper Lake you have fine views of Castle Mountain (2850 m), with the bedlam of Highway 1 in the foreground. At Smith Lake, the setting is the exact opposite – a pocket in the deep woods – the definition of tranquillity. You reach Copper Lake on a simple out-and-back jaunt from the parking area, by keeping straight ahead after you cross Altrude Creek. To reach Smith

TRAIL THUMBNAIL

Trailhead
Follow Highway 1 to Castle Junction, 30 km west of Banff, 25.5 km east of Lake Louise. Exit west for Radium and Highway 93 South. After 200 m, turn south (left) onto a gravel road that leads to the Altrude Creek trailhead in 400 m. See map, p. 35.

Ratings
- Copper Lake: easy, 700 m
- Copper Lake and Smith Lake: harder, 4.7 km return

Best lighting: anytime

Nearby trails: (15) (16) (17)

Lake, after crossing Altrude Creek turn south (right). Take the southeast (left) trail at the next junction in 100 m. The trail climbs steadily for most of the way to the lake, with a steep drop at trail's end to the lakeshore. Look for clematis and calypso orchids in the forest in early summer. Joe Smith was a resident, and later a recluse at nearby Silver City (see p. 35).

44. Bow Riverside

TRAIL THUMBNAIL

Trailhead
At Lake Louise train station on Sentinel Road in Lake Louise Village, or at the Lake Louise Campground. You may also pick up the trail at many points in between, on either side of the river.

Rating: easy or moderate. Loops of 2.5 km to 7.2 km are possible.

Special considerations: Bear warnings are frequently posted for this trail. Check at the Lake Louise information centre. Follow instructions and use caution when handling the electrified gates at the campground.

Best lighting: anytime

This trail along the banks of the Bow River near Lake Louise village is ideal for those staying at Lake Louise Campground. Bridges span the river in four places, allowing loop walks of various lengths. You may visit the historic Lake Louise train station at the north end of the loop. Mt. Temple (3544 m), the highest peak in this part of the Rockies, is prominent in the view southwest. Interpretive panels highlight the human history and the natural history of the area.

45. Fairview Lookout

TRAIL THUMBNAIL

Trailhead
From Lake Louise Village, follow Lake Louise Drive 5.5 km to the parking areas at the lake. Paved walkways lead to the lakeshore (distance included in rating). Turn south (left) at the lake outlet. The Fairview Lookout-Saddleback Pass trailhead is adjacent to the World Heritage Site monument.

You can walk to the trailhead from Lake Louise Campground/village via the Tramline trail. Inquire at the park information centre. See map, p. 40.

Rating: harder, 3.1 km loop

Best lighting: afternoon

Nearby trails: (18) (19) (20)

Follow the Saddleback Pass trail for 300 m and turn west (right). The Fairview Lookout trail ascends steadily for 700 m through a subalpine forest of Engelmann spruce and subalpine fir to a viewpoint that overlooks Lake Louise. Although trees block the view of the Chateau, interpretive panels describe the hotel's history. It's easier and shorter to retrace your route to the trailhead than to complete the loop trail, which descends steeply from the viewpoint to the lakeshore, where you will contend with rocks underfoot and water, too, when the lake level is high. It is 1.5 km from the viewpoint to the boathouse via this route, and another 300 m to the parking area.

46. Herbert Lake

Herbert Lake

TRAIL THUMBNAIL

Trailhead
West side of the Icefields Parkway, 3.1 km north of Highway 1. Park at the south end of the parking area.

Rating: easy, 50 m

Best lighting: morning and evening

The Herbert Lake picnic area was built on the site of a camp used during construction of the Icefields Parkway. The lake was probably named for one of the workers. Pick your way through the lodgepole pines to the lakeshore for a superb view of Mt. Temple (3544 m) and other peaks in the Lake Louise area. Photographers will love this location in early morning on a fair day. Look and listen for common loons on the lake.

47. Upper Waterfowl Lake

TRAIL THUMBNAIL

Trailhead
At an unnamed pull-off on the west side of the Icefields Parkway, 55 km north of Highway 1; 1.4 km south of Waterfowl Lakes Campground.

Rating: easy, 200 m

Best lighting: morning

The trail descends west from the edge of the parking area. After 40 m, you cross the bed of the "Wonder Road", the forerunner of the Icefields Parkway, and then the site of a highway construction camp from the late 1930s. You soon arrive at the shore of Upper Waterfowl Lake in a wet meadow. You may see moose here or in similar habitat on the far side of the lake. The peaks of the continental divide rise magnificently across the lake. Howse Peak (3295 m), with its two niche glaciers, is prominent, as is Mt. Chephren (KEFF-ren) (3274 m), and the Whyte Pyramid (3275 m).

If you like this area, you may also want to visit the reach of the Mistaya River between the Upper and Lower Waterfowl Lakes. Turn off from the Icefields Parkway at Waterfowl Lakes Campground, 56.4 km north of Highway 1. Don't go into the campground, but continue south (straight ahead) on the access road for 400 m. The trailhead is at the southwest corner of the parking area. Follow a gravel path that skirts the south edge of the campground. After 400 m, you reach the bridges that cross the narrows between Waterfowl lakes. Bears frequent the campground and surrounding area. Travel accordingly.

48. Warden Lake

TRAIL THUMBNAIL

Trailhead
East side of the Icefields Parkway, 73.2 km north of Highway 1; 1.7 km south of the junction with Highway 11. Park at the park patrol station. Walk 50 m south along the road's east edge to the trailhead. See map, p. 55.

Rating: moderate, 2.2 km

Best lighting: anytime

Nearby trails: ③⓪ ③① ④⑨

The trail skirts south of the Parks Canada buildings and then jogs north (left) to pick up an old jeep track along the bank of the North Saskatchewan River. This riverbank has seen traffic for millennia. For First Peoples, it was part of the Kutenai Trail, along which the Ktunaxa (toon-AWK-ah) travelled, bringing ochre, salmon, and berries to trade for bison meat and skins at nearby Kootenay Plains. Early white explorers made forays to the great peaks of the Columbia Icefield area along this route. Later, jeep enthusiasts bashed their way into the mountains.

Warden Lake

Look for moisture-loving wildflowers here in early season, including elephant-head and shooting star. From a prominent bend in the river, look back for a splendid panorama, from the Kaufmann Peaks in the south, to Mt. Amery in the north. Due west is Mt. Forbes (3617 m), 7th-highest in the Rockies. Mt. Wilson (3260 m) rises across the river. The forest on that bank was consumed in a prescribed burn in 2009. About 1.5 km from the trailhead, a metal sign nailed to a tree, points southeast (right) and indicates "Warden Lake 400 yards". You reach a smaller pond, first, with Warden Lake nearby. Both lakes are kettle ponds. Corona Ridge (3065 m) and the north peaks of Mt. Murchison (3337 m) form the backdrop. You may see moose and waterfowl.

49. Howse Valley Viewpoint

TRAIL THUMBNAIL

Trailhead
Parking area on the west side of the Icefields Parkway, 74.8 km north of Highway 1; 400 m south of the junction with Highway 11. See map, p. 55.

Rating: easy, 250 m loop. Wheelchair ♿ accessible with assistance.

Best lighting: evening

Nearby trails: ③⓪ ③① ④⑧

This trail loops through a lodgepole pine forest to the crest of a windswept river terrace that overlooks three valleys: the North Saskatchewan, the Mistaya, and the Howse. The pine trees seeded after the Survey Peak burn of July 1940.

Mt. Murchison (3337 m) dominates the view to the southeast. Stoney and Ktunaxa (toon-AWK-ah) First Peoples believed it was the highest peak in the Rockies. It isn't, but the sentiment is understandable;

the mountain towers almost 2000 m above. In the distant view west, you can see Mt. Forbes (3617 m), 7th-highest in the Rockies. The Howse Valley, part of the original fur trade route across the Rockies, stretches away to the southwest. Interpretive panels describe the fur trade in this area, and also highlight the importance of this area to First Peoples. The viewpoint includes a plaque unveiled when the reach of the North Saskatchewan River within Banff was proclaimed a Canadian Heritage River, in 1989.

50. Panther Falls

TRAIL THUMBNAIL

Trailhead
Parking area on the east side of the Icefields Parkway, 110.8 km north of Highway 1; 13.7 km south of the Columbia Icefield information centre. Park the uppermost (northerly) of the two viewpoints on the Big Bend Hill. The trail departs from the south end of the parking area. See map, p. 59.

Rating: harder, 450 m

Special considerations: Caution! Fall risk! This unfenced, water-soaked trail usually offers poor footing in the vicinity of the falls. Avoid this outing if the trail is icy, or after snow or heavy rain. Wear proper footwear with good treads. Do not approach the falls from the end of the beaten path.

Best lighting: morning

Nearby trails: ③② ③③ ⑤② ⑤③

The trail switchbacks down through cool forest into a canyon on Nigel Creek. After traversing beneath a cliff, the last 50 m of trail crosses an exposed sideslope to an unfenced viewpoint near the base of the 60-m high falls. The water cascades over colourful limestone and dolomite of the Eldon Formation. This step marks the place where the lesser valley of Nigel Creek was shorn by the greater North Saskatchewan Valley glacier in ice age times. Much of the water in Nigel Creek is thought to come from Wilcox Lake in neighbouring Jasper National Park. The creek joins the North Saskatchewan River about 3 km southeast of the Panther Falls. In 1907, Mary Schäffer named the falls after finding mountain lion tracks on the trail. In recent decades, Panther Falls have been an extreme testing ground in winter for the world's ice climbing and mixed climbing elite.

51. Lower Siffleur Falls

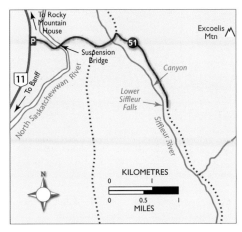

Siffleur Canyon

TRAIL THUMBNAIL

Trailhead
At Siffleur Falls parking lot in the Kootenay Plains Recreation Area on Highway 11; 26 km east of the junction with the Icefields Parkway; 99.5 km from Highway 1; 62 km west of Nordegg.

Rating: harder, 3.9 km

Special considerations: Although the established viewpoints are well fenced, there are hazardous places along the canyon. Use caution if the trail is slippery. Keep children nearby and stay within the fenced areas when near the canyon edge. You share the trail with equestrians and cyclists as far as the Siffleur River bridge.

Best lighting: anytime

The Siffleur River flows north from the northern edge of Banff National Park to its confluence with the North Saskatchewan River at Kootenay Plains. A seldom-travelled place today, the Siffleur Valley was well known to Stoney and Siksika First

Peoples. In the late 1800s and early 1900s, mountaineers heading north from Lake Louise also used the valley to approach the high peaks near the Columbia Icefield. The trail to Lower Siffleur Falls gives you a taste of the wilderness area to the south, and grants access to a classic front-range canyon.

The Kootenay Plains is a pocket of prairie within the mountains. The area is in a rain shadow of the high peaks to the west, and is raked by near constant southwest winds. In this relatively arid niche, grasslands dotted with a few spruces, pines, and aspens prevail. Interpretive panels in the first 400 m describe the area's human history and natural history. Stoney, Siksika, Piikani, and Ktunaxa (toon-AWK-ah) [Kootenay] First Peoples met here to trade bison, salmon, ochre, and berries. Fur traders also replenished their supplies by trading and hunting here. Some early white explorers referred to the Kootenay Plains as "Katoona Tinda" – Kootenay Prairie.

More than 240 species of plants have been catalogued on Kootenay Plains, including 20 species that are uncommon. Many typify the prairie. Look for showy locoweed (photo, p. 70), so called because, when consumed in large quantities, locoweeds are poisonous to cattle and other large mammals. This is partly due to phytotoxins produced by the plants, but mostly due to the fact that locoweeds concentrate selenium from the soil. *Locoism*, the resulting

Kootenay Plains

North Saskatchewan River

Lower Siffleur Falls

disease, includes a spectrum of symptoms, but not crazy behaviour. "Loco" refers to the fact that many animals keenly seek out the plant to eat it – they go "crazy" over it.

After about 600 m you reach a suspension bridge across the North Saskatchewan River. For a few years in the early 1800s, brigades of the North West Company and Hudson's Bay Company lined and poled their canoes upstream along this mighty torrent each spring, headed for the crossing of the mountains at Howse Pass. In the autumn, they tore eastward, hardly pulling a stroke. As harrowing as it may be to contemplate a crossing of this river if the bridge were not here, on a fair day you can easily wile away a few hours appreciating the setting.

Across the bridge, you traverse a sandy flat on a boardwalk. The trail cuts through a river terrace and at the 2 km mark, you cross the Siffleur River on a bridge, just upstream from its confluence with the North Saskatchewan River. *Siffleur* is French for "whistler". James Hector, doctor and geologist with the Palliser Expedition of 1857-60, gave the name when in the upper valley, on account of the hoary marmots there. When alarmed, marmots give a shrill whistle. Hector named dozens of features in the Rockies but this is the only French name that he applied. From here to the falls, you follow the east bank of the Siffleur River through a forest of lodgepole pine and white spruce, with the understory dominated by the most fragrant shrub in the Rockies – wolf willow (silverberry). Look for showy, montane wildflowers, including yellow and purple hedysarum, and brown-eyed Susans.

You may be tempted to descend to the cliff edge to have a look into the canyon but, patience, Grasshopper! Wait for the two fenced viewpoints, especially the southerly one – its view of the canyon is as spectacular as it is safe.

The third viewpoint provides a point-blank prospect of the Siffleur Falls. If your timing is fortunate and the lighting co-operates, you may see a rainbow nearby. There is a limestone "beach" just above the falls, but don't go anywhere near the river as you won't have a chance at recovering from a tumble in that direction. Look for harlequin ducks and dippers in the fast flowing water. This is the end of maintained trail. Retrace your route to the parking area.

ON STRIKE

The front range landscape provides graphic depiction of mountain creation. Huge masses of rock, called thrust sheets, piled upward, moving from southwest to northeast. The contact point between thrust sheets is called a thrust fault. In the front ranges, this will typically now be a straight-running valley, oriented southeast to northwest along what geologists call the strike of the Rockies. The easterly wall of the valley will be a slope that dips steeply to the southwest; the westerly wall of the valley will resemble a northeast-facing cliff. When a strike valley "captures" a river, the water will undercut that cliff, creating a strike canyon. There are many strike canyons in the Rockies but few match the one below Siffleur Falls for depth, length, and "textbook" quality.

Showy locoweed

Cavell Meadows

Jasper National Park

Established in 1907, Jasper is the largest of the mountain national parks. It includes 11,228 km² of the front ranges and eastern main ranges. The Jasper Walks and Easy Hikes visit an array of settings: tranquil lakes, glacial forefields, historic places, wildflower meadows, and one, truly spectacular mountain top.

Jasper town provides a full range of supplies, accommodation, and services. Jasper is 366 km west of Edmonton on Highway 16; and 230 km north of Lake Louise via the Icefields Parkway. Access is by car, passenger bus or train. The park information centres are in Jasper town and at the Columbia Icefield.

By using an excellent network of trails, it is possible to complete all of the outings near town without having to start a vehicle. You would rack-up some long days, distance-wise doing this (making them Not Quite So Easy Walks and Hikes), but if you want to give it a try, pick up a trail network guide at the park information centre and ask the staff for help in planning an itinerary. Jasper town is bike-friendly, too, so you could consider that option for getting to and from trailheads. When you see a trail number like this, #3f, in the text, it refers to the trail numbering system used by the park in its brochure and on its signs.

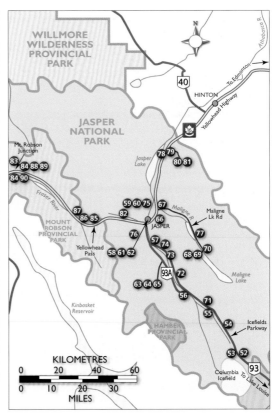

52. Wilcox Pass

Wilcox Pass

TRAIL THUMBNAIL

Trailhead
At Wilcox Campground, on the east side of the Icefields Parkway; 121.5 km north of Highway 1; 103.7 km south of Highway 16; 3 km south of the Columbia Icefield information centre. The trailhead is on the north (left) side of the campground access road. See map, p. 59.

Rating: harder, 4.0 km to pass; 5.4 km to viewpoint

Best lighting: anytime

Nearby trails: ③② ③③ ⑤⓪ ⑤③

When explorer Walter Wilcox travelled north from Lake Louise in 1896, his party hit a roadblock in the upper Sunwapta Valley. The terrific jumble of the Mt. Kitchener Slide, and the resulting gorge on the Sunwapta River, made direct travel from Sunwapta Pass into the Sunwapta Valley impossible for horses. Wilcox's guide, Fred Stephens, suggested that they detour by climbing over a pass to the northeast, to regain the Sunwapta Valley farther north. The Wilcox Pass trail retraces this historic route, offering panoramic views of the peaks and glaciers near the Columbia Icefield.

The trail initially climbs steeply in an ancient forest of Engelmann spruce. They aren't giants, but many of these trees – stunted by the glacial chill – are 300 years to 350 years old. The oldest known Engelmann spruce in Jasper National Park – approximately 700 years – grows 3 km west of here. The high stumps you see are from trees cut for bridge timbers during construction of the original Icefields Parkway in the late 1930s.

You reach treeline in just 600 m, on a cliff edge that overlooks the Icefields Parkway. In the view south, from left to right, the features are Mt. Athabasca (3442 m), Mt. Andromeda (3450 m), Athabasca Glacier, Snow Dome (3451 m), Dome Glacier, and Mt. Kitchener (3480 m). J.N. Collie and Hermann Woolley made the first ascent of Mt. Athabasca in 1898. From its summit, they claimed the "discovery" of the Columbia Icefield. Today, Mt. Athabasca is probably the most frequently ascended alpine peak in the Rockies. Look for climbers on the icy faces of this mountain, and on Mt. Andromeda.

The trail veers north from the edge of the cliff and begins a rambling ascent through stands of ragged

DISAPPEARING ICE AND DISAPPEARING WATER

For now, ice abounds in the view south and west from the approach to Wilcox Pass. Some of the glaciers are officially named, some have nicknames. Boundary and "Little A" glaciers cloak Mt. Athabasca. The "A-A glacier" lies between Mt. Athabasca and Mt. Andromeda, which sports two unnamed glaciers. Athabasca Glacier is the principal glacier in view. "Little Dome" and Dome glaciers cascade from Snow Dome. Athabasca Glacier receded 1.6 km, and decreased 57 percent in area, and 32 percent in volume between 1870 and 1971. Glaciologists estimate that in the summer of 1998, the glacier lost 5 percent of its mass.

All of these glaciers are directly or loosely connected with the Columbia Icefield – the largest icefield in the Rockies. Meltwater from this 215 km² body of ice feeds three of the continent's great river systems: the Columbia, the Saskatchewan, and the Athabasca/ Mackenzie; and thus three oceans: the Pacific, the Atlantic, and the Arctic. As the icefield disappears, so do the major rivers of western North America.

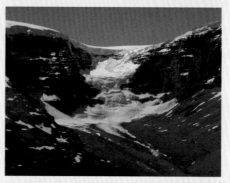

Wilcox Lake is concealed from view on the east side of Wilcox Pass, at the foot of Nigel Peak. The lake has no surface outlet, indicating underground drainage in the limestone bedrock. A large spring along Nigel Creek, 5 km south, is thought to be the emergence of the underground stream.

kruppelholz, along the principal stream that drains Wilcox Pass. Nigel Peak (3211 m) rises to the east.

Wilcox Pass is alpine tundra at its best – a broad, U-shaped valley, 3 km long. Wildflowers and wildlife abound. Flocks of bighorn sheep – often exclusively composed of rams – congregate on lingering snow patches, seeking escape from heat and bugs. I have only taken the safety off a bear spray a few times in the backcountry. Once was here, when a bighorn ram approached head down, with menace in his eye. Other wildlife species that frequent the pass include mountain goat, grizzly bear, moose, wolverine, and golden eagle. I have also seen falcons, killdeer, and green-winged teals. In early August, the showy, white tufts of the sedge, cotton-grass, decorate many of the ponds in the height of the pass. The glacially streamlined form of Wilcox Peak (2884 m) borders the west side of the pass. Walter Wilcox and his companion, R.L. Barrett, made the first ascent in 1896. Turn around at the large cairn in the height of the pass to retrace your route to the trailhead, or turn south (left) for 1.4 km to reach a viewpoint that provides a spectacular view of Athabasca Glacier.

GOOD STEW, NIGEL!

Nigel Vavasour was the cook on the 1898 expedition that made the first ascent of Mt. Athabasca. On the way north from Lake Louise, the party lost many supplies when testy pack horses plunged into the North Saskatchewan River. The larder was almost empty before serious climbing could begin. While J.N. Collie and Hermann Woolley claimed glory on the heights of Mt. Athabasca, guide Bill Peyto (PEE-toe) and Hugh Stutfield bagged bighorn sheep near Nigel Pass, in an area that they called the "Wild Sheep Hills". The sheep stew that became the party's staple for the next two weeks must have been a success, for Collie applied the cook's name to several features nearby.

Athabasca Glacier

TRAIL THUMBNAIL

Trailhead
West side of the Icefields Parkway, 124.8 km north of Highway 1; 100.4 km south of Jasper town; 300 m south of the Columbia Icefield information centre. For the Forefield trail, follow the glacier access road 100 m to the first parking area. To hike the Toe of the Glacier only, carry on along the access road for another 700 m to the second parking area. See map, p. 59.

Ratings
- Forefield trail: moderate, 1.2 km
- Toe of the Glacier: moderate, 1.4 km loop

Special considerations: Glacial stream washouts may affect portions of this trail. Check at the information centre. Warning! Keep off the Athabasca Glacier.

Best lighting: morning

Nearby trails: **32** **33** **50** **52**

53. Athabasca Glacier

The Athabasca Glacier (GLAY-seer) is the most accessible glacier in North America. Although many people drive to the parking area closest to the ice, the Forefield trail provides a more complete appreciation of this glacial landscape. You will be walking on gravel and rock, and will likely be hopping streams. Wear sturdy footwear. If the day is typical, you will also need a warm hat, gloves, sweater, and windbreaker. After crossing the forefield, this trail connects with the well-beaten loop path from the second parking area to the toe of the glacier. This second path gets longer each year as the glacier recedes, but as of 2015, it was about 1.4 km return. Although you may be tempted to join the throngs scampering about on the ice, keep off it. A year does not go by without a calamity or two caused by tumbles on the ice. Sometimes, when a person slides into a crevasse, the results are fatal.

The Ice Factory

With an area of 215 km², the Columbia Icefield is the largest icefield in the Canadian Rockies. Conditions on the icefield resemble those of the Late Wisconsin Glaciation – an ice age that held most of the northern hemisphere in its chilling grasp between 31,000 years ago and 14,000 years ago.

Columbia Icefield

Nestled on an upland plateau with an average elevation of 3000 m, the icefield is ringed by 13 of the 30 highest mountains in the Rockies. Meltwaters from the summit of Snow Dome (3451 m) flow to three oceans: the Pacific via the Columbia River; the Atlantic via the Saskatchewan river system; and the Arctic via the Athabasca, Slave, and Mackenzie river systems.

More than 10 m of snow falls on the Columbia Icefield each year, and very little melts. Over time, the fallen snow changes shape from flakes to grains. The grains begin to compact under the weight of snow layers above. Eventually, when a thickness of 30 m of compacted snow has accumulated, its lower layers become glacial ice. The maximum known ice thickness on Columbia Icefield is 365 m.

The icefield acts as a huge refrigerator, chilling the air above it. Cold air is more dense than warm air. It flows (sometimes it howls!) downhill from the icefield into adjacent valleys and collects in hollows. This chill, coupled with the ever-changing courses of glacial meltwater streams, makes it difficult for vegetation to grow. Mats of white mountain avens, clumps of snow willow, alpine willow, sedges, and mountain fireweed are all that have taken hold since the ice last covered this area.

A River of Ice

The Athabasca Glacier is a perfect example of an outlet valley glacier. From the icefield rim (on the skyline) to its terminus or ending point, the glacier descends 820 m in 6.2 km. A prominent icefall marks the steepest drop, about 1 km from the icefield rim, where the glacier attempts to conform to a cliff in the bedrock. The surface of the glacier is moving faster and is under less pressure than the ice beneath. So the surface ice accelerates over the drop and becomes heavily fissured. These cracks are called crevasses (creh-VASS-ezz). There are more than 30,000 crevasses on the Athabasca Glacier.

Towers of ice that form in icefalls or on the edges of hanging glaciers are called seracs (sair-RACKS). You can see a wall of seracs on the southeast face of Snow Dome (3451 m), just to the northwest (right) of the upper icefall of the Athabasca Glacier. Avalanches of ice from this cliff frequently crash to the glacier surface. If you think that you hear thunder on a clear day, look at this serac wall – you might see the end of an avalanche.

The purity of glacial ice affects its colour. Air and dirt tend to reflect all wavelengths of light, causing ice to appear white or gray. The uniform and minute ice crystals deep within a glacier have had most of the air squeezed out of them. They reflect the blue wavelengths of light.

In August, look for the annual snowline above the upper icefall. Snow toward the icefield rim from that point is in the accumulation zone of the glacier, and will endure the summer to become glacial ice. The glacier's ablation zone is between the annual snowline and the terminus. In the ablation zone, the mass of the glacier is melting, thus its surface is free of snow.

The Athabasca Glacier occupies a U-shaped valley, scoured when the glacier was larger. Because

HERE TODAY, GONE TOMORROW?

Glaciers and ice sheets cover 10 percent of the Earth's surface, and store 75 percent of the planet's freshwater. Between 1960 and 2005, Earth's glaciers lost 8000 km3 of ice mass – a volume with a meltwater equivalent to more than 500 times Canada's present annual water use. The Athabasca Glacier has receded 1.8 km since 1844. The Columbia Glacier, on the north edge of the Columbia Icefield, receded 1.5 km between 1992 and 2006. Glaciers in the Rockies are now at a minimum not seen in the last 3000 years.

The overall climate in the Canadian Rockies is warming, with winters warming faster than summers. Less snow is falling – the average maximum depth of the winter snowpack has decreased 61.3 percent at Banff since 1956. The overall amount of precipitation (including rain) is also decreasing; 10 percent at Banff in 100 years; 20 percent at Lake Louise in 85 years. As mountaintops warm, treeline creeps upwards, squeezing out alpine animal and plant species. This is troubling, especially because if the sources of the major rivers of western Canada continue to dwindle, the consequences will reach far beyond the mountains.

Lateral moraine

of the U-shape, the glacier is deeper along its midline than at its sides. The deepest point is 320 m, about 2 km below the lower icefall. As the glacier approaches the Sunwapta Valley, it leaves its confined side valley and widens. This, along with the melting in the ablation zone, makes the ice thinner near the terminus. The fastest moving ice on the glacier is on the surface in the centre, where it moves about 127 m a year at the lower icefall, compared to 15 m a year at the terminus.

Many meltwater streams ply the surface of the Athabasca Glacier. The water sculpts runnels in the ice, and sometimes disappears into crevasses or chutes. The chutes are called moulin (moo-LANN) or millwells. A major sub-surface stream network empties at the terminus. From year to year, glacier caves of varying dimensions mark this point.

The Rubble Strewn Path

Glaciers created the blueprint of the Rockies – they scoured the troughs of the major valleys, eroded deep cirques into mountainsides, gouged the basins of lakes, and sharpened mountain summits into horns. Glaciers have also created many landforms with the rubble bulldozed and deposited in the process. This rubble, un-layered in appearance, is called till.

Moraines are the most common till landforms. Ground moraine is till that blanketed the surface or the underside of a glacier, and was left in place when the glacier receded. The area traversed by this trail is ground moraine. One of its delights is the multitude of peach- and apricot-coloured chunks of dolomite. The most easily recognized moraine-type is an end moraine, formed at the terminus of a glacier. End moraines include terminal moraines, which are deposited at the maximum extent of a glacial advance, and annual moraines or recessional moraines that show positions of halt during glacial retreat. The road to the Athabasca Glacier cuts through a series of recessional moraines. Signs indicate the years in which they were formed. The terminal moraine of the last advance of Athabasca Glacier abutted the slopes of Wilcox Peak adjacent to the Columbia Icefield information centre. It is hard to pick out.

The most impressive moraines near the Athabasca Glacier are the two lateral moraines that flank the ice. A lateral moraine is till pushed aside by a glacier. The east lateral moraine of the Athabasca Glacier (left-hand side, photo) towers 150 m above the ice. The interior of a lateral moraine often has an ice core. Ice-cored moraines are unstable. Rocks may avalanche onto the surface of the ice. (What goes up must come down.) This is one way in which surface moraine forms. Rockfall from cliffs above is another. As the glacier carries surface moraine "downstream", the moraine spreads out, where it may cover and insulate the ice. You can see this on Dome Glacier, to the northwest (right) of the Athabasca Glacier.

There is one glacial deposition feature that will make the greatest impression on those who stray from the trail near the terminus of Athabasca Glacier – a thick, grey-black mud known as glacier goo claims many a running shoe here every summer. The goo is difficult to spot until you've taken one step too many, so it's a good idea to keep to the beaten path.

54. Beauty Creek

TRAIL THUMBNAIL

Trailhead
Parking area on the east side of the Icefields Parkway, 17.4 km north of the Columbia Icefield information centre, 82.1 km south of Highway 16. See map, p. 76.

Rating: moderate, 2.5 km

Special consideration: Caution! Fall risk! There are no fences or guardrails along Beauty Creek. Avoid this trail when it is icy or after a snowfall.

Best lighting: afternoon, but overcast days are good, too

Between 1940 and 1961, the original route of the Icefields Parkway hugged the east side of the Sunwapta Valley, with a bridge at the mouth of Beauty Creek. Motorists who stopped at the bridge naturally followed the creek upstream to its canyon. When the Icefields Parkway was re-routed to the west, the landmark of the bridge was lost, and the trail became much less visited. This is a shame because, as you will see, the creek could have no better name.

Stanley Falls

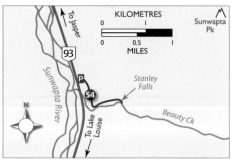

The trail crosses a drainage dyke adjacent to the Icefields Parkway and then passes through a short section of forest. Turn south (right) onto the old roadbed. After about 500 m, just before the ruin of the old bridge, turn sharply east (left) and climb into the hanging valley of Beauty Creek, and a forest of pine, spruce, and fir.

Some people count seven waterfalls along this trail; some count eight. No matter, the first one is just beneath you at the top of this climb. Beauty Creek is a tumultuous watercourse; you are never far from its cascades and riffles. The creek has exploited a joint set in the bedrock, and follows the resulting sequence of short doglegs as it plunges from its sidevalley. Note

how the opposite side of the creek is more cliff-like than the nearside, which is deeply undercut in places. This is because the sedimentary formations in the underlying rock tip slightly to the north, pitching much of the water's energy to this side of the canyon. There is also a normal fault here; the rock on the north side of the creek has dropped relative to the rock on the south side. Many of the cascades feature fine plunge pools at their bases.

The north-facing canyon walls (across the creek) feature a damp forest of spruce and fir, with feathermosses and lichens covering the rocks. Lodgepole pines are more common at trailside on the sunnier, north side of the creek. At one point, the trail

CARIBOU ROAD

The first time that I photographed a mountain caribou was on the old road bed just north of Beauty Creek. The caribou is a deer family member that has a brown coat with lighter patches on the neck, rump, belly, and lower legs. The neck is fringed on its underside. The word "caribou" is probably derived from the Micmac name for this animal, *Xalibu*, which means "the one who paws". The caribou herd of southern Jasper National Park sometimes uses Beauty Creek to move between alpine areas to the east and the Sunwapta Valley.

Male and female caribou each grow antlers that feature a forward-reaching "shovel". In summer, it is usually the females that carry antlers. Their "rack" is smaller than that of mature males. When they run, caribou carry their heads high and tilted back, and lift their legs in a distinctive prance. If you are close enough you will hear the clacking made by tendons in the animal's legs. The caribou's large hooves help to support it in deep snow, and leave a track that is more rounded than that of other deer family members. The wolf is its principal predator.

One of Jasper's three caribou herds (whose members you may see here) does not migrate out of the park, making its 10 animals the only fully protected mountain caribou in Canada. Nonetheless, the population of Jasper's herds declined more than 90 percent between 1988 and 2014. Alberta's caribou population has decreased from more than 9000 animals to less than 1000 animals since 1960.

Canada's southern mountain caribou are "endangered". Clear-cut logging and oil and gas activities on provincial lands have fragmented habitat and have destroyed large areas of the old-growth forests that provide winter range. Helicopters take people quickly into formerly remote caribou habitat. Climate change is reducing the summer snow cover that caribou require to help regulate their body temperature. When a constellation of such stresses aligns, it may trigger an "extinction vortex" – a situation in which a species' natural breeding rate cannot keep pace with deaths resulting from natural and unnatural causes. All of Canada's 27 mountain caribou sub-populations have already crossed that threshold. Time is ticking. Environment Canada released a caribou recovery strategy in 2014. A key element will be reintroducing caribou, bred from captive animals. BC and Alberta also have strategies in place, but these have so far been ineffective.

squeezes between chunks of layered limestone that appear as though they were once in the stream bed. Look and listen for dippers in the canyon.

About 2.5 km from the trailhead, you may note a change in character of the canyon that suggests there will be no more waterfalls. Stanley Falls is indeed the last cataract. Upstream, the angle of the creek diminishes and the canyon widens. Travel beyond Stanley Falls is a wilderness route; the sources of Beauty Creek are in a labyrinth of side valleys in one of the more rugged and beautiful areas of the park. Turn back here.

All of the clamour to this point has been due to a glacial step caused by differential erosion. Beauty Creek flows in a hanging valley that was not as deeply eroded by its ice-age glacier as was the Sunwapta Valley. Nonetheless, as the rounded summit of Tangle Ridge (3000 m) to the south attests, all of this area was buried by ice that was a kilometre thick during the Late Wisconsin Glaciation.

Who was Stanley? No one knows, but it is likely that he worked on the construction of the original Icefields Parkway in the late 1930s.

The second falls, upper canyon

55. Sunwapta Falls and Canyon

TRAIL THUMBNAIL

Trailhead
West side of the Icefields Parkway, 47.7 km north of the Columbia Icefield information centre; 53 km south of Highway 16. Follow the Sunwapta Falls Road 600 m to the parking area. See map, p. 78.

Ratings
- Upper falls: viewpoint, 100 m. Wheelchair 🦽 accessible with assistance.
- Lower falls: moderate, 1.4 km

Best lighting: afternoon

Nearby trail: **71**

Rushing water will always take the path of least resistance. At the end of the last ice age, at what is now Sunwapta Falls, a glacial moraine blocked the Sunwapta River's north-westerly course, forcing it to make a right-angle turn to the southwest. The river has since exploited weaknesses in the bedrock to create a classic Rockies canyon that features five waterfalls. Most people walk short paved trails on either side of the river to visit the two upper falls. The first one has a drop of 18.5 m. If you have the time, extend your visit by walking the trail along the northwest bank of the river to the lower falls and canyon. This trail is on the same side of the river as the parking area.

From the fenced viewpoint just downstream from the parking area, look upstream to see the right-angle turn in the Sunwapta River below the second falls.. The trail to the lower falls descends on a wide path through montane lodgepole pine forest. These trees probably date to 1889, when a massive forest fire scorched much of the Athabasca and lower Sunwapta valleys. In the Rockies, lodgepole pine forests generally reach maturity in about 125 years. In the absence of significant forest fires in the last century, blowdowns and infestation by mountain pine beetles have become the principal agents of change in this forest. You will see many trees that have been toppled by wind.

Where the trail draws alongside the river, and on the canyon walls opposite, note how Engelmann spruce and subalpine fir – hallmark trees of the subalpine life zone – outnumber lodgepole pines. The chilling effect of the canyon and its spray, and the shading on the opposite canyon wall, create enough of a niche to allow them to grow here.

Fenced viewpoints in the lower canyon provide wonderful views of the river, which at times will be a milky torrent, loaded with glacial silt. The principal cascade is a picture-book waterfall. Look for

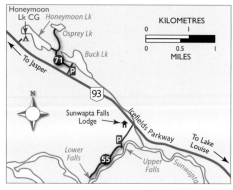

A.P. Coleman

dippers, winging through the spray. The bedrock here is Cathedral Formation limestone and dolomite. The rocks here are in the eastern arm of an anticline, a massive arch-shaped fold. Ice-age glaciers eroded the adjacent Athabasca Valley through the crest of this fold.

You can see the craggy summit ridge of Mt. Quincy (3150 m), downstream from the lowest viewpoint in the canyon. Lucius Quincy Coleman was the brother of A.P. Coleman, a geologist and an avid explorer of the Rockies between 1888 and 1907. The pair travelled in this area in 1892 and 1893, looking for two mythical peaks, Mt. Hooker and Mt. Brown. Reported to be approximately 4900 m high, the Colemans had a hand in proving the mountains to be, in reality, closer to 2700 m high.

Where the trail levels and the fencing ends, it's time to turn around. The great thing about canyons when you walk them both ways is that you are bound to see things on the return trip that you missed on the way out.

TURBULENT WATER

Early explorers often named features without having had much experience "in the neighbourhood". Yet it is sometimes the case that you wouldn't be able to improve on a name that was given in that first brush of acquaintance. *Sunwapta* is a Stoney word that means "turbulent water". A. P. Coleman gave the name in 1892 and it stuck – as this canyon attests – for excellent reasons. The river begins at the toe of the Athabasca Glacier.

WINTERGREENS

The understory in this part of the Sunwapta Valley features a characteristic pine forest mix of flowers and shrubs: dwarf dogwood (bunchberry), calypso orchid, arnica, wild strawberry, yellow columbine, twinflower, Labrador tea, buffaloberry, creeping juniper, and three wintergreens: pink, one-flowered, and one-sided. How do you tell the three wintergreens apart? Pink wintergreen is obvious. The blooms of one-flowered, and one-sided wintergreen are each a pale, creamy, green. One-flowered has one, delicate nodding bloom with five petals. (Single delight is a folk name for this flower.) One-sided wintergreen has multiple, bell-shaped blooms on a single stem, all nodding to the same side.

56. Athabasca Falls

Athabasca Falls

TRAIL THUMBNAIL

Trailhead
Follow the Icefields Parkway to its junction with Highway 93A; 29.8 km south of Highway 16; 70.9 km north of the Columbia Icefield information centre. Follow Highway 93A for 500 m to the parking area. See map, p. 80.

Rating: easy, 200 m – 700 m. Wheelchair accessible in part.

Special considerations: Warning! Fall risk! Keep inside the railings. Do not wade in the river or walk on river ice.

Best lighting: afternoon

Nearby trails: 72 73

The Athabasca River carries more water than any other river in the Rocky Mountain parks. At Athabasca Falls, the river pours over a 23 m drop. Rain or shine, don't miss the incredible sensory experience of the thundering water, the mist, and the spray, from the viewpoints at the water's edge. You can explore abandoned river courses, potholes, and the canyon downstream. Keep within the viewpoints and railings. The slick riverbank is death-on-rocks. Of the many who have fallen in here, no one is known to have survived. One person fell out of a canoe above the falls and somehow survived the trip over, down, and under.

Many waterfalls in the Rockies plummet from hanging valleys. The cascade of Athabasca Falls exists for a different reason. Here, the ancient Athabasca Glacier encountered a resistant outcrop of quartzite – the McNaughton Formation, a member of the Gog Group (see p. 40). Like a skier almost taking air from a bump and then face-planting on the landing, the glacier skipped over the outcrop and eroded a deep hollow in softer material downstream. Athabasca Falls now cascades over this glacial rock step.

The spray from the falls sustains a canyon forest of lodgepole pine, subalpine fir, and white spruce. Feathermosses and lichens thrive in this area, along with shade-tolerant shrubs and wildflowers. Nearby,

SYNCLINES

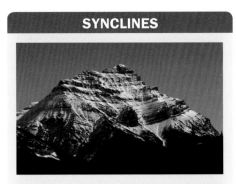

If you look at the sedimentary layers in the northwest face of Mt. Kerkeslin, you will see a shallow, downward fold. This U-shape is a syncline (SIN-cline). When the rock that now comprises Mt. Kerkeslin was deep within the Earth's crust, it was warm and pliable. The tremendous compressive forces of mountain building were able to warp it into folds. The U-shaped fold of a syncline was usually paired on either side with arch-shaped folds called anticlines. Rock at the base of a syncline was compressed and rendered more resistant to erosion. Rock at the crest of an anticline was stretched, weakened, and subsequently more easily eroded. Many major valleys in the Rockies, including the Bow and Athabasca, have been eroded by ice and water downward into anticlines, whereas the paralleling mountain ranges have endured atop synclines. The fold in Mt. Kerkeslin marks the northern end of a series of synclines that begins at Castle Mountain in Banff, and extends for 260 km.

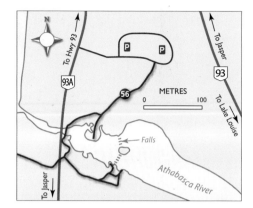

FROM ICEFIELD TO OCEAN

just north of the junction on the Icefields Parkway, you can see a stand of moisture-loving black spruce – an uncommon tree in the Rockies.

In the view east from Athabasca Falls, look for the U-shaped, syncline fold in Mt. Kerkeslin (2956 m). James Hector is often cited as the person who named the mountain. *Kerkeslin* is reportedly Stoney or Cree for "wolverine". In his journal in January 1859, Hector mentioned an "Indian" name for the wolverine: *ker-kes-shu*. In an entry made just over three weeks later, he recorded an encounter in this part of the Athabasca Valley, when one of his companions shot a wolverine. The animal dropped to the snow – "His blood spouted out." As the party approached the wounded animal, it fled. Hector's men "pressed it hard", but the wolverine ran up a bank and onto a cliff, making good its escape. So, Hector clearly was preoccupied with wolverines when in this area, but he did not place the name on the peak.

57. Valley of the Five Lakes

TRAIL THUMBNAIL

Trailhead
East side of the Icefields Parkway, 8.7 km south of Highway 16; 92 km north of the Columbia Icefield information centre.

Rating: moderate, 4.3 km loop

Best lighting: anytime

Nearby trail: 74

From its sources on the northern edge of the Columbia Icefield, the Athabasca River flows 1230 km to Lake Athabasca in north-eastern Alberta. Its waters eventually reach the Arctic Ocean via the Mackenzie river system. *Athabasca* is Cree for "place where there are reeds", referring to the delta at the river's mouth. (Unfortunately, the namesake plants are sedges, not reeds.) The name was one of the earlier to be used by Europeans in the Rockies, possibly in 1790. The 168 km section of the Athabasca River within Jasper National Park was designated a Canadian Heritage River in 1989. The Alberta Tar Sands developments on the river's northerly reach severely threaten the volume and health of this watercourse.

The Athabasca Valley is undeniably a spectacular place. Some of its wonders, however, are subtle. Tucked away in the rolling, gritstone ridge country just south of Jasper town, the Valley of the Five Lakes is one such place. There are no towering peaks nearby, no glaciers, and no plummeting cascades. What there is, perhaps, is balance; a tranquillity that smoothes some of the harsh edges of the mountains. This outing offers opportunities to see deer, elk, beaver, waterfowl, coyote, and bears. The forest is open lodgepole pine, with an undergrowth of buffaloberry, bearberry, twinflower, and juniper.

Valley of the Five Lakes

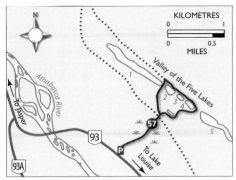

The trail (posted as #9a) crosses a gritstone ridge and then descends to "Wabasso Creek". Beavers have dammed the creek. You cross the resulting pond on a boardwalk. You may see beavers here in early morning or late evening. Look for their lodges – dome-shaped mounds of sticks and mud. Sedges and a thicket of moisture loving shrubs grow at the pond's edge. I have seen a great blue heron here.

Keep straight ahead at the intersection with trail #9 (watch for cyclists!), as you climb away from the pond onto a grassy, sunny slope – another gritstone ridge. This one supports a stand of mature

THE MIETTE GROUP

The bedrock in this part of the Athabasca Valley contains the Miette (mee-YETT) Group of sedimentary formations. Miette sediments were laid down between 740-million-years-ago and 542-million-years ago, making the resulting rocks the oldest visible in the central Rockies. The Miette Group is the thickest assemblage, too, reaching a maximum of 8 km. It is about 2.7 km thick near Jasper town.

The Miette Group contains layers of resistant gritstone, alternating with softer, recessive layers of shale or slate. (Slate was formerly shale that was transformed by heat or pressure when deep underground.) The entire assembly records episodes of erosion and deposition during the Earth's longest known glacial period. Most of the gritstone particles probably came from granite bedrock of what is now the Canadian Shield. The particles are naturally "graded" – in any given sequence, the larger particles, which would have dropped out of flowing water first to settle in the mud, will be on the bottom. These form a rock type known as conglomerate. It looks like natural concrete. The finer layers above created sandstone. The still finer layers atop that became shale and slate.

Enter mountain creation. In this part of the Athabasca Valley, the Miette formations were tipped steeply upwards, almost on edge. In the alternating sequence of resistant and recessive layers, the softer layers have been eroded, creating the pockets that now hold many of Jasper's lakes and ponds. The resistant layers endure as the ridges that separate the lakes. Travel across the valley floor, as you do on the way to the Five Lakes, and you will see (and feel!) this geology come to life; the resulting up-and-down topography is obvious.

The member of the Miette Group visible in this part of the Rockies is the McKale Formation. It is pleasing to the eye for a number of reasons. The

shales and slates contain pyrite and chlorite, with resulting crimson and green streaks and hues where these minerals have oxidized. Fissures in the gritstone layers often filled with liquefied quartz when the rock was deep underground. The white quartz veins now stand out against the coarse, buff-coloured gritstone.

Douglas-fir trees. Mt. Edith Cavell (3363 m) is prominent to the southwest, although, with its glaciers concealed, it is hard to recognize. At the top of the ridge you enter a grove of trembling aspen trees and reach a junction. If you are visiting in June, pause here and listen. The trees will be alive with wood warblers. At the junction, you want trail #9b, which angles to the northeast (left). Descend from the ridge into a damper lodgepole pine forest.

The Five Lakes owe their existence to the bedrock structure of the Athabasca Valley. The parallel, upturned ridges of resistant Miette gritstone are separated by weaker slates that have been eroded into the hollows that now contain a myriad of ponds, the Five Lakes among them. Natural dams of more resistant rock separate the lakes. Look for common loons, especially on the larger lakes (1 and 5); and for other waterfowl, including mallards, blue-winged teals, and green-winged teals.

After about 700 m the trail passes between lakes 1 and 2. At the junction just beyond, turn southeast (right) onto trail #9a. You traverse an open sideslope, dotted with Douglas-firs, above the northeast shores of lakes 2, 3, and 4 to a junction at the tip of lake 5. Wildflowers that prefer dry locations bloom here in late spring and early summer. Various short side-trails have been beaten to the best viewpoints on the lakeshores, and also to the best swimming spots. You may agree with our daughters who, during one visit on a hot, July day, christened this hike the Valley of the Five Swims. In really scorching summers lakes 2 and 3 will be almost dry.

Turn west (right), still on trail #9a, to loop back to the first junction in 700 m. Look for a bonus – a sixth lake in the trees, north of the trail, just over halfway to the junction. Retrace the first kilometre of trail to the parking area.

Twinflower

58. Jasper Discovery Trail

A rooftop wilderness

TRAIL THUMBNAIL

Trailhead

The trail loops around Jasper town. Convenient places to start are opposite the park information centre on Connaught Avenue, or on Pyramid Lake Road adjacent to the Jasper-Yellowhead Museum. About one-third of the loop is paved and is wheelchair ♿ accessible.

Rating: You can tailor the outing to your ability. The full loop is rated harder, 8.3 km.

Special considerations: You share the trail with cyclists. Use caution crossing roads.

Best lighting: anytime

Nearby trails: 61 62 75

With a network of 190 km of trails within striking distance of town, Jasper is the "urban" walking and hiking capital of the Rockies. You could easily spend a week making outings from town without ever having to start a vehicle. The crown jewel in Jasper town's trail network was set in 2007 when the Jasper Discovery Trail opened in time for the park's centennial. The trail was a combined effort of the Jasper Trails Project and Parks Canada, and is a shining example of an inspired community endeavour. As you make the loop around town (described here, clockwise), trailside interpretive panels highlight three principal themes. Use caution crossing roadways. Keep away from the railway tracks.

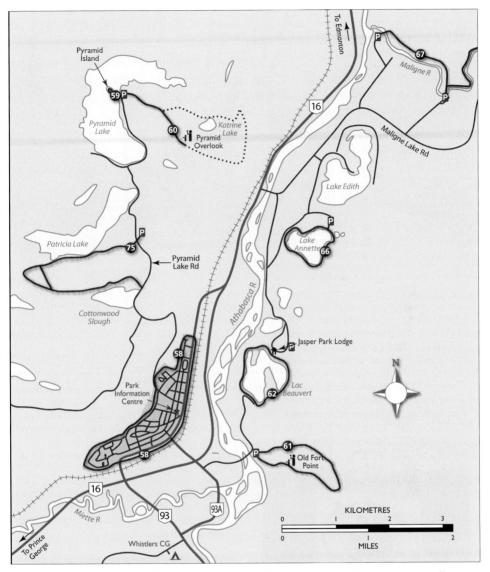

"Discover Our Peaks"

The trail is paved for just over 2 km, from its north end to the intersection of Hazel Avenue with Connaught Avenue. With few buildings in the foreground, the views to the east and south feature the mountains of the Colin Range, the Maligne Range, and the main ranges, all of them flanking the massive breach of the Athabasca Valley. Prominent are Roche Bonhomme, Mt. Tekarra, and Mt. Edith Cavell. Interpretive panels provide background on the history and geology of these mountains, and on some of the early settlers and explorers in this area.

"Discover Our Railway Ties"

The south-westerly portion of the loop focuses on Jasper's early railway history. Jasper National Park was established in 1907, before any community existed here. It was not, however, the park that gave rise to the town, but the logistics of building two transcontinental railways. In 1903, the Grand Trunk Pacific Railway (GTPR) received its charter to build a line from Ontario to Prince Rupert, crossing the Rockies at Yellowhead Pass. Three years later, the Canadian Northern Railway filed plans to construct a parallel line across Yellowhead Pass, that would then head southwest through the Thompson and Fraser valleys to Vancouver. The GTPR chose the present location of Jasper town as a divisional point, and named the

Laying track for the GTPR in 1911

siding Fitzhugh after a railway vice-president. The first train from the east reached town in August 1911. After Mr. Fitzhugh resigned, locals successfully petitioned to have the community name changed to that of the park. The Canadian Northern built its closest divisional point to the west at Lucerne, just across the border in B.C.

As the GTPR work gangs cleaved a railroad bed from the mountains, surveyors for the Canadian Northern played catch-up, working alongside them.

FOLLOW THE BEAR

The instruction "follow the bear" will generally get you around this loop without difficulty. There is only one place that you may have trouble. Walking the loop clockwise, as you leave the parking area just east of the Jasper-Yellowhead Museum, follow the bear and trail #2 for 65 m to a Y-junction. Take the right-hand trail (follow the bear!) to descend to the Pyramid Lake Road, which the trail then follows on a sidewalk. If you miss this junction, you will go for a walk in the woods on trail #2 – not necessarily a bad thing, but it will add some distance to your day by the time you figure out your mistake. Trust me.

In places, the finished railway lines were literally side by side. The GTPR completed its line in April 1914; the Canadian Northern completed its line in January 1915, and opened a station here, called Jasper Park, the following spring.

It was not, of course, a sustainable proposition for either operation. The crash came in 1916 as the Canadian government began a lengthy process of amalgamating and taking over the foundering railways. When the Canadian Northern shut down its Lucerne operations in 1924, 300 people moved to Jasper, almost tripling the town's population. The influx was so great, people slept in boxcars and tents. But Jasper got its first hospital, relocated from Lucerne, as a result. Jasper Park station became a railway bunkhouse at a location still known as Sleepy Hollow. At the southerly end of this portion of the trail, you can see a GTPR railway bridge, now abandoned, completed in 1913.

"Discover Our Wild Side"

For approximately 4.5 km, the remainder of the Jasper Discover Trail climbs onto the edge of the Pyramid Bench on the north side of town. The trail cuts in and out of ravines and gullies on this otherwise dry slope, showcasing a diversity of habitats. Douglas-fir trees dominate the forest. The bark of many trees is fire-scarred. Parks Canada has cleared trees on these slopes to help create a firebreak near town. Elk, deer, and bears use the trail as a travel route. Interpretive panels describe the key role of the bench north of town in the lives of these animal species. I have seen an American marten here.

59. Pyramid Island

Pyramid Lake

Pyramid Island shelter

Lakes and ponds abound in Jasper – there are more than 800 of them. Although relatively few of Jasper's lakes are close to present day glaciers, almost all of them owe their existence to glaciation. Many, such as Lake Annette (see p. 93), are kettle ponds, created when large blocks of ice detached from receding glaciers at the end of the last ice age. Other lakes occupy hollows scooped by ice age glaciers from softer formations in the bedrock. The Pyramid Bench, just north of town contains an assortment of more than 30 lakes created by these processes. Pyramid Lake, with an area of 1.27 km², is the largest of these. It is not, however, with a depth of 19 m, the deepest. Nearby Patricia Lake is 40 m deep.

A forest of white spruce and lodgepole pine cloaks Pyramid Island. The views of the peaks southwest of Jasper are particularly fine in the early morning and evening. But the prime view is of Pyramid Mountain (2763 m) rising above the lake's north shore. The reddish hue of the cliffs is, indeed, caused by rust. The quartzite rocks contain pyrite ("fools gold"), an element of which is iron. When the pyrite weathers, it rusts, becoming hematite.

TRAIL THUMBNAIL

Trailhead
From Jasper town, follow Pyramid Lake Road north for 6.2 km to the Pyramid Island parking area near road's end. See map, p. 83.

Rating: easy, 600 m loop. Wheelchair ♿ accessible in part, with assistance.

Best lighting: anytime, morning and evening are especially good

Nearby trails: 60 75

PYRAMID?... REALLY?

Seen from Pyramid Lake, Pyramid Mountain is impressive, rising almost a mile above. But any number of other mountains in the Rockies are more pyramid-like. It's all a matter of perspective. James Hector named the mountain in 1859 as he  pounded along the frozen Athabasca River. Seen from Disaster Point about 30 km northeast of town, the striking, pyramid-like form of the mountain is a prominent landmark.

For 80 years, Pyramid Island has been an integral part of the fabric of life in Jasper. Baptisms, weddings, memorial services, picnics, and parties – all take place on this tiny island with its picture-perfect backdrop. The shelter dates to 1933. If you are visiting in late summer or early autumn when the leaves of the aspens, birches, and poplars have turned, a visit to Pyramid Island is a must. The Friends of Jasper National Park restored the trails and shorelines in 1998. Please keep to the beaten paths.

60. Pyramid Overlook

Trailhead

As for Pyramid Island (outing 59). The trailhead is slightly north of the Pyramid Island trailhead, on the opposite side of the road. See map, p. 83

Rating: moderate, 1.6 km

Special considerations: Grizzly bears frequent the area. You share the trail with cyclists. Check yourself for wood ticks after hiking in late spring.

Best lighting: late afternoon and evening

Nearby trails: 59 75

This short outing is an excellent choice for a fair summer evening. Head southeast from the parking area on trail #2b. You pass through micro-habitats of dry lodgepole pine forest and wetter Engelmann spruce. After about 250 m you draw alongside the cliff edge with a view of Pyramid Lake. The trail cuts back into the forest. At the junction about 800 m from the trailhead, keep southwest (right) on trail #2b. You make a sidehill climb through a pocket of wet forest, complete with alders and ferns. The displays of arnica and dogwood can be superb.

At the top of the sidehill climb, a short sidetrail leads west (right) to the cliff edge, but stay on the main trail as it makes a switchbacking climb to the beginning of the overlook. Note the change to a classic montane cliff-edge forest dominated by Douglas-firs. Juniper and buffaloberry are common in the understory. I have met a grizzly bear sow and cub, here. Look for bighorn sheep on the grassy slopes below.

From the rocky terrace at the top of the climb, openings in the trees provide a panoramic view of the Miette and Athabasca valleys, Jasper town, and Pyramid and Patricia lakes. There are great views, also, at your feet: the blooms of alpine spring beauty, stonecrop, red-stemmed saxifrage, mullein, pussytoes, yarrow, and locoweed grace the thin soils atop the limestone. What is this cliff all about? It's the Pyramid Thrust, the westerly edge of the front ranges. To the northeast of here, the rock is all limestone; to the southwest, it's quartzite, sandstone, shale, and slate in the eastern main ranges.

Although it is possible to carry on along the edge of the overlook, a warren of trails in that direction makes for challenging route-finding. If you begin to descend on the main trail while heading south, it's time to turn around and retrace your route, north to the parking area.

61. Old Fort Point

TRAIL THUMBNAIL

Trailhead

Follow Highway 93A south from the intersection of Hazel Avenue and Connaught Drive in Jasper town. Cross Highway 16. In 150 m, turn east (left) onto the Lac Beauvert Road. Follow this for 900 m, across the bridge over the Athabasca River. Park on the south (right).

1. From town, follow trail #12 from the intersection of Hazel Avenue and Connaught Drive, south along Highway 93A. Cross Highway 16 with caution. Turn east (left) on to trail #14. Follow it for about 600 m to where it crosses the Lac Beauvert Road. Turn east (left) on to the road. Cross the Athabasca River to the Old Fort Point parking area. (Distances not included in outing.)

2. From Whistlers or Wapiti campgrounds, follow trail #12 north to its intersection with trail #14. Turn east (right). Follow the trail about 500 m to where it crosses the Lac Beauvert Road. Turn east (right) on to the road. Cross the Athabasca River to the Old Fort Point parking area. (Distances not included in outing.) See map, p. 83.

Rating: harder, 4.4 km loop including both summits

Special consideration: You share part of the trail with cyclists.

Best lighting: anytime

Nearby trail: 62

The Old Fort Point trail loops steeply over the crest of a rocky knoll south of Jasper, and provides an overview of the town and the Athabasca Valley. When I lead this outing as a guided hike, I find it an inspiration – it touches on almost every human history and natural history theme in the Rockies.

During the winter of 1810-11, David Thompson, an explorer and fur trader with the North West Company, established a trade route across Athabasca Pass. As Thompson set off to tackle that frigid crossing, he directed one of his men, William Henry, to build an outpost near present day Jasper town. Henry House, as it came to be known, was the first, permanent habitation built by white people on the east slope of the Rockies.

View from Old Fort Point

Athabasca River

The location of Henry House is maintained as a local mystery. Some historians have ventured that Old Fort Point is a misnomer, and that Old *Ford* Point was the original name for this feature. A ford is a river-crossing place. Explorers certainly made fords of the Athabasca and Miette rivers, nearby. However, in 1908, Mary Schäffer gave a precise description of the ruins of Henry House, placing it about 8 km downstream from here on the Athabasca River, and on the opposite bank.

Begin at the staircase at the south end of the parking area. At the top of the stairs, you may view the plaque that was unveiled when the portion of the Athabasca River within Jasper was proclaimed a Canadian Heritage River in 1989. The Athabasca River is 1230 km long. It rises at the north edge of Columbia Icefield and flows to the Arctic Ocean by way of the Slave and Mackenzie river systems. Together with its tributaries, the Athabasca drains most of Jasper National Park. *Athabasca* is a Cree name that means "place where there are reeds" – a reference to the delta at the river's mouth in Lake Athabasca.

Keep southeast (left) on trail #1 at the junction with trail #9c. You climb steadily, following an upturned edge of rock that forms the spine of "the point". This rock is a conglomerate of the McKale Formation, part of the Miette Group (see p. 81), which contains the oldest rock formations visible in this part of the Rockies. If a particular rock shimmers in the sunlight, it's probably because it contains quartz particles.

What happened to the forest? The crest of the point is a montane meadow that owes its existence to wind and to the past effects of fires. A few Douglas-fir trees, survivors of those fires, dot the slopes, along with creeping juniper and common juniper. The meadows are awash with wildflower blooms in late spring and early summer.

A short sidetrail cuts north (left) onto the summit of the point, to provide a panoramic view

ROCHE MOUTONÉE

If you read about the Miette Group of sedimentary formations (see p. 81), you will understand what Old Fort Point is made of and how the bedrock here came to be. But what explains the contrast between its streamlined, southwest slope and its craggy, northeast aspect? Old Fort Point is a *roche moutonée* (ROSH moot-on-AY). This French expression means "fleecy rock". If you are up on your European fashion of the 1700s, you will know that a *moutonée* was a wig smeared with mutton fat to stick it in place. Hang in there. This should all make sense to you after the following paragraph.

A roche moutonée requires a relatively resistant rock outcrop – in this case gritstone of the Miette Group. The shape of a roche moutonée indicates the direction that glacial ice flowed during the last ice age. The smooth, southwest slope (right side of photo) faced into the flow of ice; the cliffy side faced away. (Think of a hand, smeared with mutton fat, sweeping up over a forehead onto a wig. What happens to the hair at the back of the wig?)

Glaciers that flowed north in the Athabasca Valley, and east from the Miette Valley, merged near here. They were able to hone the southwest slope of Old Fort Point, but could not conform right away to the drop on the northeast slope, which remained out of contact with the base of the ice. Various forces of erosion have since chunked away at that cliff. The resulting topography profoundly influences life. The southwest slope of Old Fort Point, angled perfectly to catch maximum solar energy at this latitude, is home to species that prefer wind, sun, and dry soils; the northeast slope is home to those that prefer shelter, moisture, shade, and cold.

Flying high

of the Athabasca and Miette valleys, and Jasper town. If you have had enough, you can turn back here. To carry on with the loop, return to the main trail and head southeast (left). After about 600 m, another sidetrail heads north (left) onto the lower, southeast summit. Here, you have fine views of the lakes along the east bank of the Athabasca River. If you note a transition in the forest on the valley floor, you are probably looking at a fireguard – a thinning in the forest cut by Parks Canada to protect Jasper Park Lodge. The agency has carried out other forest

thinning nearby, including small prescribed burns on the south slopes of Old Fort Point.

The large block on the southeast summit looks out of place. It's a glacial erratic, a chunk of quartzite carried by the ancient Athabasca Valley glacier, and dropped here at the end of the last ice age. You can see striations – scratches caused by glacial ice, in the bedrock adjacent to the erratic.

Backtrack to the main trail and begin the descent into trembling aspen forest. The colours of the leaves are a delight in late season. At the junction in 400 m, turn north (left) to follow trail #1. Keep left at two subsequent junctions, each 600 m apart, to stay on trail #1 as it loops back to the parking area under the northeast cliff of Old Fort Point. Note how the shaded forest here is much more damp than that on the sunny slopes that you ascended a while ago. There are pockets of white spruce and subalpine fir, and a few white birch.

62. Lac Beauvert

Trailhead

🚗 1. As for Old Fort Point (61). From the Old Fort Point parking area, continue north on the Lake Beauvert Road to where it ends at the lake. The lakeshore trail is #4a.

2. Those staying at Jasper Park Lodge can access the trail from near the main lodge building.

🥾 As for Old Fort Point (61). Follow trail #7 north for 500 m. At the junction, keep straight ahead on trail #7b for 500 m to the lakeshore, where you want trail #4a. (Distances not included in outing.) See map, p. 83.

Rating: moderate, 3.7 km loop

Special considerations: Elk frequent this trail. Use caution. Please keep off the golf course and away from the outlying buildings of Jasper Park Lodge.

Best lighting: anytime

Nearby trail: 61 62

Lac Beauvert (bow-VAIR) is French for "beautiful green lake". The trail makes a circuit of this horse-shoe-shaped lake adjacent to Jasper Park Lodge. The lodge originated in 1922. Earlier accommodation at the site was a camp called "Tent City". The open, Douglas-fir forest and grasslands near the lake are important year-round range for elk. You may see Common loons and Canada geese on the lake.

MINING ITS OWN BUSINESS

The trembling aspen is the most abundant and widely dispersed tree species in North America. It occurs in every province and territory in Canada. Some aspen stands are thought to be thousands of years old, and have survived many shifts in the climatic regime. Although not a fire-dependant species, the well-being of aspens is now being affected, in part, by the relative absence of large-scale forest fires in western Canada. One thing that forest fires do is keep populations of tree pests in check, preventing them from reaching thresholds where infestations take place. While the mountain pine beetle has gained attention for its affects on the pine forests of the west, the aspen forests are being hit hard by the aspen leaf miner. This tiny moth chews away at the surface layers of aspen leaves, producing a tell-tale pattern. Over the course of a few summers in an infested area, the moths can defoliate entire aspen stands. In some cases, the trees will die; in others, they will leaf out again after the aspen leaf miner moves on.

63. Path of the Glacier

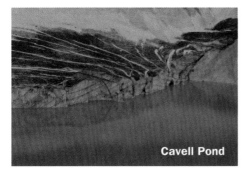

Cavell Pond

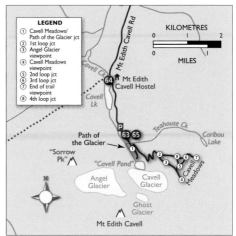

LEGEND
① Cavell Meadows/ Path of the Glacier jct
② 1st loop jct
③ Angel Glacier viewpoint
④ Cavell Meadows viewpoint
⑤ 2nd loop jct
⑥ 3rd loop jct
⑦ End of trail viewpoint
⑧ 4th loop jct

TRAIL THUMBNAIL

Trailhead

Follow the Icefields Parkway, 6.7 km south from Highway 16 to Highway 93A. Turn right and follow Highway 93A south for 5.2 km. Turn right onto the Mt. Edith Cavell Road, and follow this 14 km to the Mt. Edith Cavell parking area. The Path of the Glacier-Cavell Meadows trailhead is at the southeast corner of the parking area. Large recreational vehicles and trailers are not allowed on the Mt. Edith Cavell Road. Use the trailer drop-off opposite the beginning of the road.

Rating: easy, 1.3 km loop

Special considerations: Caution! Ice avalanches, snow avalanches, flash-floods and rockfall are significant hazards. Keep to maintained trails. Keep off Cavell Glacier and away from Cavell Pond.

Best lighting: anytime

Nearby trails: 64 65

In the deep, cirque pocket at the base of Mt. Edith Cavell, you can walk back in time to an era when ice ruled the Earth. The Path of the Glacier traverses a landscape that was buried under the combined ice of the Angel and Cavell glaciers just over a century ago. Today, hardy vegetation is taking hold. Dress warmly.

The initial climb from the parking area is over a horseshoe-shaped pile of boulders, an end moraine of Cavell Glacier. There were formerly two end moraines here, one nested inside the other, but the northerly one was destroyed when the parking area was built in the 1970s. From the crest of the moraine, you have a fine view south across the forefield – the area scoured during the last glacial advance. If you look uphill to the east (left) you will see the trimline, which indicates the depth of that ice. The trees in the forest above the trimline were alive when the ice flowed past them. Ice obliterated the forest below the trimline.

The trail climbs along the flank of a lateral moraine that consists almost entirely of quartzite boulders and fragments. Look for golden-mantled ground squirrels and for pikas. After 600 m you reach the Cavell Meadows junction. Keep straight ahead and descend slighlty to the Cavell Pond viewpoint. In 2012, an ice avalanche from Ghost Glacier plunged into Cavell Pond, creating a deluge that swept the valley to beyond the parking lot. The event happened in the middle of the night. No one was injured.

From studies carried out in this valley, the period of cooling in the Rockies that lasted from 1200 to 1850 AD has been named the Cavell Advance. During this interval, glaciers in the Rockies advanced significantly – some as much as 3 km beyond their present positions. When the first explorers arrived in the Rockies in the late 1880s, most of the glaciers were just backing off from those maximums. So for many glaciers, there exists a fine photographic record of the changes since. What have glaciologists learned about Cavell Glacier? Between 1888 and 1975, the glacier receded 988 m. The maximum of the Cavell Advance here took place in 1705. This was the greatest advance of Cavell Glacier during the previous 2600 years.

The pinnacles of ice on the upper cliffs of the Angel Glacier are called seracs (sair-RACKS). Angel Glacier formerly descended to the valley floor and merged with the ice of Cavell Glacier. In the 1940s Angel Glacier broke contact and began to recede.

Angel Glacier

64. Cavell Lake

MT. EDITH CAVELL (3363 m)

Mt. Edith Cavell is the highest mountain near Jasper town. First Peoples knew it as the "White Ghost", probably because of the snow-covered mountain's appearance in moonlight. The voyageurs of the fur trade called it *La Montagne de la Grande Traverse* ("The Mountain of the Great Crossing"). When they saw Mt. Edith Cavell from the northeast, it meant that the long approach to Athabasca Pass was almost over, and that the "great crossing" of the Athabasca River and the mountains lay just ahead.

Locals originally knew the mountain as Mt. Fitzhugh after a vice-president of the Grand Trunk Pacific Railway. In 1915, the Geographic Board of Canada asked surveyor A.O. Wheeler to recommend a mountain to commemorate Edith Cavell, an English nurse who had worked behind the lines with the Belgian Red Cross in World War I. She tended to the injured of both sides, but was executed for allegedly assisting the escape of captive Allied troops. Wheeler chose "the beautiful mountain facing the Athabasca Valley". The Board made the name official the following year. A memorial service is held for Edith Cavell each summer at St. George's church in Jasper. Mountain guide Hans Fuhrer took a cross to the summit. According to Edith's brother, their family name is properly pronounced and emphasized to rhyme with "gravel".

Mt. Edith Cavell has long been popular with mountaineers. Its first ascent was made in 1915. The east ridge (left-hand skyline), first climbed in 1924, is considered one of the classic alpine rock climbs in the Rockies. The first ascent of the spectacular north face in 1961 marked the beginning of extreme alpine climbing in the Rockies. If you're wondering which is the mountain's highest point, it's the central bump on the nearly horizontal summit ridge.

The quartzite rock layers in Mt. Edith Cavell angle upward to the northeast. They are the western arm of a massive arch-shaped fold – an anticline. Ice age glaciers eroded downward through this fold, removing the crest of the arch.

Trailhead

Initially as for Path of the Glacier (outing 63), but park opposite the hostel at km 12.2 on the Mt. Edith Cavell Road, at the Astoria River trailhead. See map, p. 89.

Rating: easy, 250 m

Best lighting: early morning and evening

Nearby trails: 63 65

This road-width trail descends to the bridge at the outlet of Cavell Lake, revealing a postcard view of Mt. Edith Cavell (3363 m).

If conditions favouring glacial retreat persist, the "body" and "wings" of Angel Glacier may disappear. The hanging glacier frequently avalanches ice and snow onto the valley floor.

Snow does not usually bond to slopes steeper than 40 degrees, so most of the snow that falls on the north face of Mt. Edith Cavell slides off in avalanches. Couloirs and gullies funnel these avalanches onto the valley floor. In the near perpetual shade cast by the mountain, the snow accumulates and consolidates into the ice of Cavell Glacier. The remnant glacier above and slightly to the left of Cavell Glacier is Ghost Glacier – a reference to Mt. Edith Cavell's original name – "White Ghost".

You may take advantage of short alternate trail sections on your return. Although the forefield of Cavell Glacier initially appears devoid of vegetation, hardy plants grow here. The process of transformation – in this case the primary succession from moraine to subalpine forest – may take more than a thousand years. Less than one percent of the area covered by ice a century ago is presently vegetated.

Cavell Meadows

returns via the Path of the Glacier. The Friends of Jasper National Park and Parks Canada completed an extensive restoration of the Cavell Meadows trail in 2004. To spare the meadows and to honour the work, please keep to the maintained trail.

The trail initially climbs over an end moraine and works its way south through the quartzite rubble of the glacier forefield. Life is slowly taking hold. A cottonwood poplar grows from the rocks, right on the trail. At the junction in 600 m, turn east (left). The Cavell Meadows trail climbs steeply over a lateral moraine. Cavell Glacier created this landform, and the end moraine that you crossed earlier, during the glacier's most recent advance. The coarse, quartz sand underfoot has been eroded from the quartzite boulders. Least chipmunks, golden mantled ground squirrels, and pikas live in the nooks and crannies of this moraine. Please don't feed them.

The top of the moraine marks an abrupt transition to subalpine forest. This is the trimline of Cavell Glacier. A century and a half ago, the ice of the glacier was thick enough to reach this far up the side of the valley, obliterating mature forest. Some trees near trimline show evidence of roots and trunks damaged by the moving glacial ice. You can see where two, lesser moraines nest within the outer moraine. Together, they record three glacial advances of nearly equal magnitude.

Dwarf false asphodel, cotton-grass, and red-stemmed saxifrage grow in wet areas, competing for your attention with the views of Angel Glacier. After paralleling the moraine crest for a few hundred metres, the trail switchbacks east (left) into the trees. The forest here is an ancient one, dominated by Engelmann spruce and subalpine fir. One fir is half a metre thick at its base. In the winter of 1990-91, a snow avalanche from the north face of Mt. Edith Cavell created a windblast strong enough to topple some of these trees. One tree cut from the debris by chainsaw showed 232 concentric rings, each recording a year's growth. Arnica and valerian comprise most of the ground cover. Red-breasted nuthatches and Clark's nutcrackers are common, along with red squirrels.

65. Cavell Meadows

TRAIL THUMBNAIL

Trailhead
As for Path of the Glacier (outing 63). See map, p. 89.

Rating: harder, 7.7 km loop

Special considerations: Parks Canada closes this trail until the snowcover has melted. Dogs are not permitted. See also the Special considerations for the Path of the Glacier (63).

Best lighting: morning

Nearby trails: 63 64

On the rolling alpland of Cavell Meadows, Angel Glacier and the precipitous north face of Mt. Edith Cavell (3363 m) provide the backdrop for a stunning mid-summer display of wildflowers. This loop outing begins on the Cavell Meadows trail and

Pink mountain heather   Yellow mountain heather   White mountain heather

Keep right at the first loop junction. At km 2.4, you reach a viewpoint that provides an excellent view of Angel Glacier. The ice cliffs are 40 m thick. Angel Glacier formerly merged with Cavell Glacier. Glacial recession caused it to break contact in the 1940s. After a few decades when the Angel hovered in equilibrium, it began winging up the cliff. You can see the lichen trimline of Angel Glacier clearly to the north of the hanging body of ice. The Cavell Advance of the glacier (see below) scoured the lichens from the rock.

Cavell Meadows

The forest soon becomes a patchwork of tree islands separated by glades of subalpine meadow. Although the elevation here (2060 m) is low for treeline, the chilling effects of glacial ice, the north-facing slope, and the winter-long shade of Mt. Edith Cavell, combine to inhibit the growth of trees. Soon the trail emerges onto tundra. Fleabane, paintbrush, Sitka valerian, western anemone, arnica, alpine veronica, bracted lousewort, groundsel, everlasting, and white mountain-avens are just a few of the many species that grow here. Amateur botanists are particularly fond of these meadows for their displays of mountain heather – pink, yellow, and white (see also p. 99). In most years, the blooms peak in late July.

At km 2.8, you reach the Cavell Meadows viewpoint. If you are tired, turn back here and retrace your steps to the trailhead. For those wanting to go higher, please refer to the map. Keep right at junctions after you leave this viewpoint, to reach the end-of-trail viewpoint in 1.1 km. As you ascend the quartzite screes of the ridge, you may have the pleasure of placing your feet in the "Sasquatch tracks" – footprints made by the many thousands of hikers who have preceded you.

The upper meadows are part of the alpine life zone and are occasionally visited by grizzly bears and mountain caribou (hence the dog ban). Some hollows here may hold snow until mid-August. The trickle of snowmelt on warm days provides water for moisture loving plants such as leather-leaved saxifrage, white globeflower, and red-stemmed saxifrage. The reddish tinge in snowbanks is watermelon snow, caused by algae with a red pigment. Some of the steep slopes above the meadows contain rock glaciers – accumulations of rock that contain just enough ice to allow the whole mass to creep downhill.

The Path of the Glacier

Descending from the end-of-trail viewpoint, keep straight ahead (west) at the next three junctions to reach the Path of the Glacier junction in 2.7 km. Turn south (left) to descend to the Cavell Pond viewpoint in the cirque at the base of Mt. Edith Cavell. Please refer to pages 89-91 for more information.

THE LITTLE ICE AGE: COOL DETECTIVE WORK

The most recent advance of Cavell Glacier took place during what is often called the Little Ice Age, a period of cooling in the northern hemisphere that lasted from 1050 AD to the mid 1840s. Glaciologists have gained much of their understanding of that recent glaciation in the Rockies from studies carried out here, so they often refer to the Little Ice Age as the "Cavell Advance".

Glaciologists use vegetation near glaciers to help them assign dates to glacial events. In a process called dendrochronology (Greek for "tree-time-knowledge"), they take core samples from mature trees near trimline. By counting the tree rings in the core they can determine the approximate ages of the trees. By sampling many trees close to a glacier, the date and extent of the most recent glacial advance can be plotted. Trees that grow on moraines formed during the Cavell Advance, or those obviously damaged by glacial ice, are particularly useful in this process.

Rock lichens also provide an accurate means for dating glacial events. The rock lichen known as map lichen (*Rhizocarpon geographicum*, see p. 46), grows at a known rate. These lichens have been growing on boulders in the forefield since the ice withdrew. By measuring the diameter of the lichens, glacier detectives can determine how long it has been since the adjacent area was covered by ice.

What have those cool sleuths learned about Cavell Glacier? Between 1888 and 1975, the glacier receded 988 m. The maximum of the Cavell Advance here took place in 1705. This was the greatest advance of Cavell Glacier during the previous 2600 years.

66. Lake Annette

Lake Annette

Douglas-fir forest

TRAIL THUMBNAIL

Trailhead
Follow Highway 16 northeast from Jasper for 3.7 km to the Maligne Lake Road. Turn east (right). In 500 m turn south (right) onto to the Jasper Park Lodge road. Follow this for 1.4 km. Turn east (left) and drive another 600 m to the second parking area. See map, p. 83.

Rating: easy, 2.4 km paved loop. Wheelchair accessible with assistance.

Special consideration: A section of trail on the north shore may be closed seasonally to protect bald eagle nesting habitat.

Best lighting: anytime

Nearby trails: 62 67

The paved trail around Lake Annette is one of a few in the Rockies designed to allow wheelchair access. Trail construction was made possible by a grant from the Clifford E. Lee Foundation in 1981, the International Year of Disabled Persons. A trail rebuild was in the plans for 2016-17.

There are more than 800 lakes and ponds in Jasper National Park. Many occupy glacially-scoured hollows in bedrock. Others are beaver ponds or backwaters of rivers. Lake Annette and the other lakes on the east bank of the Athabasca River near Jasper town are kettle ponds, created when large blocks of ice detached as ice age glaciers retreated

12,000 years ago. As the ice blocks slowly melted, they created depressions in the underlying glacial rubble. Silts then accumulated in the bottoms of the depressions, plugging cracks in the rubble, allowing the lakes to form. It is thought Lake Annette resulted from the joining of three kettle ponds.

Where does the water in Lake Annette come from today? Rainfall, runoff, and springs account for most of the inflow. However, studies of the Maligne Karst System (see p. 96) have shown that some of the water that disappears underground at Medicine Lake emerges at Lake Annette and other lakes nearby. Lake Annette has no surface outlet.

TAKING WING

For decades, bald eagles have nested atop a Douglas-fir snag on the north shore of Lake Annette but, until 2011, eagles had never been known to successfully raise nestlings here. Wildlife staff with Parks Canada suggested closing the trail near the nest to see if human disturbance in the area might have been a factor in the failure of the eagles to produce offspring. This was done in 2011 and... success!... one eagle fledged. Please respect any seasonal closures here and elsewhere in the national parks. In doing so, you may contribute to the preservation of species and natural processes.

Western wood lily

ROCHE BONHOMME (2495 M)

Roche Bonhomme (ROSH bun-OMM) in the Colin Range is prominent in the view east from Lake Annette. The mountain's name is French for "good fellow rock". The ridgecrest resembles the profile of a man's face, looking skyward. On the upper slopes you can see the spar trees of a 1985 forest fire. Locals call the peak "Old Man Mountain". Once you have spotted this old man, you will probably see dozens of others on the ridgelines near Jasper. Voyageurs of the fur trade bestowed many of the French names in the Athabasca Valley between 1811 and the 1840s. The name, Roche Bonhomme, first appeared in print in the book, *Ocean to Ocean*, published in 1878.

There are many kettle ponds in the Rockies. Most will eventually fill with aquatic vegetation. Soils will collect among the growth, allowing trees to take root. You can see this process of succession happening in the area around Ochre Lake, just east of Lake Annette. The bottom of Ochre Lake is quicksand. For your safety, keep out of the water.

From the south shore of Lake Annette, the view north shows the division between the front ranges, to the east (right) and the eastern main ranges, to the west (left). The Pyramid Thrust, which separates the dull grey limestone peaks of the front ranges from the more colourful quartzite peaks of the main ranges, is slightly west (left) of the massive cliff of the Palisade.

Douglas-fir trees dominate the forest near the lake. You may see elk. Common loons nest on the shore. These birds are masterful swimmers. If a loon surfaces near you, wait and watch for it to dive and you may get to see it swimming underwater. The arid meadow near the parking area features many colourful wildflower blooms in early summer, including brown-eyed Susans and prairie smoke. On hot summer days, Jasper locals flock to the lake to take a dip. The surface temperature may reach 20°C – scorching for the Rockies! The lake commemorates Annette Rogers, the wife of an early superintendent of Jasper National Park.

COMMON LOON

Nothing says "Canada" more than the call of the common loon. You won't be surprised to learn that this bird is found in every Canadian province and territory, but perhaps you will be surprised to hear that it has also been reported from every state in the U.S.A., except Hawaii. This is a large bird – up to 60 cm long, with a wingspan of up to 1.5 m. Plumage is identical in both genders. The loon has a black head and red eyes. Two collars - one white, one black – circle its neck. The remainder of the body is an attractive pattern of black and white. There may be as many as 500,000 Common loons in Canada.

Although larger lakes can be home to more than one pair of loons, the bird is territorial - on smaller lakes you will only find one pair. Both adults take part in rearing the young. A birding highlight is to see the young (usually two in the Rockies) riding on an adult's back - either mom or dad. They do this for the first 2-3 weeks, being flightless until 10-11 weeks old. Loons eat aquatic insects, invertebrates, and small fish. They are expert swimmers, diving deeply and travelling up to 100 m underwater, often remaining submerged for more than a minute.

Loons cannot take off from land – they need to run across water to gain sufficient speed to become

airborne. This dictates the size of lake that they can inhabit - one source says that 20 hectares is the minimum to provide a runway and suitable habitat. Loons nest at the water's edge, preferring islands, if available. They winter on the Pacific and Gulf coasts.

About that call... Recent research indicates that the "crazy" call of the loon changes slightly if a particular bird is moved from one lake to another. Inflections in the calls of individual birds may be in response to local topographic features. That's right; the bird is singing about its home. Not so crazy after all.

67. Maligne Canyon

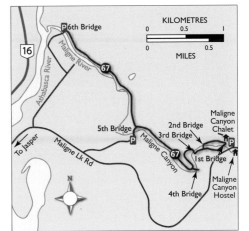

Maligne Canyon

TRAIL THUMBNAIL

Trailheads
Follow Highway 16, 1.7 km east from the Jasper east exit to the Maligne Lake Road. Turn east (right). There are three trailheads for the canyon: Sixth Bridge (turnoff at km 2.3), Fifth Bridge (turnoff at km 3.1), and Maligne Canyon (turnoff at km 6.3).

Ratings
- Sixth Bridge: harder, 3.7 km
- Fifth Bridge: moderate 2.7 km
- Maligne Canyon: easy, 0.8 km loop.
  Wheelchair ♿ accessible in part.

Special considerations: You share the first 1.3 km with bikers; the first 1.6 km with equestrians. If you take young children on this hike, hold their hands. Although the trail is fenced in many places, the route is often alongside the swift-flowing river or along the maw of the canyon – places not without hazard.

Best lighting: Cloudy days provide the best detail in the canyon.

Nearby trail:

Maligne (mah-LEEN) Canyon is one of Jasper's "must see" places. If you hike the full length, it rates as a stellar natural history walk. From the parking area, cross the bridge to the northeast bank of the Maligne River. Turn southeast (right) on trail #7. Jesuit missionary, Pierre-Jean De Smet, referred to the river in 1846, using the French word "maligne", which means "wicked". Imagine the bridge removed; contemplate the crossing, and you can appreciate the sentiment.

The next 800 m along the riverbank is on a wide, flat trail through a montane forest of white spruce, lodgepole pine, trembling aspen, and a few Douglas-firs. The fire-scarred trunks of the Douglas-firs testify to their ability to withstand moderate ground fires. I have met a black bear here. Prickly juniper, buffaloberry, wild onion, bearberry, and very tall, Scouler's willow make up most of the sparse ground cover. Red squirrels chatter from the trees. Short spur trails lead to pleasing views of the river. Look for dippers. The building on the opposite bank of the river was formerly the warden office and, before that, the park fish hatchery. In the early 1930s, park staff transplanted fish fry raised in this building into the fish-less rivers of the Maligne Valley above this canyon. Sigh.

The pleasant preamble done with, you soon reach the mouth of the canyon. Note the change in the character of the forest. Dampness and chill prevail; Engelmann spruce, subalpine fir, and lodgepole pine dominate. The trail climbs over a jumble of limestone boulders, from which issues a bit of the mystery and magic of the Maligne Valley. Yes, it's a spring, but it also has been proven to be an outlet for the underground drainage of Medicine Lake, 17 km southeast. This outlet, called an emergence, is one of more than twenty between here and Fourth Bridge. The emergences gush when Medicine Lake is full; they trickle as the lake level drops.

Horsetails – a favourite springtime food of bears – grow alongside the first emergence. I have seen

Maligne Canyon fossils

Upper Maligne Canyon

bear scats and tracks in the sand nearby. White birch also grows here. Please don't peel the bark. At km 1.3 the bike trail veers left. Keep straight ahead. At km 1.6, the trail from Fifth Bridge comes in from the west (right). Angle left, upstream, and turn right at the horse-hiker separation in 50 m. You want trail #7.

The trail traverses an exposed till bank that is being colonized by trembling aspen, juniper, and wild rose. Across the river, you can see the sedimentary layers of the bedrock. They dip slightly to the north, but what is more important to the creation of the canyon is that the bedrock on the west side of the river is higher than that on the east side – by about 3 m. This offset is a normal fault – a fracture in the bedrock that occurred after mountain building. A lateral moraine deposited by the ancient Maligne Glacier diverted the Maligne River onto the fault, where the flowing water readily exploited the weakness. In no time, geologically speaking – less than 10,000 years – Maligne Canyon came into being.

That's one canyon-creation theory. Another proposes that Maligne Canyon is itself the course of an ancient underground stream, exposed to daylight by glacial erosion during the Late Wisconsin Glaciation.

The trail descends into the damp forest at riverside. This is my favourite part of the canyon. Two of the larger emergences enter beneath an overhang on the opposite bank. Beaten paths lead to the riverbank in places, but the wet, silt-covered rock is certain death if you misplace a step. The canyon winds; the trail makes brief climbs and descents, passing from open slope to confined chasm – a patchwork of micro-habitats. On the opposite bank, a waterfall cascades from the ancient lateral moraine on the canyon rim, scouring away the soils to reveal a complete exposure of the bedrock. Fourth Bridge takes you across the canyon but the trail does not continue on that bank.

Fourth Bridge to Trail's End

The bedrock geology changes above the Fourth Bridge. The canyon narrows dramatically as a result. Downstream, the river is eroding the relatively weak shales of the Banff Formation. Upstream, the river

has a tougher time with the more resistant limestone of the Palliser Formation. This limestone is fossil-rich, containing snail-like gastropods, clam-like brachiopods, squid-like cephalopods, crinoids (related to sea-stars), and corals.

The Maligne River takes a mighty drop beneath Third Bridge, where the canyon's depth is 10 m and you cross to the opposite bank. The air also changes. Below the bridge, it's cool and damp where you've been hiking within the canyon. From here on, you climb along the canyon rim, where the air is noticeably warmer. If you've had any solitude on the trail to this point, you probably won't now, as many people walk here from the upper parking area. Note how the bedrock has been polished smooth in places by the shuffling of millions of feet, some, amazingly, clad in

THE INVISIBLE RIVER

Two rivers flow through Maligne Canyon. If you were to compare the volume of flow at Sixth Bridge with the volume at First Bridge in mid-summer, you would see that the lower canyon contains much more water (eight times as much) as the upper canyon. The emergences of the Maligne karst system pump 24,000 litres per second into the canyon. This underground river may be the largest in the world. The entrances to the karst system – called sinks – are upvalley on the floor of Medicine Lake. It has been proven that it takes 70 hours for the water to travel from there to Maligne Canyon. Other emergences of the underground river feed some of the lakes near Jasper town.

high heels. The large boulders at trailside are glacial erratics, dropped here when the Maligne Valley glacier last receded, some 12,000 years ago.

Nooks and crannies on the opposite wall of the canyon are nesting places for ravens. Maligne Canyon is also one of three known nesting places in Alberta for black swifts. Look for them on the wing in the evening. They are easy to recognize in flight, having been described as "cigars with wings". I have seen a dipper flying through the canyon.

Maligne Canyon is deepest – 55 m – at Second Bridge. It's so deep, it's hard to grasp the scale. Locals know the pocket of ice on the wall below as "The Icebox". (If you are wondering… yes, people venture onto the canyon floor on guided walks in the winter.) A damp, canyon forest of spruce and subalpine fir grows on the shaded, south side of the river, whereas a drier forest of lodgepole pine and Douglas-fir grows on the sunny, north side of the river.

Don't cross Second Bridge but carry on to First Bridge, where the canyon is 38 m deep and the entire river is forced through a 1 m slot. A chockstone spans the canyon just downstream; you get to cross on a bridge. Although the canyon is shallow from here on, it features wonderful potholes – circular depressions drilled into the limestone by boulders caught in eddies – a process that requires thousands of years. Some of the potholes now lie in abandoned channels. The depressions are gradually filling with soils to become miniature gardens. Alas, the upper canyon is showing the abuses of heavy visitation. Graffiti has appeared on rocks in the river bed, and a fenced area that displays fossils has been walked on so much, the outlines of the fossils have been obliterated.

Return

I recommend that you walk back down the canyon, as you are certain to see things that you missed on the way up. Loop around the parking area and pick up trail #7f. Recross the canyon at Second Bridge to get back on trail #7. If nothing else, you get to spend more time in the company of the lower Maligne River, a ribbon of blue-green beauty.

Common raven

68. Bald Hills

Maligne Lake from the Bald Hills

TRAIL THUMBNAIL

Trailhead
Follow Highway 16, 1.7 km east from the Jasper east exit to the Maligne Lake Road. Turn east (right). Follow the Maligne Lake Road 44 km to the bridge over the lake's outlet. Cross the bridge and follow the road 250 m to the parking area on the west shore of the lake. There are two trailheads west of the parking area. The one for Bald Hills is to the south (left). See map, p. 99.

Rating: harder, 5.2 km

Special considerations: You can make a loop to and from the lookout site by ascending the fireroad and descending the shortcut trail, or vice versa. The loop will be 1.3 km shorter than the out-and-back distance along the fireroad. If you use the shortcut trail up and down, your outing will be 2.6 km shorter. You share the trail with equestrians. Dogs are not permitted. The trail may be closed until the snowcover is melted.

Best lighting: anytime

Nearby trails: 69 70

On a fair day, it would be difficult to pick a finer destination than the Bald Hills. Few viewpoints in the Rockies, reached in so short a distance, offer such a great panorama. Adding to the attractions are interesting geology and tremendous wildflower displays.

The forest near the trailhead is thick with lodgepole pine, which indicates an intense forest fire in the not-too-distant past. You can see charred logs and stumps. Golden-crowned kinglets and black-capped chickadees buzz through the trees. Two plants prevalent in pine forests are everywhere in the understory – twinflower and Labrador tea. Arnica, fleabane, buffaloberry, dwarf dogwood, northern sweet-vetch, and various willows are also common. Ruffed grouse and spruce grouse make occasional trailside appearances. Fritillary butterflies – smallish, with orange wings dotted with black – seem partial to this fireroad; perhaps attracted by various goodies in the horse dung.

You reach the Maligne Pass junction in 300 m. Keep southwest (straight ahead). Ahead, you have a glimpse of the ultimate destination. Looking back, you can see the mountain known as the "Sinking Ship", on the east side of Maligne Lake. The fireroad veers north and winds through an area of rocky hummocks. The debris came from the vicinity of the Opal Hills on the east side of the valley, in a series of monumental landslides that followed the retreat of the main valley glacier after the Late Wisconsin Glaciation. Some of the debris dammed the outlet of Maligne Lake.

The fireroad levels just before the shortcut trail junction at km 2.5. The shortcut trail is steeper than the fireroad, and is rockier and rooted. It is a toe-jammer and knee-cruncher on the way down, but if you use it on the ascent, it cuts the remaining distance to the lookout site from 2.7 km to 1.4 km.

Beyond the shortcut junction, the fireroad undulates for 700 m to the Evelyn Creek junction. Keep west (left) for the Bald Hills. I have seen the tracks of moose and deer here. The steepest section of fireroad follows, yielding a fine view back to the Opal Hills. Note the transition in the understory; pink mountain heather and yellow mountain heather are now common, marking the lower subalpine life zone. Views to the north begin to open, with the Queen Elizabeth Range visible across the Maligne Valley, and Little Shovel Pass in the Maligne Range visible to the north. This snippet of view encapsulates the two great themes of the local geology – younger, gray, front range limestone to the east; older, colourful, main range quartzite underfoot. Mona Lake, named for Mona Harrigan, Jasper's first female trail guide, is revealed as a blue gem in the green mantle of the valley floor.

The grade moderates as the fireroad curves southwest to enter treeline glades. You pass a small pond. White mountain avens and white mountain heather are common. In this transitional forest, I have heard a surprising chorus of birdlife: juncos, hermit thrushes, a golden-crowned sparrow, ruby-crowned kinglets, and a Cooper's hawk.

A hitching rail marks the lookout site. Prompted by extensive forest fires in 1936, Parks Canada constructed a fire lookout system in the national parks in the late 1930s and early 1940s. With only a few exceptions, the structures – which saw use until the

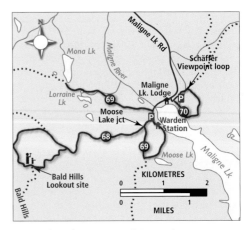

1970s – have been removed. But without exception, all were well sited, as this view attests. To the southeast, you see most of the length of Maligne Lake. From north to south, the peaks in view on the east side of the lake are: Opal Hills, "Sinking Ship", Leah Peak (2801 m), Samson Peak (3801 m), Maligne Mountain (with glacier, 3200 m), Mt. Paul (2850 m), Monkhead Mountain (3219 m), and Mt. Warren (3362 m). Mt. Charlton (3217 m) and Mt. Unwin (3268 m), on the near shore, complete the visible lakeside peaks.

Mary Schäffer named many of the peaks during her explorations of the lake in 1908 and 1911. Mt. Brazeau (3470 m), highest mountain in the front ranges, is concealed from view at the south end of the lake.

MOUNTAIN HEATHER

Plants of the heath family are emblematic, evergreen shrubs of the alpine life zone, creating extensive mats above treeline. Botanists often refer to such areas as heath tundras. There are four species of heather in the Rockies; two white, one yellow, and one pink (see p. 92 for other photos). All have nodding, urn-like flowers, but none bear fruit. If you see small berries on a heath-like plant in these meadows, you are looking at either grouseberry (also in the heath family) or crowberry.

Maligne Lake

69. Mona, Lorraine, and Moose Lakes

Trailheads

As for Bald Hills (68). There are two trailheads adjacent to this parking area. The trail to Mona Lake and Lorraine Lake uses the Skyline Trail, to the north (right). The trail to Moose Lake begins at the Bald Hills trailhead, to the south (left).

Ratings

- Mona Lake: moderate, 2.4 km
- Lorraine Lake: moderate, 2.1 km
- Moose Lake: easy, 2.4 km loop

Best lighting: anytime

Nearby trails: 68 70

The landslide that dammed Maligne Lake was a biggy – the second-largest measured in the Rockies. It ran across the valley floor and partway up the western side. Depressions in the rockslide debris have become natural hollows in which small lakes have formed. To reach two of these, Mona Lake and Lorraine Lake, hike the Skyline Trail through open pine forest to the short spur trails that lead, respectively, southwest (left) to Lorraine Lake, and north (right) to Mona Lake. Mona Lake commemorates Jasper's first female trail guide.

To reach Moose Lake, follow the Bald Hills trail and branch south (left) at the first junction in 300 m. In another kilometre, turn east (left) to reach Moose Lake in 100 m. Either backtrack to the parking area or make a loop by descending the trail from Moose Lake's north shore to Maligne Lake. Follow the lakeshore trail north (left) past the park patrol cabin and boat launch, to the parking area.

70. Schäffer Viewpoint

Trailhead

Follow Highway 16, 3.7 km east from Jasper to the Maligne Lake Road. Turn east (right). Follow this road 44 km to the parking areas on the east side of Maligne Lake. Descend any trail to the lakeshore and head south (left).

Rating: moderate, 2.8 km loop

Best lighting: anytime

Nearby trails: 68 69

The trail to Schäffer Viewpoint on Maligne (mah-LEEN) Lake follows the lake's east shore to a prominent bay, where interpretive signs describe the exploration of the lake in 1908 by the party of Mary Schäffer. An aristocrat from Philadelphia, Schäffer took to the backwoods life of the Rockies with passion, and eventually settled in Banff. On the way to the viewpoint, you pass the boathouse built by outfitter Donald Phillips in 1928. Maligne Lake is the largest lake in the Canadian Rockies. It is 22 km long, has an area of 20.66 km², and a maximum depth of 96 m. The average width is about 1 km. *Maligne* is a French word that means "wicked". Father Pierre-Jean de Smet named the river in 1846, when he had trouble crossing it near its confluence with the Athabasca River. From Schäffer Viewpoint, return to the parking area either along the lakeshore, or by carrying on around the loop. At the intersection with the Opal Hills trail on the loop, turn west (left) to reach the parking area.

71. Buck, Honeymoon, and Osprey Lakes

TRAIL THUMBNAIL

Trailhead
Parking area on the east side of the Icefields Parkway, 50 km north of the Columbia Icefield information centre; 50.7 km south of Highway 16. See map, p. 78.

Rating: easy, 1.3 km

Best lighting: anytime

Nearby trail: 55

When glaciers receded from the floor of the Athabasca Valley at the end of the Late Wisconsin Glaciation, huge blocks of ice detached and melted into the rubble. The lakes that resulted are known as kettle ponds. These three lakes are great examples. Buck Lake is 250 m straight ahead (east) from the parking area. The trail to Honeymoon Lake and Osprey Lake branches north (left), about half way to Buck Lake. It visits the south shore of Honeymoon Lake before heading east through a black spruce bog to Osprey Lake. Wear rubber boots or beater running shoes. Spotted orchids and tall white bog orchids grow at trailside. Moose and osprey frequent the area.

72. Horseshoe Lake

Horseshoe Lake is a gem that sits in a deep pocket in the quartzite rubble of a rockslide. A maze of beaten paths leads to the lakeshore. It's best to stay on the "inside" of the horseshoe, so keep straight ahead at the first obvious junction. Then follow the lakeshore south (right) before looping back to the parking area. Cliffs at the south end of the lake are a favourite diving and swimming place for locals who can brave the chill waters. If you are going to make the leap, be sure you check out the landing area first! Always swim with a buddy.

Horseshoe Lake

TRAIL THUMBNAIL

Trailhead
Parking area on the east side of the Icefields Parkway, 26.6 km south of Jasper town, 74.1 km north of the Columbia Icefield information centre.

Rating: moderate, 600 m loop

Special considerations: Fall hazard! Cliffs at the lakeshore pose a hazard. Use caution, especially with children.

Best lighting: afternoon

Nearby trails: 56 73

73. Goats and Glaciers Viewpoint

TRAIL THUMBNAIL

Trailhead
Parking area on the west side of the Icefields Parkway, 36.1 km south of Highway 16; 64.6 km north of the Columbia Icefield information centre.

Rating: viewpoint, 100 m

Best lighting: morning and evening

Nearby trails: 56 72

Mountain goats

The Goats and Glaciers Viewpoint sits atop an outcrop of glacial till adjacent to the Athabasca River. Mountain goats that range on Mt. Kerkeslin congregate here to lick the sulphur-bearing minerals in the till. They come here most often in late spring. If you see goats, please keep at least 30 m away. Across the river, you can see classic examples of hanging valleys, and the turreted form of Brussels Peak (3161 m, see photo, p. 14.).

74. Wabasso Lake

TRAIL THUMBNAIL

Trailhead
Parking area on the east side of the Icefields Parkway, 86.6 km north of the Columbia Icefield information centre, 14.1 km south of Highway 16.

Rating: moderate, 3.1 km

Best lighting: anytime

Nearby trails: 57

Until mountain bikes were permitted on the trail, Wabasso was a seldom-visited lake in the rolling, gritstone ridge country of the Athabasca Valley. It's a busier place now, but few people make the trip on foot. The trail (#9) undulates over a series of gritstone ridges. At km 1.5 it skirts a slough created by beavers. Keep left at all trail junctions. After climbing over another ridge – with views southwest to Mt. Edith Cavell (3363 m) – the trail drops to a cascade that drains the marshes below Wabasso Lake, which you reach in another 700 m. Although views are limited, you can see the Maligne Range on the east side of the valley. The osprey that nest nearby are probably grateful to the generations of beavers whose handiwork has created and maintained the lake. *Wabasso* is a Cree word that means "rabbit".

75. Patricia Lake Circle

Cottonwood Slough

TRAIL THUMBNAIL

Trailhead
Park at Pyramid stables on the east side of the Pyramid Lake Road, 3.3 km north of Jasper town. See map, p. 83.

Rating: moderate, 4.6 km loop

Special considerations: You share the trail with equestrians. Use caution crossing the road.

Best lighting: afternoon and evening

Nearby trails: 59 60

Looping through the forest south of Patricia Lake, this outing offers views of that lake and of Cottonwood Slough. The entire outing traverses excellent birding habitat. Look and listen for warblers, loons, and waterfowl.

From the stables, follow trail #6c. Cross Pyramid Lake Road with caution. You reach the junction with trail #6 in 150 m. Turn west (right). Ascend through stands of trembling aspen and then descend to the shore of Patricia Lake. The lake commemorates the daughter of the Duke of Connaught, Governor General of Canada from 1911-16. Keep west (straight ahead) at the junction with trail #6b, or use trail #6b to reduce the outing length by 1 km. Trail #6 loops south from the outlet stream of Patricia Lake, and then east, travelling through montane forest. From the high bank of Cottonwood Creek, you have fine views to its wetland – Cottonwood Slough. Look for beavers and their lodges. You may also see moose, muskrats, ducks, and great blue herons. Listen for common yellowthroats: *witchety-witchety-witchety*. Keep on trail #6 at all junctions to loop back to trail #6c just before the Pyramid Lake Road. Cross the road with caution to reach the parking area.

76. The Whistlers

The Whistlers summit

TRAIL THUMBNAIL

Trailhead
Follow the Icefields Parkway, 1.8 km south from Highway 16 to Whistlers Road. Turn west (right). Follow this road 4 km to the Jasper Skytram. The trailhead is at the upper terminal. Call 780-852-3093, 866-850-8726 for prices and schedule. www.jasperskytram.com

Rating: moderate, 1.2 km. The boardwalk at the upper terminal is wheelchair ♿ accessible with assistance.

Best lighting: anytime

In its seven minute ride, the Jasper Skytram climbs 937 m, whisking you from the montane life zone to the stark, mountain top environment of The Whistlers. From the upper terminal, if you are well-shod and warmly-clothed, you can walk the summit trail. This is the easiest way to a mountain top in the Rockies, and at 2464 m, is the highest point on any trail in this book. Hardy wildflowers – miracles of life in this harsh terrain – dot the screes and boulders. The panorama from The Whistlers includes the Miette and Athabasca valleys, Jasper town, many lakes, and on clear days, Mt. Robson (3957 m), the highest peak in the Canadian Rockies, 78 km distant. Please keep to the marked trails to spare the vegetation.

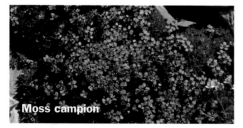

Moss campion

77. Beaver Lake

TRAIL THUMBNAIL

Trailhead
Follow Highway 16, 1.7 km east from the Jasper east exit to the Maligne Lake Road. Turn east (right). Follow the Maligne Lake Road 28.2 km to the Beaver Creek picnic area at the south end of Medicine Lake.

Rating: easy, 1.6 km

Special consideration: You share the trail with cyclists.

Best lighting: afternoon

The short walk to Beaver Lake follows a wide, well-graded gravel path, ideal for families. The glacially-fed waters of the lake reflect the steeply tilted, sawtooth mountains of the Queen Elizabeth Ranges.

78. Jasper House

Jasper House in 1872

Jasper House was a fur trade outpost built by the Hudson's Bay Company near this location in 1830. It replaced an outpost with the same name that had been located downstream on the Athabasca River at Brulé Lake. The earlier post commemorated Jasper Hawse, who directed its operations in 1817. The name migrated upstream when the new post was built.

Jasper House was a resupply point for brigades, a gathering place for those bringing in furs to trade, and a stopping place for travellers, many of whom were not connected with the fur trade. The Hudson's

Trailhead
Pull-off on the west side of Highway 16, 33.1 km northeast of the east exit from Jasper town.

Rating: easy, 350 m

Best lighting: anytime

Nearby trail: 79

Bay Company closed the post twice – once for a year in 1857, and finally in 1884. Early settlers of the Athabasca Valley refurbished and used the buildings. Surveyors for the Grand Trunk Pacific Railway built a raft from the remaining lumber in 1909, erasing the building from the landscape. Charles Horetzky's photographs of Jasper House, taken in 1872, are the earliest photos known of the Canadian Rockies.

The trail takes you away from the bustle of Highway 16 and leads through an open white spruce forest to a viewing platform that overlooks the Athabasca River. Jasper House National Historic Site – where the post formerly stood – is on the opposite bank. Interpretive panels feature a series of maps, paintings, and photographs that invoke the days of the fur trade and early settlement in the Athabasca Valley. Roche Ronde and the peaks of the De Smet Range are prominent in the view.

79. Pocahontas

Trailhead
Follow Highway 16, 40.9 km northeast of Jasper town to Pocahontas. Turn south (right) onto the Miette Hot Springs Road. Turn west (right) into the trailhead parking area in 150 m.

Rating: easy, 1 km loop. Wheelchair ♿ accessible with assistance.

Best lighting: anytime

Nearby trail: 78

The paved Coal Mine Trail at Pocahontas explores the ruins of the industrial and commercial sections of an abandoned mining town. Prospector Frank Villeneuve discovered coal on the lower slopes of Roche Miette (ROSH mee-YETT) in 1908. Villeneuve named his mine Jasper Park Collieries, and the community that evolved nearby, Pocahontas, after the successful coal mining town in Virginia.

Mining began in 1910. A residential upper town and a commercial lower town developed. The upper town, on the east bank of Mountain Creek, reportedly housed more than 2000 people, making it far larger than Jasper. Most of the miners were immigrants from Britain, Italy, and eastern Europe.

World War I created a huge market for coal, but, due to poor management and a series of accidents, affairs at Pocahontas were far from happy. After the mine lost rail access, a strike in 1919 sealed its fate. It closed permanently in April 1921.

80. Miette Hot Springs Boardwalk

Trailhead
Follow Highway 16 east of Jasper, 42.9 km to the Miette Hot Springs Road. Turn south (right), and follow this road 19 km. Park at the south end of the Miette Hot Springs parking area, near the picnic area. Trailers and large RVs are not permitted on this road. Park them at the trailer drop-off, 150 m from Highway 16.

Rating: easy, 800 m

Best lighting: anytime

Nearby trail: 81

From the parking area, walk south to the old hot springs building. Constructed in 1937, this facility saw use until deemed unsafe in 1984. The boardwalk beyond the old building leads to the outlets of the springs, the hottest (53.9°C) and most pungent in the Rockies. You may see bighorn sheep at the parking area. Please do not feed them

81. Utopia Pass

Sulphur Creek

TRAIL THUMBNAIL

Trailhead
As for Miette Hot Springs Boardwalk (80).

Rating: harder, 2.6 km

Special consideration: Utopia Pass is an excellent pocket of bear habitat.

Best lighting: anytime

Nearby trail: 80

Beyond the Miette Hot Springs boardwalk, the trail ascends within the canyon of Sulphur Creek. About 850 m from the trailhead, cross the creek on a bridge to its east bank. (This crossing may not be possible at high water). The trail climbs, steeply at times, in damp forest with wonderful wildflower displays. The tiny meadows on Utopia Pass are lush with blooms in early summer. The shattered slopes of Sulphur Ridge rise to the northeast of the pass. Where the trail begins to descend into the Fiddle River Valley, it's time to turn around and return.

Virl Lake

82. Dorothy, Christine, and Virl Lakes

TRAIL THUMBNAIL

Trailhead
At Meadow Creek, north side of Highway 16, 11.1 km west of the junction with the Icefields Parkway.

Rating: harder, 10.0 km return

Special consideration: The trail crosses the CN Railway main line. Trail numbers in the text match park trail signs.

Best lighting: anytime

If you are looking for a get-away hike with a bit of a wilderness feel, you will likely be happy with this outing. Although it can be wet in places, the trail is generally snow-free by late May. Follow the railway access road for 125 m. Cross the double tracks with caution. Descend to a bridged crossing of the Miette River. On the far side, the trail (#60) angles sharply north, paralleling the river.

On the way to its destinations, the trail rambles up and down, cutting across the grain of the local geology. Steeply tilted rocks of the Miette Group of formations (see p. 81) form the bedrock here. The lakes sit in the relatively soft pockets of shale and slate, while the harder gritstones endure as the surrounding ridges. You can see a fine exposure of Miette slate near the railway tracks.

The forest in this part of the Miette Valley is classic montane. Note how the aspens, Douglas-firs, and lodgepole pines prefer the sunnier, southwest slopes of the ridges, where juniper and buffaloberry are also common. On the shaded northeast slopes, a damper forest prevails. Arnica, dwarf dogwood, calypso orchids, and western columbine colour the margins of the trail.

Keep northeast (right) at the Elysium Pass junction at km 2.7. A fire succession forest of lodgepole pine now surrounds you. Look for ruffed grouse. At km 3.7, trail #60a branches southeast (right) to Virl Lake. It's 400 m to the north shore, which grants views of The Whistlers and Indian Ridge. Back on the main trail, carry on for 450 m to a bay on the shore of Dorothy Lake, with views of Mt. Tekarra in the Maligne Range. In another 250 m, you reach the south shore of island-dotted, Christine Lake, along which the trail fades after another 200 m. A surveyor named H. Matheson christened the three lakes in 1914, but did not record for whom. You may see or hear common loons on the lakes, or flying between them.

Mt. Robson, Kinney Lake trail

Mt. Robson Provincial Park

While many of the mighty peaks of the Canadian Rockies are tucked away in remote corners, through a happy quirk of topography, Mt. Robson, the highest peak in the range, towers majestically near roadside. This impressive mountain was the sole reason that B.C. established Mt. Robson Provincial Park in 1913. But, fortunately, the park was made large enough (2172 km²) to include a chunk of the headwaters of the Fraser River.

You will find the park information centre, two frontcountry campgrounds, and your roadside view of Mt. Robson on Highway 16 at Robson Junction, 83.3 km west of the Icefields Parkway, 16 km east of Highway 5. You will find another frontcountry campground at Lucerne, 33 km west of the Icefields Parkway, 50.3 km east of Robson Junction. The park is in the Pacific time zone, one hour behind Jasper and Banff. You can easily spend 2-3 days exploring the lush forests, riverbanks, lakes, and waterfalls reached on these Walks and Easy Hikes. If you need to top up supplies, your closest choice is 36 km distant at Valemount; west then south from Robson Junction via Highway 16 and Highway 5.

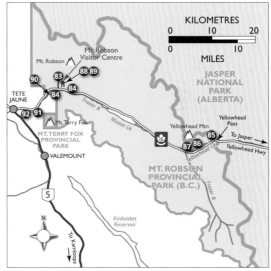

83. Kinney Lake

Kinney Lake

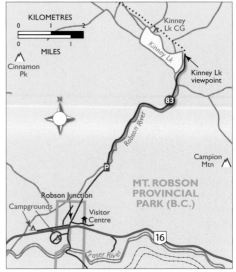

TRAIL THUMBNAIL

Trailhead
Follow Highway 16, 83.3 km west of the Icefields Parkway; 16 km east of the junction with Highway 5, to Robson Junction. Turn north and follow the paved sideroad 2 km to its end at the Berg Lake trailhead parking area.

Rating: moderate, 4.2 km to lake, 5.2 km to viewpoint

Special consideration: You share the trail with cyclists.

Best lighting: anytime

Nearby trails: 84 88 89 90 91 92

The broad trail to Kinney Lake is always within sound, and usually within sight, of the Robson River. The glacial river, with its pleasing hues and cataracts, are reasons enough to make this outing, but the forest along the way makes this one of the better nature walks in the Rockies. Look for harlequin ducks and dippers in the fast-flowing water. About 1 km from the trailhead, the trail crosses the base of an avalanche slope. Here, in late June, you will find one of the best wildflower displays at trailside in the Rockies. Look for western columbine, common fireweed (photo, p. 128) paintbrush, harebell, spotted saxifrage, false Solomon's seal, wild rose, wild strawberry, white geranium, calypso orchid, and cow parsnip.

THE REVEREND MOUNTAINEER

Kinney Lake commemorates Reverend George Kinney, who was in the first mountaineering party to attempt Mt. Robson. In 1907, Kinney and A.P. Coleman (see p. 78) approached the mountain on horseback from Lake Louise – a journey that took six weeks. Poor weather and a shortage of food put an end to the exploration before they could set foot on the mountain. Kinney returned in 1908 and again in 1909 when, with outfitter Curly Phillips, he nearly reached the summit by a difficult route on the west face. Given their scant equipment and Phillips' lack of mountaineering experience, it was a bold and remarkable achievement, later tainted by the fact that Kinney claimed to have reached the summit while Phillips admitted his doubt in the matter.

Cedar-hemlock forest

The forest in this valley features species that typify B.C.'s Western Interior Hemlock Forest zone – western redcedar (B.C.'s provincial tree), western hemlock, western white pine, thimbleberry, and devil's club. The trail passes through an old-growth stand of western redcedars about 2 km from the trailhead. Scan the forest for B.C.'s provincial bird – the hooded, blue and black, Steller's jay. At km 3 the trail bisects a mineral lick used by elk, deer, moose, and mountain goats. Look for their tracks. We have seen a moose in the Robson River just beyond this point.

About an hour from the trailhead, you reach the outlet of Kinney Lake – sometimes referred to as "the mirror of the mount". Just downstream from the outlet, a creek that drains the basin between Mt. Robson and Mt. Resplendent has created an alluvial fan in the Robson River. This fan holds back some of the river's energy, helping to create Kinney Lake. In recent years, the shoreline and trail near the lake have often been flooded. Whitehorn Mountain (3399 m) is framed in the view north down the lake. For a better view, carry on to the viewpoint on the lake's southeast shore, 1 km beyond the outlet bridge. Avalanche slopes on Cinnamon Peak extend to waterline on the opposite shore.

THE MOUNTAIN OF THE SPIRAL ROAD

Mt. Robson (3957 m) towers 2972 m above Kinney Lake, yet the summit is only 3 km away. This staggering vertical relief is hard to grasp. By way of comparison, Mt. Temple rises slightly more than 2000 m from the floor of the Bow Valley near Lake Louise, and Mt. Stephen rises 1900 m above the Kicking Horse Valley at Field.

Mt. Robson is 216 m higher than Mt. Columbia, the 2nd-highest mountain in the Rockies, and 549 m higher than Resplendent Mountain (3408 m), the next highest peak nearby. Why is Mt. Robson so high? Its rock is not particularly tough. The secret is that the layers are flat-lying through the centre of the peak. Flat-lying layers are more difficult for glaciers to erode than tilted layers. This rock sandwich – almost 4 km thick – is one of the more complete, unbroken assemblages of Cambrian Period rock exposed anywhere on Earth.

The strata bend slightly upward from the centre of the mountain toward the east and west, revealing a broad syncline. This creates the illusion of spiral ramps. Secwempc (Shuswap) First Peoples from the interior of B.C. knew Mt. Robson as *Yuh-hai-has-kun* – "mountain of the spiral road". As impressive as it is, Mt. Robson is not the highest mountain in British Columbia, nor is Mt. Waddington (4019 m), the other popular guess. The honour belongs to Mt. Fairweather (4671 m), on the boundary with Alaska.

The quest to find the definitive origin of Mt. Robson's name has been a bane for scholars of Rockies' history. You might think that the monarch

mountain of the range was named to honour a politician, official or dignitary. Elsewhere in B.C., the name "Robson" appears frequently, commemorating John Robson, provincial premier from 1889-92. However, there is no connection here.

The name "Mt. Robinson" may have been in use for the mountain as early as 1827. Scholars agree that the strongest candidate to lay claim to the name is Colin Robertson, an officer with the North West and Hudson's Bay companies. In 1820, Robertson dispatched a group of Iroquois fur traders to the area immediately west of Mt. Robson. They may have applied his name, which was subsequently corrupted – twice – through use.

84. Overlander Falls

Overlander Falls

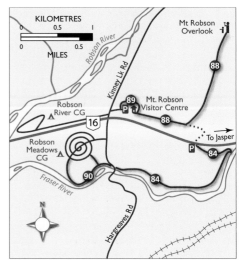

TRAIL THUMBNAIL

Trailheads

1. Parking area on the south side of Highway 16, 81.8 km west of the Icefields Parkway; 1.5 km east of Robson Junction; 17.5 km east of the junction with Highway 5.
2. On the north side of the Fraser River bridge, 500 m south of the entrance to Robson Meadows Campground. Easily reached on foot from the campground.

Ratings

- From Highway 16: easy, 500 m
- From the Fraser River bridge: moderate, 2.3 km

Special consideration: Fall risk! Stay within the fenced viewpoints.

Best lighting: afternoon

Nearby trails: 83 88 89 90 91 92

Overlander Falls commemorates the epic journey of a group of gold seekers who crossed Canada in 1862. You can reach this 10 m-high waterfall on the Fraser River by two approaches. For those with ample time (and especially for those staying at the campground), take the trail that begins on the north side of the Fraser River bridge, south of Robson Meadows Campground. It winds along the steep banks of the Fraser River, and visits the ruins of a camp used during construction of the Grand Trunk

Pacific Railway. For those who desire a shorter outing, follow the trail downhill from Highway 16.

The 1368 km long Fraser River ranks 10th in length among Canadian rivers, and 105th in the world. It begins in glaciers high on the west slopes of The Ramparts, and drains an area of 220,000 km² – 23 percent of the province of B.C. It has the second-greatest mean annual flow of any Canadian river, and is the core of the most productive, free-flowing salmon river system on the planet. Simon Fraser was a fur trade partner with the North West Company. In 1808, his party became the first to descend the river now named for him, travelling in a harrowing journey from Fort George (now Prince George) to its mouth. Fraser's report on that trip nixed his namesake river as a subsequent trade route.

In 1858, reports of the gold rush in the Cariboo Mountains reached eastern Canada and Europe. In the spring of 1862, a group of emigrants, recently arrived from England, departed Toronto for the gold country. The agent who had arranged their travel deserted them at Fort Garry (now Winnipeg). So they hitched up with a group of westbound settlers and carried on. They soon became known as the Overlanders because they were crossing the continent by land rather than by journeying by boat around Cape Horn.

At Edmonton, the Overlanders traded their wagons for horses and cattle, and engaged the services of a knowledgeable guide. A party of 125, including one pregnant woman, set out to cross the Rockies – a journey fraught with hardship and peril. The Overlanders soon ran short of food, and resorted to shooting skunk and butchering their cattle. At Tête Jaune Cache they traded with Secwempc (Shuswap) First Peoples, who provided salmon and berries.

With winter approaching, the party split. Many built rafts and ran the Fraser River to Quesnel (kwuh-NELL). At least six drowned. Thirty-six others set off on foot along the North Thompson River for Fort Kamloops. The pregnant woman gave birth soon after her arrival – the first recorded birth of a white person in the interior of what would later become B.C.

There was gold in the Cariboo Mountains. Miners struck more than $10 million worth in 10 years. However, the ore was confined to a small area, and the tale of many prospectors was one of hard luck. The Overlanders had set out equipped for a life of prospecting in western Canada. At the conclusion of the journey one of them commented: "Our mining tools were the only articles that we found to be unnecessary." A few of the Overlanders took up residence in Kamloops, Quesnel, and Barkerville. Most never prospected, but continued their journey to the west coast the following year.

Overlander Falls is an insurmountable barrier to chinook salmon returning from the Pacific Ocean. You may see them here in late August and early September. Were it not for the falls, the Fraser salmon run might extend to the river's headwaters.

DWARF DOGWOOD

Dwarf dogwood (*Cornus canadensis*) is a common and attractive wildflower in damp, mossy areas of shaded forests in the Rockies. The prominent white "petals" are not part of the flower, but are modified leaves called bracts. The true petals of the minuscule flowers are pale green. The flower yields a brilliant cluster of red berries in late summer, providing another folk name: bunchberry. Look for dwarf dogwood near Overlander Falls, along with three other common wildflowers of the coniferous forest: wild strawberry, queen's cup (photo, p. 112), and twinflower. B.C.'s provincial flower is that of the shrub, Pacific dogwood – *Cornus nattallii* – not of this plant.

85. Portal Lake

Portal Lake

TRAIL THUMBNAIL

Trailhead
North side of Highway 16 at the picnic area in Yellowhead Pass, 23.1 km west of the Icefields Parkway, 60.2 km east of Robson Junction.

Rating: easy, 500 m

Best lighting: anytime

This short loop is an ideal leg-stretcher for travellers on Highway 16. The trail follows the lake's northeast shore for 350 m, then climbs onto a rocky knoll covered in a doghair forest of lodgepole pine. Carry on to the south and then loop back to the highway, in part along the provincial boundary cut-line. Yellow pond lilies grow in the lake. The surrounding outcrops feature slate and gritstone of the McKale Formation, part of Miette Group of sedimentary rocks (see p. 81).

Yellowhead Pass was an important place in the 1870s during the survey of the Canadian Pacific Railway, and again in the early 1900s during the surveys of the Grand Trunk Pacific Railway and Canadian Northern Railway. Mountaineer, A.P. Coleman (see p. 78), stopped here in 1907 on his way to Mt. Robson. Coleman wrote: "Before we knew it we were on the watershed on Yellowhead Pass, where clear streams flowed over gravel beds among the timber, and three bench-marks made by the engineers of three great railway lines announced the summit. They did not agree very well to level, showing 3,747, 3,682, and 3,722 feet…" Today's accepted elevation at the lake, which is slightly above the true level of the pass, is 3750 feet (1143 m).

86. Yellowhead Mountain Lookout

TRAIL THUMBNAIL

Trailhead
Turn onto the Lucerne Station Road on the north side of Highway 16, 31.4 km west of the Icefields Parkway, 51.9 km east of Robson Junction. Follow the road to its end at trackside in 1.1 km.

Rating: moderate, 1.2 km

Special consideration: The trail crosses the twinned tracks of the CN Rail main line.

Best lighting: anytime

It seems like the back of beyond today, but Lucerne Station was, between 1913 and 1924, a thriving railway centre. More than 500 people lived nearby during the construction and early operations of the Canadian Northern Railway. When the railway folded in 1924, most residents moved to Jasper. Many took their buildings with them. Today's railway tracks use the grade cleared for the Grand Trunk Pacific Railway. At this location, the Canadian Northern's right-of-way was on the south side of today's Highway 16. The Yellowhead Mountain trail originated in the railway days.

Carefully cross the railway tracks (watch for grease underfoot and trains above-foot) and angle north to pick up the trail (marked by a wooden sign in 2011). The trail takes the slope head-on, climbing through a forest of aspen and lodgepole pine, with a few birches. Arnica and dwarf dogwood are common on the forest floor. The trail soon swings east to contour the cliff edge. At the third opening, a small log bench marks the turnaround point. Views south include Yellowhead Lake and the densely forested Selwyn Range. Late summer visitors will be treated to marvellous splashes of tree colour in the stands of aspen, poplar, and birch.

Labrador tea

87. Labrador Tea

TRAIL THUMBNAIL

Trailhead
North side of Highway 16 in Lucerne Campground, next to site 3; 33 km west of the Icefields Parkway, 50.3 km east of Robson Junction.

Rating: easy, 1.2 km loop

Best lighting: anytime

The Labrador Tea trail loops through a shaded lodgepole pine forest to the shore of Yellowhead Lake. Wildflower species include arnica, calypso orchid, and dwarf dogwood. Labrador tea is an evergreen shrub with showy white flowers. First Peoples and explorers made a strong tea from its leaves. This is not recommended on two counts: the resulting brew contains an alkaloid that is relatively poisonous, and picking plants is illegal in provincial and national parks. The trail ends at a beach on the lakeshore. Retrace the route (400 m longer), or walk along campground roads to the trailhead.

88. Mt. Robson Overlook

TRAIL THUMBNAIL

Trailhead
Turn north off Highway 16 at Robson Junction, 83.3 km west of the Icefields Parkway, 16 km east of Highway 5. The trailhead is at the east end of the parking area. See map, p. 108.

Rating: harder, 2.9 km

Special consideration: Caution! Fall hazard! The upper viewpoint is near an unfenced cliff edge.

Best lighting: anytime

Nearby trails: 83 84 89 90 91 92

Walk Through Time

L et it be said right away that this trail does not provide a fantastic view of Mt. Robson. Views of the main attraction are better, on a fair day, from the parking area at the visitor centre. What the trail does provide is a solid workout, climbing 400 m, most of it in the last 1.8 km; as well as a fine walk in the woods, replete with a multitude of wildflowers and birdsongs.

Head east from the parking area on a road-width trail that narrows to a single track after about 400 m. The forest here is a bit drier than is typical for the Fraser Valley. Trees include Douglas-fir, Engelmann spruce, western redcedar, white birch, Douglas maple, and trembling aspen. The understory is a positive riot of blooming flowers and shrubs in late spring and early summer: false Solomon's seal, queen's cup, dwarf dogwood, wild rose, cinquefoil, twinflower, devil's club, and thimbleberry. At 1.2 km, you reach a junction where a trail descends south (right) to Highway 16 and Overlander Falls. Turn north (left) and begin the switchback climb to the overlook. Listen in the forest for the songs and calls of Townsend's warblers, red-breasted nuthatches, and Swainson's thrushes.

You'll know that you're nearing trail's end when rocks become common underfoot. A bench provides a place to rest and enjoy the views south and south-west. Stonecrop and juniper grow on this modest summit. You can look down onto the parking area and to Overlander Falls on the Fraser River. Across the valley to the south, Overlander Mountain (2687 m) is the prominent peak with three summits. Locals know them as (l-r) Faith, Hope, and Charity. In the southwest, the view includes the Cariboo Mountains. Walk a short distance north for a different and much quieter view. A spur ridge blocks most of Mt. Robson, but Whitehorn Mountain (3399 m) stands clear. If something goes crash in the woods nearby, it might be a bear. It might also be a moose – I've seen moose droppings on the summit.

89. Walk Through Time

TRAIL THUMBNAIL

Trailhead
Turn north off Highway 16 at Robson Junction, 83.3 km west of the Icefields Parkway, 16 km east of Highway 5. See map, p. 108.

Rating: easy, 900 m

Best lighting: anytime

Nearby trails: 83 84 88 90 91 92

B egin on the west side of the information centre and walk clockwise around the meadow that has been cleared to allow views of Mt. Robson. Nine interpretive panels describe aspects of the geology, glaciology, vegetation, First Peoples history, and the exploration history of the Mt. Robson area. The meadow features an abundance of montane flower and shrub species. I often see or hear an uncommon bird species here; once it was a cedar waxwing eating huckleberries, another time a northern shrike screeched from a treetop.

90. Fraser River

TRAIL THUMBNAIL

Trailhead
Turn south off Highway 16 at Robson Junction, 83.3 km west of the Icefields Parkway, 16 km east of Highway 5. Follow Hargreaves Road for 200 m. Turn west (right) into the campground. Park just inside the entrance. The trail begins at site 39. See map, p. 108.

Rating: easy, 2 km loop

Special consideration: Use caution at the river edge.

Best lighting: anytime

Nearby trails: 83 84 88 89 91 92

MOUNT ROBSON PROVINCIAL PARK

This nature walk along the banks of the Fraser River is an ideal outing for those staying in Robson Meadows Campground. It serves as both an introduction to the montane forest that cloaks the valley floor here, and to the Fraser River. Tree species include: Douglas-fir, trembling aspen, cottonwood poplar, western hemlock, western redcedar, Engelmann spruce, and lodgepole pine. Many of the trees have been thrown by the wind. Early summer visitors will be treated to prolific wildflower blooms. The songs of red-breasted nuthatches, Swainson's thrushes, robins, and yellow-rumped warblers fill the treetops. The trail concludes with a perfect kid-friendly destination – the campground playground and sandbox.

92. Rearguard Falls

Rearguard Falls

TRAIL THUMBNAIL

Trailhead
South side of Highway 16; 95.3 km west of the Icefields Parkway; 12 km west of Robson Junction; 4 km east of Highway 5.

Rating: easy, 300 m

Special consideration: Fall risk! Stay within the fenced viewpoints.

Best lighting: afternoon

Nearby trails: 83 84 88 89 90 91

91. Mt. Terry Fox Viewpoint

TRAIL THUMBNAIL

Trailhead
On Highway 16; 92.1 km west of the Icefields Parkway; 7.2 km east of Highway 5; 8.7 km west of Robson Junction.

Rating: easy 110 m

Best lighting: anytime

Nearby trails: 83 84 88 89 90 92

Walk on pavement through the picnic area to reach the fenced viewpoint on a short section of natural trail. Mt. Terry Fox commemorates the young Canadian who, after having lost part of a leg to cancer, ran 5373 km of the distance across Canada in 1980 to raise money for cancer research. Fox, who was a resident of B.C., died the following year. Before being named, Mt. Terry Fox (2643 m) was reportedly the highest unnamed mountain in B.C. visible from a paved highway. Eastbound travellers obtain their first view of Mt. Robson here. On a fair day, it's a show-stopper.

Rearguard Falls is a spectacular, river-wide rapid on the Fraser River, and is the penultimate obstacle on that river for chinook salmon returning to spawn. You can see them here from late August to mid-September, at the culmination of their 11-week journey from the Pacific Ocean. Only one in 2500 eggs results in an adult salmon that returns to these headwaters, four years after its birth. If you are here at the right time and would like to see the salmon close-up, visit the Swift Creek salmon viewing area at Valemount, 19.7 km south of Highway 16 on Highway 5.

Queen's cup

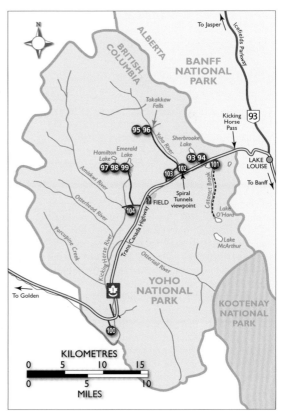

Takakkaw Falls

Yoho National Park

Founded in 1886 as Canada's second national park, Yoho includes 1313 km² on the western slopes of the Rockies in B.C. *Yoho* is a Cree expression of awe and wonder – sentiments affirmed by many hikers who cherish the park's trails.

The village of Field is in the centre of the park, 85 km west of Banff; 26 km west of Lake Louise; and 57 km east of Golden on Highway 1. Access is by car or by passenger bus. Accommodation and basic supplies are available, but campers should stock up before arriving. The park information centre is on Highway 1 at the Field junction. Yoho is in the Mountain time zone – the same as Banff and Jasper national parks.

93. Paget Lookout

Paget Lookout

TRAIL THUMBNAIL

Trailhead

On the north side of Highway 1 at the Wapta Lake picnic area, 11 km east of Field; 15 km west of Lake Louise. For safety, eastbound travellers should make a U-turn at West Louise Lodge, 500 m east of the trailhead, and approach westbound. The trailhead is adjacent to the picnic shelter.

Rating: harder, 3.5 km

Best lighting: anytime

Nearby trails: 94 101 102

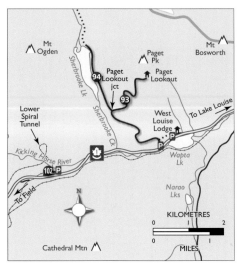

In the aftermath of large forest fires in 1936 and 1940, the Dominion Parks Branch surveyed the mountain national parks to determine suitable sites for fire lookouts. The sites chosen each possessed unrestricted views of major valleys and were in line of sight with adjacent lookouts in the system. Connected by telephone to warden stations in the valleys below, lookout staff would phone in reports of smokes and fires. The upper slope of Paget (PADGE-ett) Peak was one of three sites chosen in Yoho National Park. Paget Lookout saw use until the late 1970s. The access trail is still maintained and the lookout building is open as a day-use shelter. From the lookout, you are rewarded with a grand overview of much of eastern Yoho National Park.

Hike northeast from the picnic area for 80 m to a junction. Make a sharp turn west (left). The next 1.3 km of trail ascends through subalpine forest, notable for its inclusion of cottonwood poplars and Douglas-firs; both species are near their altitudinal limits. In early summer, you may spot the blooms of evergreen violets and calypso orchids. Some trees still sport insulators from the lookout telephone system. You'll

also see old stumps – evidence of logging during railway construction in the 1880s.

Turn northeast (right) at the junction at km 1.4. The trail crosses and recrosses an avalanche slope beneath Paget Peak. I've seen spruce grouse here and at the lookout. The cliffs to the north contain a sequence of Cambrian rocks – five formations in all – that dip toward the southwest.

Where the trail begins its switchback ascent through the cliffs of Paget Peak, whitebark pine trees become common. The whitebark pine grows in the upper subalpine life zone and prefers windswept locations. On younger trees the bark is smooth and silvery-gray; on older trees, it is gray and scaly. The needles are in bunches of five.

The switchbacks provide glimpses of Mt. Niles (2967 m) and Sherbrooke Lake – the third largest lake in Yoho. Mt. Ogden (2703 m) rises from the

BEAUTY CONCEALED

Calypso **is Greek** for "concealment". You'll find the exquisite calypso orchid tucked away in damp, shaded woods, such as those along the trail as far as Paget Lookout junction. The calypso blooms soon after winter's snow melts. The bloom fades, but can endure until early August.

94. Sherbrooke Lake

Sherbrooke Lake

Trailhead
As for Paget Lookout (outing 93).

Rating: moderate, 3.0 km or 4.4 km

Best lighting: anytime

Nearby trails: 93 101 102

With an area of 35 ha, Sherbrooke is the third largest lake in Yoho. It is 12 m deep, and is usually frozen until late June. Surveyor J.J. McArthur named the lake in 1887 after the town of Sherbrooke, near his home in the province of Quebec. This outing shares the first 1.4 km of the Paget Lookout trail.

At the Paget Lookout junction, keep north (straight ahead). Sections of trail have been gravel-capped. Pressure-treated wood decking has been installed to bridge boggy areas. Look for the blooms of orchids here in early summer, including tall white rein-orchid and hooded ladies'-tresses. You can see Mt. Stephen (3199 m) and Cathedral Crags (3073 m) through the trees to the southwest. Just before Sherbrooke Lake, the trail passes through the first of the valley's blowdown areas. Many of these Engelmann spruce and subalpine fir trees were uprooted during a thunderstorm in August 1984. A few of the toppled spruces were roughly 300 years old.

Sixty metres beyond the first blowdown, a short sidetrail leads west (left) to the shore of Sherbrooke Lake. Early morning visitors often find the lake a tranquil mirror, reflecting the colourful slabs of Mt. Ogden (2703 m) opposite, and the thumb-like form of Mt. Niles (2967 m) at the north end of the valley. If you would like to extend this outing, follow the trail along the east shore for another 1.4 km. When you start to climb along the lake's inlet stream you are heading into wilder terrain, so it's best to turn around.

western shore. The mountain commemorates Isaac Ogden, a vice-president of the Canadian Pacific Railway. The Lower Spiral Tunnel is in the opposite flank of the mountain. I've often seen boreal toads on these switchbacks, hike-hopping along. At the top of the switchbacks the grade eases as the trail heads northeast to the lookout. Early season hikers will be treated to displays of glacier lilies.

Paget Lookout commands a 180° panorama, from Mt. Richardson, the Slate Range, and the Bow Valley in the northeast; to the lofty peaks that surround Lake Louise and Lake O'Hara in the south; and to the Van Horne Range and the middle reach of the Kicking Horse Valley in the southwest. Narao Peak (nah-RAY-owe) (2973 m) peak is across the valley to the southeast. The mountain's name is Stoney for "hit in the stomach", probably a reference to when James Hector of the Palliser Expedition was kicked by his horse, near Wapta Falls in 1858 (see p. 121). The

KETTLES AND SINKS

Most of the major east-west passes in the Rockies (Kicking Horse, Vermilion, Yellowhead, and Crowsnest) have lakes near their summits. The massive ice sheets of the early Pleistocene glaciations scoured these passes, 1.9 million-years-ago. At the end of the most recent glaciation, the Late Wisconsin, huge blocks of rubble-covered ice came to rest atop the passes. As the ice blocks melted, the rubble slumped, creating hollows. The resulting lakes are known as kettles. Wapta Lake is a kettle, as are Summit Lake and Sink Lake farther east in Kicking Horse Pass. Sink Lake has no visible surface outlet, and may drain underground into Wapta Lake. When Highway 1 was constructed through Yoho in 1956, crews excavating a road cut near Wapta Lake found permafrost – evidence of the remnant glacial ice. *Wapta* is a Stoney word for "river". It was the original name of the Kicking Horse River.

forested slopes of Narao Peak show different shades of green, indicating tree stands dominated by different species. Most of the upper Kicking Horse Valley burned in 1889 in fires caused by railway operations. The lighter green canopy indicates stands of lodgepole pine that date to those fires. The darker, taller canopy indicates more ancient stands of Engelmann spruce and subalpine fir.

You may see some of Yoho's estimated population of 400 mountain goats near the lookout. For decades, bighorn sheep were thought to be absent from the park. However, since the early 1990s sheep have made regular appearances at a mineral lick on the lower slopes of Paget Peak, adjacent to Highway 1. The peak (2580 m) was named for Reverend Dean Paget of Calgary, a founding member of the Alpine Club of Canada, who climbed the peak in 1904. Surveyor J.J. McArthur made the first ascent in 1886.

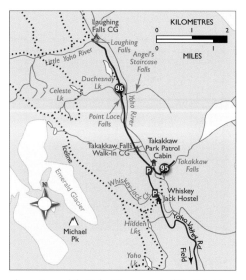

95. Takakkaw Falls

TRAIL THUMBNAIL

Trailhead
Follow Highway 1 to the Yoho Valley Road, 3.7 km east of Field; 22.3 km west of Lake Louise. Turn north and follow this road 13 km to the south end of the Takakkaw Falls parking area.

Rating: easy, 600 m. Wheelchair ♿ accessible in part.

Special considerations: The Yoho Valley Road is not ploughed between October and June. Vehicles longer than 7 m, and vehicles pulling trailers cannot negotiate the switchbacks. Use the trailer drop-off opposite Monarch Campground.

Best lighting: afternoon and evening

Nearby trail: 96

The Yoho Valley exemplifies the park's theme of "rockwalls and waterfalls" better than any other place. Glaciers carved the massive U-shaped valley. The tributary valleys were also filled with ice, but were not as deeply eroded. When the ancient Yoho Glacier receded, the tributary valleys were left hanging above the main valley floor. Their streams now

plunge toward the Yoho River as waterfalls. Takakkaw (TAH-kah-kah) Falls is the greatest of them.

The waterfall's Cree name means "It is magnificent!" William Cornelius Van Horne, President of the Canadian Pacific Railway gave the name on a visit in 1901. German explorer Jean Habel (AHH-bull) made the first recorded visit to the falls, in 1897. Habel's account of the wonders he saw in the Yoho Valley prompted Van Horne's visit, and was instrumental in the valley being added to the original 16 km^2 Mt. Stephen Reserve.

You may have heard that Takakkaw Falls is the highest waterfall in Canada. Whether you measure the single highest drop or the total of all the drops, it isn't. Canada's highest waterfall measured by total drop is Della Falls on Vancouver Island, with a height of 440 m. It's single highest drop is unmeasured. The highest as measured by single drop is Hunlen Falls in South Tweedsmuir Provincial Park, B.C., with a height of 260 m. Helmet Falls, in Kootenay National Park, has a total drop of 352 m. It's single greatest drop is unmeasured. The total drop of Takakkaw Falls is 384 m, 2nd to Della Falls; its single greatest drop is 254 m, 2nd to Hunlen Falls. So, until someone packs gear in to survey the single greatest drop of Helmet Falls, proponents can claim Takakkaw Falls to be Canada's second-highest waterfall. All straight?

The amount of water in Takakkaw Falls varies with the season and with the time of day. It will be at maximum on hot afternoons in July and August. You can often hear boulders carried in the stream's flow, tumbling down the cliff. There have been occasions when boulders plugged the falls, temporarily stopping the flow of water. If you arrive in late afternoon or early evening on a sunny day, you may see a rainbow in the falls.

In winter, the volume of the falls drops. A broad shield of ice forms lower down, with a series of narrow pillars higher up. A team of four Calgarians made the first ascent of the frozen falls in January 1974, heralding the arrival of waterfall ice climbing as a significant winter activity in the Rockies. The ascent took two days. The frozen waterfall has since been solo-climbed in two hours.

The mountains immediately above Takakkaw Falls are part of the Waputik (WAH-poo-tick) Range. *Waputik* is a Stoney word that means "white goat". With luck you may see mountain goats at the base of the cliffs near the falls.

UP ABOVE

The landscape above Takakkaw Falls is truly spectacular. The water that feeds the falls empties from a marginal lake at the toe of Daly Glacier, one of five outlet valley glaciers of the 32 km² Waputik Icefield. The photo shows a mountaineer's view of the lake, Daly Glacier, and Mt. Balfour (3272 m) – the highest mountain in the area. You may obtain a distant view of this scene from the Yoho Pass and Iceline trails, across the valley from Takakkaw Falls.

Takakkaw Falls

96. Laughing Falls

Trailhead
As for Takakkaw Falls (outing 95), but park in the first parking area on the left, for the Yoho Valley trailhead.

Rating: moderate, 4.6 km

Special considerations: As for Takakkaw Falls (outing 95)

Best lighting: morning

Nearby trail: 95

The Yoho Valley trail departs from the north edge of Takakkaw Falls Campground and heads across alluvial flats into forest. This trail originated after the expansion of the Mt. Stephen Reserve – the forerunner of Yoho National Park – as a corduroy carriage road, constructed between 1903 and 1909. You can still see sections of old corduroy at trailside.

At km 2.3, short sidetrails branch east to the bank of the Yoho River and a view of Angel's Staircase Falls, and southwest to Point Lace Falls. The Yoho Valley trail continues north and climbs Hollingsworth Hill, named for a district warden who used dynamite to widen the right of way. The Duchesnay Lake junction is at km 3.7. The sidetrip is less than half the 400 m indicated on the park sign. In most years, the lake is dry by late summer. Moose frequent this area. Back on the main trail, you draw alongside the Yoho River at a small canyon. The tilted and potholed rock exposed in the riverbed is Sullivan Formation limestone.

Laughing Falls Campground is situated just beyond, on an alluvial fan at the confluence of Twin Falls Creek, the Little Yoho River, and the Yoho River. For the best views of the falls, follow beaten paths along the north bank of the Little Yoho River. Laughing Falls was named because they brightened up the otherwise glum surroundings during the rain-plagued, first exploration of the Yoho Valley in 1897.

97. Emerald Lake

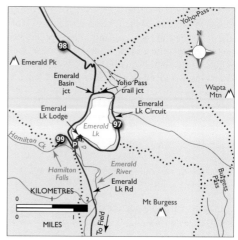

Emerald Lake

TRAIL THUMBNAIL

Trailhead
Follow Highway 1 to the Emerald Lake Road, 2.0 km west of Field. Turn north and follow the road 8 km to its end at the Emerald Lake parking area. The trailhead is at the north end of the parking area, to the west (left) of the bridge.

Rating: moderate, 4.8 km loop. Wheelchair accessible in part.

Best lighting: anytime

Nearby trails: 98 99 104

With an area of 1.16 km² and a depth of 28 m, Emerald Lake is the largest and deepest of Yoho's 61 lakes and ponds. The circuit of the lake ranks as one of the finer nature walks in the Rockies. I have walked this trail at least 50 times, and never tire of it. The first 500 m is paved, and wheelchair access is possible for an additional 1.5 km. Walk the circuit in a clockwise direction, and keep right at all trail junctions.

Emerald Lake sits in a deep pocket, surrounded by high mountains. This arrangement results in frequent rain in summer and heavy snows in winter. Coupled with the low elevation of the lake, the moisture supports trees more typical of B.C.'s Interior Cedar-Hemlock forest zone: western redcedar, western yew, western hemlock, Douglas-fir, and western white pine.

Amateur botanists will love this outing. I have counted more than 60 species of wildflowers and flowering shrubs in bloom on a single visit in late

June. Wildflowers thrive on the alluvial fan on the northeast shore of the lake. This place is orchid-central. You may see the blooms of yellow lady's slipper, tall white bog orchid, hooded ladies'-tresses, spotted orchid, and a rarity – mountain lady's slipper.

Emerald Lake is also a great place to see wildlife, including species not often observed. American martens frequent the ancient stand of Engelmann spruce just north of the trailhead. I have had an eye-to-eye encounter with one as it clung to a tree trunk as I walked by. Woodpeckers nest in tree cavities right beside the trail. On a visit in 2010, after we had completed a circuit of the lake, we watched a grizzly bear descend the avalanche path to the trail. Wolverines lumber across the alluvial fan from time to time. Look for moose on the lakeshore in the south bay, especially late in the day. Osprey and common loons nest at the lake. Beavers have built lodges along the northeast shore. Cougars have been sighted often in recent years. Rainbow trout, cutthroat trout, eastern brook trout, and slimy sculpin are the recorded fish species. Some of the trout spawn in the gravels along the alluvial fan.

Emerald Lake is frequently described as having a "dry side" and a "wet side". The "wet side" includes the east and south shores that lie at the base of shaded mountain slopes. The upper parts of these slopes hold snow most of the summer, and also receive a lot of rain. This cool, damp environment allows growth of a lush forest, more typical of wet coastal and interior forests in B.C. The "dry side" of the lake (west shore) features a normal variety of vegetation for its location and elevation. It is only "dry" in a relative sense to the "wet side".

Five hundred metres from the trailhead, the trail crosses a swath in the forest – an avalanche slope that runs from the summit of Emerald Peak to the lakeshore. The snow on this slope can release with such mass and force that it punches through the frozen surface of the lake. The avalanche slope provides excellent habitat for moose, elk, and bears. Although you will no doubt be looking across the lake at the view of the lodge and Mt. Burgess (2599 m) as you cross the avalanche path, keep your head up and make some noise here. A scene depicting Mt. Burgess and Emerald Lake appeared on the verso side of the Canadian ten dollar bill between 1954 and 1971.

The peak to the east (left) of Mt. Burgess is Mt. Field (2635 m). Farther east (left) is Wapta Mountain (2782 m), connected to Mt. Field by Fossil Ridge – where Charles Walcott of the Smithsonian Institution discovered the 530-million-year-old soft bodied fossils of the Burgess Shale in 1909. You may be able to pick out the tents of researchers high on the ridge. Other white dots might be mountain goats.

The trail swings east (right) onto the alluvial fan at km 1.4. Rubble carried by glacial melt streams has created this landform. The rocky soils, cold air drainage, ever-changing courses of the streams, and high water table hinder the growth of vegetation. Trees include lodgepole pine, white birch, and gnarled white spruce. Juniper and willows grow beneath them. The trees are exposed to the full brunt of winds from across the lake. Some of the trees near the lakeshore "flag" the prevailing southwest wind. They have branches only on their northeast sides.

In summer, the alluvial fan can be transformed from ice box to furnace. Intense light and heat result when sunlight reflects off the rocks. Many of the mat-like plants are pale on the undersides of their leaves, in order to reflect the light and heat coming from beneath.

As harsh as the environment on the alluvial fan sounds, nature decorates it with many wildflowers and flowering shrubs. Yellow mountain avens, bearberry, and twinflower hug the ground in the drier areas. The wetter areas support cotton-grass, sedge meadows, blue-eyed grass, and orchids. White camas and paintbrush are common at trailside.

In the view west across the lake from the alluvial fan, the horn mountain shapes of the Van Horne Range are prominent. The highest peak visible is Mt. King (2892 m), with a small niche glacier on its north flank. Farther south (left), the other glaciated peak is Mt. Vaux (VOX) (3310 m) in the Ottertail Range.

ALL IN A SUMMER'S WORK

The year 1882 was momentous for Tom Wilson. In his work with the railway survey, he discovered Lake Louise, crossed Bow Pass and Howse Pass, and found ore on the slopes of Mt. Stephen. At the end of the summer he topped it off by discovering Emerald Lake. Wilson had left horses in a pasture near the present site of Field. The horses went looking for better feed, and Wilson tracked them across Natural Bridge to Emerald Lake.

"Emerald" is an obvious name for the lake, but was not the one given by Wilson. He had already used "Emerald" to name the lake now known as Lake Louise. When the name of Lake Louise became official in 1884, the name "Emerald" came west to Wilson's other gem of a discovery.

THE ABLEST RAILWAY GENERAL

The Van Horne Range (visible from the alluvial fan) commemorates William Cornelius Van Horne, appointed General Manager of the Canadian Pacific Railway (CPR) in 1881, and later its President and Chairman. Van Horne's career was the ultimate success story. After dropping out of school, in a span of twenty years he worked his way from telegraph operator of the Illinois Central Railroad to become chief of one of the largest railway undertakings. At the age of 38 he was touted as "one of the ablest railway generals in the world".

Van Horne was a bear of a man with a remarkable memory and no apparent requirement for sleep. In his meteoric rise he took no rest either from learning about his profession, preferring to acquaint himself with railway jobs by working them on his days-off. As a result he knew every aspect of railroading, from yard work, to scheduling, to driving locomotives. It was reported that he could decipher the background clatter of a telegraph transmission while simultaneously carrying on a conversation. In all matters, Van Horne paid tenacious attention to detail, saving pennies here and minutes there, making railroads profitable.

Van Horne's crowning achievement with the CPR was the creation of a hotel business, and the establishment of working relationships with an array of mountaineers, artists, and scientists who visited the Rockies. These travellers publicized their exploits, thus repaying the CPR by generating more tourist business. Van Horne was forthright in his support of proposals to establish Banff and Yoho national parks. Although he was motivated by commerce, we can be thankful to this dynamic man for the role he played in helping to create Canada's national park system.

The bridge at the far side of the fan crosses one of the main inlets to the lake. This stream deposits fine sediments, building a delta. Emerald Lake is one of a few places in the Rockies where a delta and an alluvial fan are found together. Pondweed, horsetail and sedges grow here, providing cover for waterfowl and food for moose. Wheelchairs cannot proceed beyond this point.

Across the bridge, the forest immediately becomes damp. Shrub-like western red cedar are interspersed among ancient white spruce, subalpine fir, and a few western hemlock and Douglas-fir. Intense forest fires have not occurred on this side of the lake for more than three hundred years, allowing this old-growth forest to develop. In the undergrowth, green alder, ferns, thimbleberry, devil's club, horsetails, queen's cup, and foam flower are common. At time of publication, the slick boardwalks on this side of the lake were slated for replacement.

The circuit finishes with a short climb to the crest of the moraine that dams the lake and the site of Emerald Lake Lodge. The main lodge building includes part of the original chalet that was built in 1902. The lodge was completely redeveloped in 1985-86.

To reach the parking area, walk through the lodge grounds to the bridge at the lake's outlet. The

98. Emerald Basin

Trailhead
As for Emerald Lake (outing 97). See map, p. 118.

Rating: harder, 4.3 km

Best lighting: anytime

Nearby trails: 97 99 104

Emerald Basin is a glacial valley north of Emerald Lake, hemmed by the summits of the President Range. The first 1.4 km of this outing follows the Emerald Lake trail. (See outing 97.) The trail then veers north (left) for 600 m along the edge of the alluvial fan, and then northwest (left) into the forest. After a steep climb, the trail levels in a pocket of old-growth forest, featuring western redcedar, western hemlock, and Douglas-fir. After traversing the growth of an avalanche slope on the flanks of Emerald Peak, the trail becomes indistinct. Ahead is a hanging glacier, notched in the cirque between The President (3123 m) and The Vice President (3077 m). The peaks were named for officials of the Canadian Pacific Railway. To the south, you can see Mt. Burgess (2599 m) and the summit of Mt. Stephen (3199 m).

Hamilton Falls

99. Hamilton Falls

Trailhead
As for Emerald Lake (outing 97). See map, p. 118.

Rating: easy, 700 m

Best lighting: morning

Nearby trails: 97 98 104

This outing is located in the deep basin that surrounds Emerald Lake; a place that traps storm systems and creates abundant precipitation. Vegetation contains species typical of the B.C.'s Western Interior Cedar-Hemlock "rainforest": western redcedar, western hemlock, western yew, thimbleberry, and devil's club. Queen's cup, western meadowrue, foam-flower, and dwarf dogwood are common wildflowers. The white flower of queen's cup (see p. 112) yields a striking blue-coloured berry in late summer, hence its other folk name – "bluebead". You may see black bears and moose here.

The trail draws alongside Hamilton Creek and follows it to some large Douglas-fir trees at the shaded base of Hamilton Falls. The damp environment here gives rise to brilliant yellow tree lichens. The features named "Hamilton" honour a prospector who discovered the falls while in quest of more material rewards. Hamilton Creek was formerly the water supply for Emerald Lake Lodge. You may see artifacts associated with the water intake system and pipeline. The falls are at the mouth of a hanging valley, and are being eroded into Chancellor Formation limestone. To get a better view of the falls, follow the trail (destined for Hamilton Lake, 4.6 km distant) a few switchbacks upward onto a drier slope.

massive, glacier-capped cliffs of The Vice President (3077m, named for a vice-president of the CPR) loom to the north. To the south, Mt. Burgess may be reflected in the lagoon that has formed behind the moraine. Cliff swallows fly overhead, and fish rise occasionally below. In the evening, the bridge is a good place to watch the rapid comings and goings of little brown bats. These winged mammals swoop over the lake, feeding on insects. During daytime, they congregate under the eaves of the lodge.

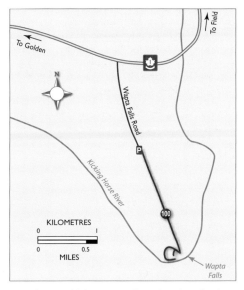

100. Wapta Falls

Wapta Falls

TRAIL THUMBNAIL

Trailhead
On the south side of Highway 1, 24.7 km west of Field. (There is no sign for westbound travellers.) Follow the Wapta Falls Road 1.6 km south to the trailhead. Early and late in the season, the access road may be closed, in which case, park in the parking area at the highway and walk the access road to the trailhead.

Rating: moderate, 2.4 km (4.0 km if access road is closed)

Best lighting: afternoon

Wapta Falls is Yoho's Niagara. Most of the surface runoff and glacial meltwater in the park passes over the brink of this 30-m high cataract, with a peak summer flow of 255 m^3 per second. Unlike many waterfalls in the Rockies, which are located within canyons or at the mouths of hanging valleys, Wapta Falls is a straight-ahead product of mountain building. The river cascades over a steeply upturned fold of shales of the McKay (muck-EYE) Formation.

The initial kilometre is along the edge of a clearing originally intended for a road to the falls. The open montane forest here is typical of the drier, low elevations in south-western Yoho National Park, and features an abundance of tree species: trembling aspen, black cottonwood poplar, western redcedar, lodgepole pine, subalpine fir, white birch, Engelmann/white spruce hybrids, and Douglas-fir. Mountain pine beetles have affected the lodgepole pines, as have strong winds. Deadfalls and windfalls dot the forest floor. Wood lilies, pink wintergreen, bearberry, and juniper are common in the undergrowth. Black bears, wolves, ruffed grouse, and white-tailed deer frequent the forest. Osprey, bald eagles, and kingfishers make use of the wetland just east of the trail.

As the trail narrows, it enters a damp pocket of forest. A short climb leads to the viewpoint above the falls. Please keep within the fence. Just upstream, you can see the confluence of the Beaverfoot River and the Kicking Horse River. For a closer view of the falls, continue downhill for 400 m to a gravel beach on the riverbank. At low water, you can walk toward the falls. Look for a rainbow in the spray on sunny days. The outcrops in the river below the falls indicate the former locations of the cataract.

Hector's Close Call

The Palliser Expedition of 1857 to 1860 explored central and western British North America (now Canada) for the British government, to appraise the region for future settlement, resource wealth, and transportation routes. It was a daunting undertaking in an unknown land. Expedition leader, John Palliser, was fortunate that one of his charges, James Hector, a 23 year-old Scots doctor and geologist, was up to the task. Many of the expedition's findings regarding the topography of the Rockies were the result of Hector's ambitious travels. He pounded along his share of tracks and trails – 900 km in one 57-day stint in 1858 alone – and made the first recorded crossings by a European of four passes – Vermilion, Kicking Horse, Pipestone, and Howse.

After crossing Vermilion Pass, Hector's native guide chose not to lead the party down the Vermilion and Kootenay rivers on a certain route to the Columbia River. They turned west over the Beaverfoot Divide to the Kicking Horse Valley. Near Wapta Falls, Hector's horse kicked him in the chest. The blow knocked him out. His men assumed him dead, and were preparing to bury him when to their astonishment

James Hector

(and his!), Hector revived. Two days later Hector noted that his men were calling the river along which they travelled, the Kicking Horse.

Following the Palliser Expedition, Hector served as Director of the Geological Survey and Colonial Museum of New Zealand, and was knighted. In August 1903, he returned to Canada with his son, Douglas, intending to visit the site of his mishap near Wapta Falls, and to cross Kicking Horse Pass by train. Douglas became ill at Glacier House, and died soon after at Revelstoke. Hector departed immediately for New Zealand, never to return. He died in 1907.

CAPTURED

A few hundred metres downstream from Wapta Falls, the south-westerly-flowing Kicking Horse River makes an abrupt 90° turn to the northwest. Why the change of course? The massive glacier that carved the Kicking Horse valley during the Late Wisconsin Glaciation undoubtedly carried on along its south-trending course, flowing through today's Beaverfoot valley. At the conclusion of that ice age, the ancient Kicking Horse River briefly followed the same course. But as the river eroded downwards, something on the valley floor near the present site of Wapta Falls – perhaps a moraine or a landslide – blocked the river's course. The valley of a tributary stream coming in from the northwest provided an escape route for the impounded water. The river made the turn in that direction, easily cutting down through the underlying weak shales to create today's Golden Canyon. Geologists refer to these two processes as diversion and capture.

Wapta is a Stoney word that means "river". So, you ask, was the original name of the Kicking Horse, "River River"? Probably not. Something must have been lost in the translation because, elsewhere in the Rockies, the Stoney word "Wapta" is usually coupled with another word, i.e.: Sunwapta ("turbulent river"), Washmawapta ("deep snow river").

BEARBERRY

Bearberry is an evergreen shrub, common in the ground cover of the montane life zone. It grows as a trailing vine, and forms mats on dry slopes. The delicate, urn-shaped flowers bloom in early summer. They are white with pink edging, and hang downward from the stem. Glossy red berries replace the flowers by August. In late summer the foliage turns brilliant hues of red, yellow, and orange. As the plant's name suggests, the berries are a favourite food of black bears, which seem to prefer eating them in the spring, after they have spent a winter on the vine.

Bearberry is also known as *kinnikinnik* (kin-IH-ki-nick), Algonquian for "a mixture that is smoked". First Peoples fashioned a primitive tobacco from its dried leaves, fruits, and bark. Bearberry is a member of the heath family of plants that includes blueberries and mountain heather. There are three bearberry species in the Rockies, two of which occur at higher elevations.

101. Ross Lake

TRAIL THUMBNAIL

Trailhead
Follow Highway 1 to the junction with Highway 1A, 12.6 km west of Lake Louise; 13.4 km east of Field. Turn onto Highway 1A and cross the railway tracks. Either park next to the concrete barricade or turn west (right) to the Lake O'Hara parking area. From the barricade on Highway 1A, walk or bike 2 km east along the road to the Ross Lake trailhead.

Rating: moderate, 3.2 km (including access road)

Special consideration: Bikes are not allowed on the trail.

Best lighting: anytime

Nearby trails: 93 94 102

Ross Lake is a glacial tarn, scoured from the bedrock by a glacier that once flowed from the hanging valley above. After reaching the trailhead by pavement, you carry on to the lake by a pleasant walk through subalpine forest, following the route of a logging trail used during construction of the Canadian Pacific Railway in the 1880s. The limestone cliffs that back the lake are 400 m high. Look for mountain goats. James Ross was the western construction superintendent during the original construction of the Canadian Pacific Railway. As one of the more successful railway builders of his era, he became one of the wealthier people in Canada. If you look carefully in the asphalt of Highway 1A near the trailhead, you may see the outlines of railway ties from a spur line, buried when the highway was surfaced in the late 1950s.

102. Lower Spiral Tunnel Viewpoint

The original line of the Canadian Pacific Railway (CPR) descended from Wapta Lake to Field with a grade that reached 4.5 percent. Wrecks occurred when trains ran-away. In 1909, the CPR completed the two Spiral Tunnels, adding 7 km to the length of the line, and reducing the maximum grade east of Field to 2.2 percent. One thousand workers

TRAIL THUMBNAIL

Trailhead
North side of Highway 1, 7.4 km east of Field; 18.6 km west of Lake Louise. See map, p. 114.

Rating: easy, 100 m, wheelchair ♿ accessible

Best lighting: anytime

Nearby trails: 93 94 101

and 700,000 tonnes of dynamite were required in the tunnels' construction. You can see the Lower Spiral Tunnel in Mt. Ogden from this viewpoint. Approximately 30 trains a day pass through the tunnels, so have patience if you want to see a train loop over itself. If you would like to learn more about the railway history of Yoho, pick up a copy of *The Spiral Tunnels and the Big Hill*. Mountain pine beetles have killed many trees in the forest near the viewpoint.

103. A Walk in the Past

TRAIL THUMBNAIL

Trailhead
Follow Highway 1 to the Yoho Valley Road, 3.7 km east of Field; 22.3 km west of Lake Louise. Follow this road 1 km to Kicking Horse Campground. Enter the campground and drive to the interpretive theatre parking area. The trail begins at the display nearby.

Rating: moderate, 1.2 km

Best lighting: anytime

Special considerations: The trail crosses the Yoho Valley Road and the double tracks of the Canadian Pacific Railway. Use caution. A brochure may be available at the trailhead or at the park information centre at Field, or visit the *Walks and Easy Hikes* page at mountainvision.ca, and use the download link.

The Big Hill in 1884

104. Natural Bridge

Natural Bridge

The seven interpretive stops along A Walk in the Past explore the history of the Canadian Pacific Railway (CPR) at the bottom of Yoho's notorious "Big Hill". You can also visit the stone bake oven in the campground 100 m west of the trailhead. The oven served a railway construction camp in 1884.

After crossing the Yoho Valley Road, the trail ascends through a damp, shaded forest that features Douglas-fir, western redcedar, baneberry, cow parsnip, thimbleberry, foamflower, false Solomon's seal, horsetails, white geranium, wintergreens, devil's club, and a veritable carpet of dwarf dogwood and queen's cup. The trail is following the route of a tote road, cleared in 1884 to pack supplies for railway construction.

After a switchback, where you leave the route of the tote road, the trail emerges at trackside at Yoho Siding. Look for deposits of coal soot and cinders beside the double set of railway tracks. These deposits accumulated during the 72 years of coal-fired railway operations that preceded the arrival of diesel locomotives in 1956. Watch for oil and grease underfoot. Do not linger near the tracks.

Across the tracks, the trail climbs to stop #5 and the original 1884 railway grade, here, near its maximum steepness of 4.5 percent. Part of this grade was subsequently used in The Kicking Horse Trail, the first road completed from Lake Louise to Golden in 1927. You can see the upper portal of the Upper Spiral Tunnel if you look upslope. Turn west (right) and follow the road 150 m. Stop #6 marks the location of the lowest of the three runaway tracks on the Big Hill. Veer southwest (left) to stop #7, where you will see the wreck of a narrow gauge locomotive, scrapped after its use in the construction of the Spiral Tunnels. For more information on Yoho's railway history, pick up a copy of *The Spiral Tunnels and the Big Hill*.

TRAIL THUMBNAIL

Trailhead
Follow Highway 1 to the Emerald Lake Road, 2.0 km west of Field. Turn north (right), and follow the road 1.5 km. Turn west (left) into the paved parking area.

Rating: easy, 100 m. Wheelchair ♿ accessible.

Best lighting: afternoon

Special consideration: Fall risk! Keep within fenced viewpoints.

Nearby trails: 97 98 99

Natural Bridge marks the point where the Kicking Horse River encounters an outcrop of Chancellor Formation slate. The rock here has been tipped vertically and has been compressed into a U-shaped syncline, making it relatively resistant to erosion by water. Formerly, the river cascaded over the lip of rock as a waterfall. But over time it has eroded downward into a crack behind the lip, creating the dog-leg "bridge". At high water, the Kicking Horse River will flow completely over the bridge.

Paintbrush, Stanley Glacier trail

Kootenay National Park

Established in 1920, Kootenay National Park includes 1406 km² on the west side of the continental divide, in B.C. The park features tremendous diversity, incorporating Rocky Mountain and Columbia Valley climates, three geologic landscapes, 256 animal species, and 993 species of plants – including 22 species of orchids. It is the only national park in Canada that is home to both cacti and glaciers.

The Walks and Easy Hikes in Kootenay visit a twice-burned forest, a dolomite canyon, the valley of an alpine glacier, and the outlets of three mineral springs. The Sinclair Canyon trail, in the south-western corner of the park, introduces you to the drier, warmer climate of the Columbia Valley. You have excellent opportunities to see wildlife on these trails: elk, deer, moose, bears, mountain goats, and bighorn sheep.

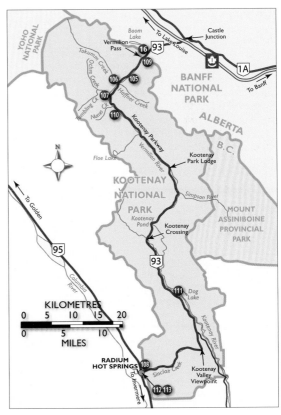

125

105. Stanley Glacier

The 2003 burn

Stanley Glacier

TRAIL THUMBNAIL

Trailhead
Parking area on the south side of the Kootenay Parkway (Highway 93 South), 13.4 km west of Highway 1; 91.5 km east of Highway 95.

Rating: harder, 4.2 km

Special consideration: Due to the hazard of falling trees, avoid this hike during windy weather.

Best lighting: anytime

Nearby trails: 16 106 107 109 110

The Stanley Glacier trail explores a hanging valley and offers close-up views of three processes that have shaped the landscape of the Rockies: fire, avalanches, and glaciation. The trailside displays of wildflowers are spectacular, so if you are hiking in mid- to late-July, consider this outing even if the weather is not great. You may see moose, mountain goats, white-tailed ptarmigan, and hoary marmots.

From the parking area, the trail descends to the Vermilion River and switchbacks up into a forest that has burned twice in recent decades. The Vermilion Pass burn (see p. 133) consumed 2360 ha of subalpine forest in July 1968. The Kootenay fires of 2003 burned 17,715 ha; 12.6 percent of the park's area.

The trail climbs steadily through the burned forest, gaining 220 m of elevation in the first 2.4 km. With the forest canopy removed by the fires, a profusion of sun-loving wildflowers blooms. Many are

species that fare well on disturbed ground – camas, fleabane, pink wintergreen, yellow columbine, yellow hedysarum, groundsel, and paintbrush. The hues of the paintbrush along this trail are particularly vibrant. Until the forest canopy closes in again, the arnica and common fireweed displays here will likely remain unmatched in the Rockies. Damp areas feature rein-orchids and gentians. The buzzy calls of varied thrushes resonate. After you crest a small rise, the trail descends slightly to a footbridge. From here on, you hike out of earshot of the highway.

The 2003 fire killed many small lodgepole pines that had grown after the 1968 fire. You can now see thousands of tiny lodgepoles that date to the later burn, but note how, near the creek, some of the older saplings survived. This patchwork of tree ages helps to create a forest with more diversity than if most of the trees were the same age.

The colossal cliff that flanks the west side of the valley is known as "The Guardwall". The lower 300 m of cliff is Cathedral Formation limestone and dolomite. It contains a number of solution caves – caverns eroded by naturally acidic rainwater. The upper cliff

SNOW AVALANCHES

The slopes on the east side of the valley feature steep avalanche paths. At trailside, you can see the sun-bleached remains of trees uprooted by sliding snow, and by the wind blasts it generates. Snow avalanches occur when one or more layers within a snowpack release from other layers, or when the entire snowpack separates from the underlying slope. Avalanches are caused by a complex interplay of temperature, humidity, wind, snow depth, slope aspect, and steepness. People and animals travelling on a susceptible slope may trigger an avalanche; loud noises cannot. Avalanches are probably the leading cause of death for mountain goats.

Although destructive in one sense, avalanches are simply another of nature's tools for ensuring biodiversity. Avalanches remove large vegetation, creating open habitat that supports shrubs and wildflowers. These are important foods for moose, elk, bears, and deer.

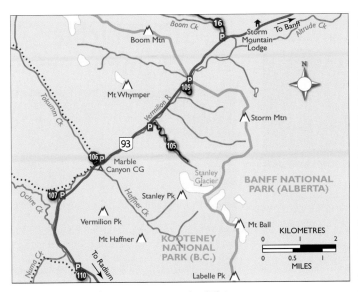

on cliffs. Less than two centuries ago, the glacier flowed over these cliffs to reach valley floor. You may hear the creaking and groaning of the ice as it creeps forward and, with fortune, see an ice avalanche. Meltwater that cascades over the cliffs is sometimes caught in updrafts, creating waterfalls that seem to disappear in mid-air.

Toward Stanley Glacier the valley is a barren world of boulders and screes that is home to mountain goats, hoary marmots, pikas, and white-tailed ptarmigan. The summit of Stanley Peak (3153 m) is concealed from view.

is Eldon Formation limestone. Between the cliffs is a fossil-rich ledge of Stephen Formation shale. These formations date to the Middle Cambrian. The dark streaks on the cliffs are water seeps and rock lichens. In the perpetual shade of winter, the seeps freeze into sheets of ice that become a destination for waterfall ice climbers. In some years, the ice endures into July.

As you near the end of trail, note how the 2003 burn did not go as far up the valley as did the 1968 burn, and how the earlier burn reached almost to the very last tree. On the west side of the trail, there is a stand of mature forest that escaped both burns. Listen for hermit thrushes. A sign on a knoll marks the end of the maintained trail, from where you can study Stanley Glacier. Several lobes of ice terminate

James Hector originally named the mountain "Mt. Ball" in 1858. However, that name subsequently came into use for a higher mountain to the southwest. Edward Whymper gave the name, Stanley Peak, in 1901, to honour Frederick Stanley, then Governor General of Canada. Lord Stanley's name also adorns the ultimate prize in North American hockey – the Stanley Cup.

Looking north, you can see the U-shape of this hanging valley. Valleys in the Rockies were originally V-shaped, the products of erosion by streams and rivers. As Stanley Glacier advanced through this valley – most recently during the Late Wisconsin Glaciation – it undercut the surrounding mountainsides. When the glacier receded, the mountainsides collapsed, widening the valley floor.

EDWARD WHYMPER: GREAT EXPECTATIONS

Edward Whymper was in the first party to climb the Matterhorn, in 1865. Whymper made five trips to the Rockies in the early 1900s. The first three were under arrangement with the Canadian Pacific Railway. In return for free rail passage and an outfit of mountain guides, Whymper was to pen magazine articles and to make suggestions regarding the location and construction of trails and facilities. The railway hoped to capitalize on Whymper's illustrious reputation, and to make the Rockies into a "new Switzerland".

Whymper had a dour temperament and a legendary capacity for alcohol. He rapidly alienated his mountaineering guides and packers, and accomplished few of his objectives. Perhaps the greatest disappointment for the railway was that, during his first visit, Whymper did not even attempt to climb Mt. Assiniboine, "the Canadian Matterhorn". The moguls of the railway soon tired of his scheme. Whymper's only significant Canadian mountaineering – accomplished at the prompting of his guides – was completed during the 1901 trip, when the group made first ascents of Mt. Whymper, Stanley Peak, and a number of mountains in what is now Yoho National Park. Mt. Whymper (2844 m) is framed by the valley walls in the view north from Stanley Glacier viewpoint.

UNCOMMONLY BEAUTIFUL

Among the silvery skeletons of the burned forest, common fireweed is sure to catch your eye. A pioneering plant on disturbed ground, fireweed often grows in thickets. Since the 2003 fire, the Stanley Glacier trail has been the fireweed capital of the southern Rockies. Each plant features a multitude of pink flowers atop a stem that may reach 2 m in height. The lowest flowers open first, and it is usual for flowers, buds, and purple` seedpods to be present on the same plant in late summer. The flowers shed a thick, yellow pollen. Common fireweed is the territorial emblem of the Yukon. Mountain fireweed (river beauty) is a smaller, equally beautiful plant that grows at higher elevations and along glacial melt streams.

MOUNTAIN MAGIC

The 15 species of arnica in the Rockies span the life zones from valley bottom to near mountain top. You will most often encounter arnica blooming from early July onwards, in the understories of lodgepole pine forests on lower mountainsides. The deep yellow blooms are easy to recognize, making arnica an "easy" genus for non-botanists (like me). However, keying out the individual species can be a problem – they hybridize.

Almost any botany guidebook will tell you that arnica is poisonous if eaten. True. But some fail to mention the plant's powerful medicinal properties if properly prepared. Tinctures and ointments made from arnica roots have well-proven capacities to reduce bruising, swelling, and inflammation. We carry arnica tincture in our first-aid kit, and apply it immediately to any harsh bruise or sprain where the skin is not open. Presto! No bruising; no pain. Some homeopathic formulations can be taken internally – I use them instead of Ibuprofen to reduce joint pain after long days on the trail. Arnica is literally magic for the inevitable tumbles and bumps that kids take on the trail and elsewhere.

106. Marble Canyon

Marble Canyon

TRAIL THUMBNAIL

Trailhead
North side of the Kootenay Parkway (Highway 93 South), 17.2 km west of Castle Junction; 88 km east of the junction with Highway 95. See map, p. 127.

Rating: easy, 800 m

Special considerations: Caution! Fall risk. Keep within the fencing. Avoid this outing during high winds as there is a risk of falling trees.

Best lighting: late morning and early afternoon

Nearby trails: 16 105 107 109 110

It has been said that in the Rockies, "The sound of rushing water is the sound of a canyon growing." After you have walked the Marble Canyon trail, you will probably agree. The trail follows the route of a "migrating" waterfall, one of several agents in the canyon's creation.

As with most canyons in the Rockies, Marble Canyon is at the mouth of a hanging valley – in this case, at the confluence of Tokumm Creek and the Vermilion River. *Tokumm* is reportedly a Stoney word that means "red fox". At the first bridge across the creek, you will be greeted by a blast of cold air – a potent illustration of the canyon's effect on local climate. The temperature on the bridge can be 10°C colder than on the trail 20 m away. Glaciers 20 km up the valley chill the air that settles on the valley floor. The shaded depths of the canyon cool the air more.

The trail crosses the canyon seven times on sturdy bridges. At the second bridge, you can see a natural arch – a lip of rock that resisted erosion. This arch may mark the waterfall's location, 9000 years ago. Please don't attempt to cross it. People have died from falls at this spot. The large sedimentary boulder near the fifth bridge is a glacial erratic, deposited here when the glacier that carved the Tokumm Creek valley receded. Cracks in its surface have filled with soil, and a tree has taken root.

Spray from the canyon saturates the thin soils on the canyon rim, causing the soils to creep toward the abyss. Only mosses, lichens, and plants with mat-like characteristics can anchor these soils and grow here. Before the 2003 fire, the complement of plants on the canyon rim included some species normally found north of the Arctic Circle. With most of the damp, canyon forest consumed by the fire, the vegetation cohort has shifted to include species associated with

The old and the new

drier, lodgepole pine forests. Countless thousands of lodgepole pines now grow amid the charred spars of the old forest. Wildflowers thrive and colour the area around the canyon in late spring and early summer.

Marble Canyon's gradual, north-westward curve resulted from the water enlarging a crack system in the bedrock. The canyon's deepest point is the 39 m-drop beneath the seventh bridge, the present location of the waterfall. The constant pounding at the base of the waterfall creates a plunge pool, which enlarges over time and begins to undercut the rock above. Eventually, gravity, the shattering effects of frost, and the sheer hydraulic force of the water prevail. The hanging, dolomite lip of the waterfall collapses into the plunge pool, and the brink moves a few metres upstream. This process has helped Marble Canyon's waterfall to "migrate" more than 600 m upstream in 11,000 years.

Some geologists speculate that another process has been at work here, and that the canyon may have existed as an underground stream, perhaps even prior to the last ice age. The massive Tokumm Valley glacier of the late Wisconsin Glaciation eroded the roof from the cave passage, exposing the "canyon".

Marble Canyon is eroded into rock of the Cathedral Formation. Most of the rock that you see is actually the mineral, dolomite, created when calcium in limestone was replaced by magnesium. Technically speaking, the rock is not true marble, but when wet, the stream-polished dolomite looks the part.

Slightly downstream from Marble Canyon, you can see potholes eroded into another exposure of highly polished dolomite. You can view them on your return by taking the branch trail to the southwest (right), just before you recross the first bridge.

BLOW-UP!

The summer of 2003 was the third-driest in the Rockies in a record that goes back more than a century. On a single day in July, lightning started five forest fires in Kootenay National Park. Firefighters extinguished three of these but, by early August, the two other fires had united to create a blaze that eventually consumed 12.6 percent of the park's area. One of these fires had started in the north reaches of the Tokumm Valley. On August 20, this firefront "blew-up" and made a 6 km southward run into the Vermilion Valley. The fire consumed a backcountry hut, most of the bridges in Marble Canyon, and the buildings of a nearby warden station. Due to the hazard posed by fire-damaged trees and the expense of rebuilding the bridges, the Marble Canyon trail was closed for four years.

107. Ochre Beds and Paint Pots

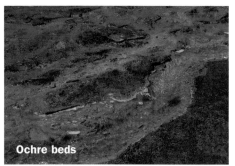

Ochre beds

TRAIL THUMBNAIL

Trailhead
Parking area on the north side of the Kootenay Parkway (Highway 93 South), 19.7 km west of Castle Junction; 85 km east of the junction with Highway 95. See map, p. 127.

Rating: easy, 1 km

Best lighting: anytime

Nearby trails: 16 105 106 109 110

The walk to the Ochre Beds and Paint Pots leads to colourful deposits of clay and the outlets of three mineral springs. On the way, you are treated to a suspension bridge crossing of the Vermilion River. Wildlife is common here. Look and listen for owls, woodpeckers, and Steller's jays in the ancient forest. You may see the tracks of wolves, coyotes, deer, elk, moose, American martens, and bears in the clay.

Sediments deposited on the bottom of an ancient glacial lake at the end of the Late Wisconsin Glaciation became the clay of the Ochre Beds. The remarkable colours result from saturation of the clay with iron-rich water. This water percolates to the surface nearby at the outlets of three mineral springs – the Paint Pots. The iron compounds in the water have also stained rocks and vegetation in the Vermilion River, providing its name.

The Ktunaxa (toon-AWK-ah) First Peoples knew the Ochre Beds as, "The place where the red earth spirit is taken." The Ktunaxa gathered the colourful clay, formed it into cakes and baked it

in fire. They ground the resulting compound into powder and mixed it with animal fat or fish grease to create a body paint, used in rituals.

The Ktunaxa discovered that the "red earth" was a valuable trading commodity. Once or twice a year, they would cross the Rockies to hunt bison and trade with the Stoney and Siksika (Blackfoot) First Peoples at Kootenay Plains on the North Saskatchewan River (see p. 69). One of their trade and travel routes, the Kutenai Trail, went north from the Ochre Beds over Goodsir Pass or Ottertail Pass, then over Amiskwi Pass and Howse Pass. Ochre and bison bones have been found at archaeological sites along this route in Yoho and Banff national parks.

In the early 1900s, the Ochre Beds were developed as a source of pigment for paint. The clay was excavated and hauled overland to Castle Junction, then shipped to Calgary by train. The enterprise soon failed. Equipment remains at the Ochre Beds, rusting beside mounds of clay collected for a harvest that was never completed.

What once was considered sacred still is. Please keep to the beaten path and do not to walk in the ochre deposits or remove any of the material. The clay will stain clothing and shoes. Disturbances take many years to fade away.

THE PAINT POTS

The Paint Pots are cone-shaped, mineral spring outlets, where water emerges at 10.7°C. Either the water does not filter far enough underground to become super-heated, or it becomes mixed with cold water on its return to the surface. The combined volume of flow is 330 litres per minute.

The cones around the Paint Pots are accumulations of iron oxide, precipitated from the spring water as it emerges. As the iron rim grows in height, the pool of the spring becomes deeper. Eventually the depth of water will create a back pressure greater than the pressure of the flowing spring water. The spring will be forced to seek another outlet where the resistance is less, leaving behind an abandoned or "choked" cone. You can see several choked cones near the Paint Pots.

The two largest Paint Pots contain a mixture of spring and surface water, and are greenish in colour. The water of the smallest Paint Pot is clear. Cotton-grass and tall white bog orchids grow in the moist area nearby.

108. Sinclair Canyon

Sinclair Canyon

TRAIL THUMBNAIL

Trailheads

1. At the parking area for the Radium Hot Springs pools, on the north side of the Kootenay Parkway (Highway 93 South), 102 km west of Castle Junction; 2.7 km east of the junction with Highway 95; 1.7 km east of the Kootenay Park gate. The trail departs from the north side of the parking area.
2. At the Juniper trailhead parking area on the north side of the Kootenay Parkway, 1.5 km west of trailhead 1; 200 m east of the Kootenay Park gate.
3. At the Redstreak Campground trailhead at Loop H in Redstreak Campground. See map, p. 132.

Ratings

- Juniper trail only: harder, 3.2 km
- Sinclair Canyon trail only: harder, 1 km
- Redstreak Campground trail only: moderate, 1.9 km
- Full loop: harder, 6.4 km

Special considerations: Use caution when crossing roadways. Stay within fenced viewpoints.

Best lighting: anytime

Nearby trails: 112 113

The Sinclair Canyon loop incorporates three separately named trails as it explores the diverse area around Radium Hot Springs. You may hike each leg as an out-and-back outing, or combine the three trails to make a rewarding loop. In this description we make a counter-clockwise loop, beginning at trailhead 1.

From the trailhead kiosk, walk the paved roadway for 175 m to where the trail branches west (left). The trail climbs moderately onto the north rim of Sinclair Canyon, reaching the high point in about 700 m. It's dry here. The montane grasslands in this area are one of the more endangered landscapes in B.C., and provide critical year-round habitat for bighorn sheep. Please keep at least 30 m away if you see these animals.

Look west to Mt. Farnham (3493 m) – the 27th-highest peak in B.C. – and Farnham Tower (3387 m) in the Purcell Range of the Columbia Mountains. Wetlands to the north in the Columbia Valley are important stopovers and nesting areas for migratory birds. More than 200 species have been recorded.

During the next 1.5 km the trail loses 220 m as it dives into the depths of Sinclair Creek. You pass two

THE COLUMBIA RIVER

The 2044 km long Columbia River is the fourth-largest river system (by drainage area) in North America, and is the continent's largest river (by volume) that empties into the Pacific Ocean. It drains 670,000 km² in B.C. and the north-western U.S.A. – an area roughly the size of France. With such a large watershed, the Columbia has several distinct sources. Its most southerly source is Columbia Lake, 45 km south of Radium. From Columbia Lake, the river flows north for 305 km before making a hairpin turn to flow south past Revelstoke, through the Arrow Lakes, and across the U.S. border. It reaches the Pacific Ocean beyond Portland, Oregon.

The Columbia River Treaty of 1961 changed the river forever. Three dams were constructed on

Canadian reaches of the river. Including those in place before the treaty, 11 dams were constructed in the U.S.A. Eighteen dams were also constructed on primary U.S. tributaries – the Kootenai, the Snake, the Spokane, the Clearwater, and the Flathead. The dams stabilize water flows and minimize the risk of flooding on the lower Columbia River, and allow hydroelectric generation. But these advantages came at a dear price – the dams killed one of the world's great salmon runs and submerged vast areas of pristine forest in B.C.

American Captain, Robert Gray, became the first American to circumnavigate the globe in 1790. He named the Columbia River for his ship, *Columbia Rediviva*, when he anchored at the river's mouth on May 11, 1792.

viewpoints en route. At the bridge over Sinclair Creek, you are surrounded by a damp forest that contains Douglas-fir and western redcedar. Feathermosses carpet the forest floor. After crossing the bridge, head 200 m east (left) on a rough trail to the base of Sinclair Falls. Backtrack to the main trail. Keep south (left) at the next junction and begin a steep climb to the Kootenay Parkway.

When you reach the road, turn east (left) onto the sidewalk. If you are looking for Sinclair Creek, creator of the canyon, you won't see it. When the road was paved here, engineers put the creek into a culvert underground. After 200 m, cross the road with care to the Sinclair Canyon trailhead. (If you want to curtail the outing, don't cross the road but carry on along the sidewalk for 1.2 km back to the parking area.) The trail climbs steeply to Redstreak Campground, offering two viewpoints over Sinclair Canyon and the Columbia Valley. You make portions of this ascent on staircases.

To complete the loop, keep straight ahead at the campground junction to carry on along the Redstreak Campground trail. More staircases lead to the highpoint, from which you descend through a damp forest of Douglas-fir and western redcedar. About 500 m from trail's end, you reach the "Place of Silence Peace Park" in a cedar grove. This location is one of hundreds in Canada intended to help foster a commitment to world peace.

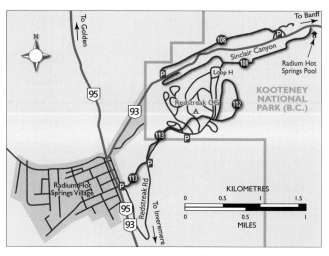

Fenced switchbacks lead down to the hot springs complex. The young trees here grew after a 1967 forest fire. Ascend the stairs that lead to a tunnel under the Kootenay Parkway, to return to the trailhead. Of course, you will probably want to take a dip in the hot pool, first.

BACKYARD BIGHORNS

The area around Radium is home range for about 250 bighorn sheep. Although many people associate bighorns with mountains, the animal's range is governed by viable winter habitat – grasslands that are free of snow – a rare commodity in the Rockies. The sun-exposed terraces low on the east slope of the Columbia Valley are the best bighorn sheep habitat in the Rockies. Unfortunately, this habitat is under siege from development and human interference. Drivers kill 10 percent of the Radium flock each year in vehicle strikes. Poaching is another serious problem.

In response, Parks Canada and the Village of Radium helped to create a public education project: Bighorns in Our Backyard. The project aims to educate residents and visitors about sharing habitat with the sheep, with the aim of minimizing the pressures on their population.

JUNIPER

Juniper is an evergreen, cypress-family shrub, with three species in the Rockies. Prickly juniper (also called common juniper) grows in circular patches. Creeping juniper grows from a trailing vine. Rocky Mountain juniper may reach 5 m in height. Creeping juniper and Rocky Mountain juniper have shreddy bark and scaly leaves, like their enormous cypress cousin, western redcedar. Hybrids with characteristics of all three species occur, so unless the specimen that you are looking at is distinctly tree-like, it can be difficult to tell which species it is.

Prickly juniper is the most common juniper species in the Rockies, and is aptly named. Contact with the spiky needles produces a skin rash in some people. All junipers produce berries that vary in colour from green to gray to purple, depending on age. The berries may stay on the plant for two summers, and provide food for birds ¬– particularly grouse and waxwings – and squirrels. In the past, the berries were used to flavour gin.

109. Fireweed

Trailhead
Parking area on the south side of the Kootenay Parkway (Highway 93 South) at the continental divide, 10.2 km west of Highway 1; 94.5 km east of the junction with Highway 95. See map, p. 127.

Ratings
- lower loop, easy, 0.8 km
- upper loop, moderate, 1.6 km

Best lighting: anytime

Nearby trails: 16 105 106 107 109

The Fireweed loops explore the Vermilion Pass Burn, providing a close-up view of the rebirth of a forest, half a century later. The summer of 1968 was hot and dry across most of western Canada. On the afternoon of July 8, the temperatures in Banff and Kootenay climbed to 30°C, and winds were strong. At 4:30 pm, a bolt of lightning struck the slopes of Mt. Whymper, just west of Vermilion Pass. Fanned by the winds, the lightning spark kindled quickly. In three minutes, the mountainside was in flame.

Although 65 firefighters were on the fireline within six hours, the fire burned for three days. On July 12 the weather began to cool. The following day, rain fell. By July 18 the fire was out after having consumed 26.3 km² of subalpine forest. The Kootenay Fire of 2003 came close to burning this area again.

Forest fires kill diseased tree stands, reduce competition for moisture and sunlight, create stable seed beds by burning off loose soil layers, trigger the mass release of seeds, and return minerals to the soil. They enhance the mosaic of habitats in an ecosystem, and promote biodiversity.

Within four years of the burn, there were nearly twice as many species of vegetation within the burned area, as in the adjacent unburned area. The number of bird and wildlife species using the burned area also increased, relative to before the fire. Avalanche terrain in Vermilion Pass has doubled in area since the burn, due to the removal of large tree stands that formerly prevented the snow from sliding. Three slide paths that post-date the fire now cross the Kootenay Parkway.

110. Numa Falls

Numa Falls

Trailhead
At Numa Creek picnic area on the west side of the Kootenay Parkway (Highway 93 South); 24.5 km west of Highway1; 100.5 km east of the junction with Highway 95. See map, p. 127.

Rating: easy, 125 m

Best lighting: anytime

Special consideration: Fall risk! Stay on the bridge. Keep off the riverbanks.

Nearby trails: 105 106 107 108 109

Follow the Numa Creek trail south from the parking area to the bridge over the Vermilion River. Although Numa Falls is a minor drop, it is nonetheless spectacular. The river constricts to about 4 m wide as it surges through a short, strike canyon eroded into Chancellor Formation slate. Some of the rock is wonderfully sculpted, other exposures appear as if cleaved by an axe. On a hot day, the water is choked with glacial sediment. This canyon separates the eastern main ranges, to the east, from the western main ranges. The Vermilion River empties into the Kootenay River, farther south and west in Kootenay National Park.

Columbia Valley

111. Dog Lake

TRAIL THUMBNAIL

Trailhead
Parking area on the east side of the Kootenay Parkway (Highway 93 South), 78 km west of Castle Junction; 27 km east of the junction with Highway 95; 500 m south of McLeod Meadows Campground.

Rating: moderate, 2.6 km

Best lighting: anytime

The trail to Dog Lake is an ideal excursion for campers staying at McLeod Meadows Campground. From the picnic area, the trail skirts the rear of the campground and crosses the Kootenay River on two bridges. It then climbs away from the river through a Douglas-fir forest. Western wood lilies bloom here in early summer. After you cross a low ridge, the sounds of the highway disappear and the trail descends to the lakeshore. Dog Lake's outlet shows evidence of a beaver dam. By crossing a footbridge, you can follow a rough and wet track to the lake's east shore. Many of the lodgepole pine trees in this part of the Kootenay Valley have been afflicted by mountain pine beetle – hence the discoloured foliage.

By taking sediment cores from the lakebed, and analyzing the pollen types and carbon content, researchers have produced a fire and vegetation history going back 10,000 years. From 9000-8200 years ago, a dry, open forest covered this area area. From 8200-4000 years ago, this area was its driest in the past 10,000 years, and experienced the most intense forest fires. From 4000 years ago to present, this area has been covered in a closed, relatively wet forest. There has been a slight drying trend during the last 2000 years.

112. Redstreak Loop

The Redstreak loop climbs onto a dry slope to provide tremendous views of the Columbia Valley and the Purcell Mountains to the west. Early season hikers will be treated to wonderful wildflower displays in the grassy openings beneath the Douglas-firs.

TRAIL THUMBNAIL

Trailhead
Just north of loop E in Redstreak Campground. See map, p. 132.

Rating: easy, 2.2 km

Best lighting: anytime

Nearby trails: 108 113

113. Valleyview

TRAIL THUMBNAIL

Trailhead
Adjacent to the information centre on Main Street East, at the south end of Radium Hot Springs village. See map, p. 132.

Rating: harder, 1.2 km

Best lighting: anytime

Nearby trails: 108 112

Beginning on a staircase that climbs steeply onto the arid benchlands on the east slope of the Columbia Valley, the Valleyview trail traverses grassy slopes that support an open Douglas-fir forest. Red squirrels, pileated woodpeckers, and ruffed grouse are common forest residents. Look also for bighorn sheep. In late spring and early summer, wildflowers proliferate on these sunny slopes.

The trail ends near loop E in Redstreak Campground, where you may connect with the Redstreak Loop (outing 112). You may also walk north through the campground for 500 m to pick up the Sinclair Canyon trail or Redstreak Campground trail (outing 108). By using these trails and sidewalks, you can make a half-day outing. Pick up a village map at the information centre.

Ptarmigan Cirque trail

Kananaskis Country

Opened by the Alberta government in 1978, Kananaskis Country is a 4200 km² parcel of provincial land that lies south of Highway 1 between Cochrane and Canmore. K-Country incorporates wildland provincial parks, forestry reserves, ecological reserves, mining and petroleum leaseholds, resorts, and recreational developments. It's a limestone paradise; packed with lakes, passes, and meadows. Opportunities for birding are exceptional. You can pick up a free birding checklist at park information centres, or visit the *Walks and Easy Hikes* page at mountainvision.ca for a link.

Kin-e-a-kis was a hard-headed Cree warrior, reportedly struck by an axe but not killed. It may also be that *Kin-e-a-kis* is a Stoney word that means "meeting of the waters". The park information centres are on Highway 40 near Barrier Lake, 6.8 km south of Highway 1; on the Kananaskis Lakes Trail, 3.5 km south of the junction with Highway 40; and on Highway 66, southwest of Bragg Creek.

The epic flood of June 2013 affected many trails in K-Country. Most rebuilds and re-routes are now complete. There may be slight differences between the trail descriptions and what you find on the ground.

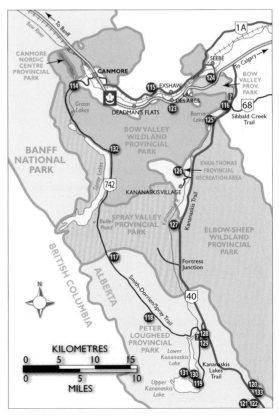

114. Grassi Lakes

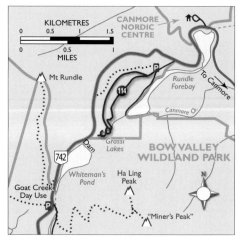

Upper Grassi Lake

TRAIL THUMBNAIL

Trailhead

From the west end of Main Street in downtown Canmore, follow signs for the Canmore Nordic Centre and the Smith Dorrien-Spray Trail (Route 742). Follow this road 4.7 km to the Grassi Lakes Day Use Area, on the left, 1 km past the Canmore Nordic Centre.

Rating: harder, 4.0 km loop, or 4.2 km loop

Special consideration: Caution! Fall risk! Keep within the viewpoint and on the beaten path at the waterfall overlook. Climbing on the cliffs above the lakes is for properly equipped and experienced climbers only.

Best lighting: anytime

Although almost every view seems to contain a penstock or a building or a powerline or a rock climber or a road, the Grassi Lakes trail is a classic, close-to-town outing. From the soils underfoot, to the plants that grow on them, to the hydro-electric development, to the sport climbing – this trail is – whether in-your-face or in a subtle way – all about limestone.

The trail begins at the gate on the power company access road. At the junction in 150 m, keep left. The trail climbs at first gradually, then steeply, through a forest of lodgepole pine and Engelmann spruce with wonderful wildflower displays in the understory: paintbrush, arnica, harebell, yellow columbine, pussytoes, twinflower, butterwort, western wood lily, and yellow lady's slippers. Prickly wild rose, Labrador tea, prickly juniper, and buffaloberry are common shrubs. Look and listen for yellow-rumped warblers. After passing through a few wet areas, at about km 1 the trail reaches a viewpoint that looks out onto the limestone rampart of Ha Ling Peak (2408 m), the waterfall on the outflow stream beneath the Grassi Lakes, and the peaks of the Fairholme Range across the Bow Valley. Don't wander off the cliff edge.

A series of rock steps and railings get you up the steepest part of the hike on the headwall below the lakes. This rock staircase was the handiwork of Italian immigrant, Lorenzo (Lawrence) Grassi. Arriving in Canada in 1912 at age 22, Grassi worked on a railway section gang near Lake Superior before transferring to Hector siding in the Rockies. By 1916, he was working in the Canmore Mines, an occupation he continued for 29 years.

While fellow miners sat idle during a strike in the 1920s, Grassi went to work, roughing out the trail to the Grassi Lakes, building a log swimming pool there, and enlarging caves nearby to use as shelters. At other times he would ramble off to climb mountains alone. As his knowledge of the mountains became recognized, climbers sought Grassi to guide them. Wearing work boots and suspenders, Grassi led hundreds of climbs. He is said to have climbed Mount Louis (in Banff) 32 times, and to have made the first solo ascent of Mt. Assiniboine, 8th-highest peak in the Rockies, in 1925. In 1936, Grassi participated in the first ascent of Mount Waddington – a formidable peak in B.C.'s Coast Mountains.

Grassi's physical strength is the stuff of legend – he carried a cast iron cook stove, 12 km, from the railway line to the Elizabeth Parker Hut in Yoho – but enduring proof lies in the trails that he built. Look at the rock steps that he placed without help on this trail – still in use 90 years later. Similar rock staircases and walkways exist near Skoki Lodge in Banff, and near Twin Falls and Lake O'Hara in Yoho, where Grassi served as an assistant park warden.

In a tribute to Grassi, delivered in 1938 at the House of Commons, M.P., James Shaver Woodsworth, said: "The world needs Grassis... men who will seek new paths; make the rough places smooth; bridge the chasms that now prevent human progress; point the way to higher levels and loftier achievements." Based on Woodsworth's recommendation, the Twin Lakes, as they had been known, were renamed Grassi Lakes. Grassi died at Canmore in 1980 at age 90. You may see a plaque that commemorates him, near the lower lake.

The grade relents where you regain the power company access road. Follow signs to reach the south shore of the lower lake. You can make a figure-eight circuit of the two lakes which, despite all the nearby manipulation of water for hydro-electric development, are fed by spring water and drain naturally. The lakes have pleasing blue-green hues.

After you spend time at the lakes, you have two options for return. Either retrace your route of ascent, or use the power company access road, by turning north (left) from the east end of the lower lake. The trail sign there (2011) describes the choices respectively: "More Difficult" and "Easy". The road makes a steady descent. About halfway down, look for the ruin of a cabin on the right. Many of the pine trees in this forest have twisted trunks – pines on neighbouring Ha Ling Peak are similarly afflicted.

ROCK ART

The Grassi Lakes are one of a few sites in the Rockies where ancient rock art has been discovered. Continue west past the upper lake, climbing steeply into a canyon. Soon after the trail levels, look on your right for a boulder that contains the pictographs. The paintings show two figures, each holding a hoop in their right hands, and other images which have been described as depicting a caribou and bighorn sheep. Various sources attribute these rock paintings to Stoney or Ktunaxa (toon-AWK-ah) (Kutenai) First Peoples. How old are the images? There is no agreement: ages of 200 years, 1000 years, and 8000-10,000 years have been suggested. Whoever painted the images probably used ochre and their fingers, and must have stood on a rock or a ladder of some sort. Please do not touch the paintings. This sidetrip will add about 400 m to the outing.

REEF ON THIS

The cliffs above the Grassi Lakes contain dolomite of the Cairn Formation. This late-Devonian rock (373 million to 370 million years old) preserves a classic prehistoric reef that formed in shallow water, in this case built from the remains of stromatoporoids - (strome-at-oh-PORE-oids) - crusty, spongy, blobby, and stringy creatures - the spaghetti and meatballs of the Rockies' fossil buffet. The Devonian reefs contain the oil-rich, gas-rich beds sought by petroleum companies. When broken, the rock actually smells like oil. *The Amphipora* fossils of the Cairn formation appear rice-like against the dark rock. When other stromatoporoid species weathered out of the rock, they left behind hollows known to geologists as vugular porosities, to rockhounds as vugs, and to rock climbers as jugs. These abound on the cliffs above the Grassi Lakes, giving the rock a rough texture much appreciated by the climbing crowd. Imagine: climbing on the outlines of 370-million-year old, sea creatures. Could anything be more bizarre?

115. Grotto Canyon

Grotto Canyon

Trailhead
At Grotto Pond Day Use Area on Highway 1A; 12 km east of Canmore; 16 km west of the junction with Highway 1X.

Rating: harder, 2.5 km

Special consideration: Flash flood warning! Avoid this hike during or after heavy rains.

Best lighting: anytime

Nearby trail: 124

This outing skirts the Baymag magnesite processing plant and then follows the floor of Grotto Canyon, providing – when you are out of earshot of the industry – the most Utah-like hiking experience on a developed trail in the Rockies. Wear sturdy footwear.

The first 600 m of trail is along an old roadbed carpeted with the minuscule evergreen wildflower, yellow mountain avens. Its nodding blooms are replaced in July by twisted seedpods that resemble those of dandelion. The rubble along the roadbed is material eroded from upstream in the canyon and deposited here during flash-floods, creating a landform called an alluvial fan. You can best appreciate the shape and height of the fan in the view west from the canyon mouth. The view also takes in the Bow Valley, Gap Lake, Mt. Lougheed (3107 m), and Pigeon Mountain.

The trail drops into the canyon and swings north (right). This is the end of a well-defined trail. In the canyon you will be walking on water-worn rock slabs, rubble, and boulders. Keep to the canyon floor. For your safety, if the creek is running, especially if it has been raining, you should turn back here.

Grotto Canyon is dry most of the time. How did the canyon become so deep with so little water typically flowing through it? A glacial meltwater stream probably sculpted the original canyon just after the Late Wisconsin Glaciation, 12,000 years ago. Evidence shows that the climate in this part of the world was relatively warm from 8000 to 5000 years ago. The remnant ice age glaciers melted rapidly, cleaving the remaining depth of this canyon in a few thousand years. Today, the major forces at work are frost shattering of the cliffs, and flash-floods of debris after heavy rains.

About 1 km into the canyon, you reach "the forks". The right-hand branch climbs to a small waterfall. The left-hand branch winds toward a more open valley, where limber pines and Douglas-firs grow. You may see the large hoodoo formation that contains a remarkable cave. This marks your turnaround point. Grotto means "cave", but the canyon does not take its name from this feature. Eugene Bourgeau of the Palliser Expedition named the mountain west of the canyon in 1858, after he explored a massive cave (not since rediscovered) in its slopes. Grotto Canyon is popular with sport climbers. In winter, waterfall ice climbers practice their craft on frozen seeps along the canyon walls.

Grotto Creek alluvial fan

116. Prairie View

Barrier Lake from Prairie View

THINK OUTSIDE THE CANYON

Given their long association with the Rockies, First Peoples left behind relatively few examples of rock art. Pictographs, most of unknown origin, have so far been found at only a handful of locations: Grotto Canyon and Grassi Lakes (see p. 136) in the Bow Valley, Zephyr Creek in the Highwood Pass area, Sinclair Canyon in Kootenay, Devona Cave in Jasper, Cataract Creek, and one site in Banff. As with many other rock paintings, those in the Rockies depict human and animal figures – often in a stylized form. Ochre was the preferred medium.

The pictographs at Grotto Canyon, first noticed in the 1960s, took on a greater significance in 1992 when a visiting archaeologist realized that one of the images depicts the Hopi character, Kokopelli; commonly known as "the Flute Player". This particular depiction is more than 1000 km north of any other yet found. Hopi legend tells of a migration, a time when these First Peoples travelled the four directions in search of what would become their home. In the north, the Hopi ventured to the land of ice and rock. After they tried unsuccessfully to melt the ice, their guardian spirits directed them to travel south, where they found their home in what is now Arizona. The legend states that the Hopi left images of "the Flute Player" in the land of ice and rock. The Grotto Canyon pictographs would seem to authenticate the legend. Similar Hopi images from Arizona have been dated to between 200 and 600 A.D.

If you find the pictographs, please do not touch them.

TRAIL THUMBNAIL

Trailhead
Follow Highway 40 (Kananaskis Trail), 8.6 km south from Highway 1 to the Barrier Dam Day Use Area. Turn west (right) and follow the sideroad 300 m to the parking area. See map p. 140.

Rating: harder, 4.6 km

Best lighting: anytime

Nearby trail: 🌀

It's been a sentinel position for centuries. The Stoneys called it *Tokyapebi ipa*: "lookout point for the Blackfeet". From the upper slopes and summit of this front range outlier, in the clearer air of pre-industrial times, Stoneys would keep watch over the prairies for the approach of their enemies. Since 1960, from two locations on the modest mountain reached on this hike, employees of the Alberta government have looked more intently into the mountains than away from them – watching for lightning strikes and scanning for the telltale smokes of forest fires.

From the parking area, keep left and head west to pick up the gravel road that crosses the Barrier Dam. If it's a windy day, you may have to hang on to more than your hat as you cross. Not a lake but a reservoir, Barrier Lake came into being in 1947 following construction of this dam. Prisoners of war had cleared the reservoir site in 1945. The power generated by the 13MW installation is added to the Alberta grid during peak periods. The reservoir has an area of 3.08 km^2.

Across the dam, either follow the road or a trail just to its right; each climbs and veers north (right) across a small meadow. There are wonderful displays of paintbrush here. Keep straight ahead (north) at the first junction at km 1.1. You enter an ancient aspen forest with a few scattered lodgepole pines and white spruce, and many wildflowers in the understory, including clematis and calypso orchids. After 500 m, you reach the east Stoney Trail junction. Jog right northeast (right) a short distance and then north (left) into forest, still on a road-width trail. You will see where shortcut trails circumvent some of the 11 switchbacks on the ensuing climb. You won't save much distance or anytime by taking them, and the walking is easier on the main trail.

About 3.6 km from the trailhead, you gain the

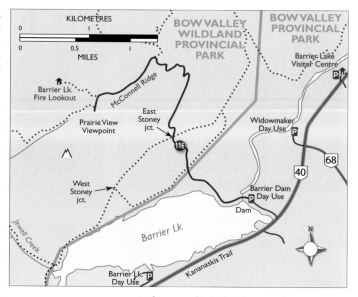

northeast end of McConnell Ridge, which you ascend, heading southwest. After about 600 m the trail levels at the former site of Pigeon Mountain fire lookout. The building is now gone, but the vista remains – a wonderful panorama over Barrier Lake, with Mt. Baldy (2192 m) to the south. A Stoney sacred site is nearby. The trail turns northwest (right) and climbs steeply toward Yates Mountain. No, a few prairie wildflower

species have not climbed with you to this point – you are looking at subalpine variations of two common grassland species: showy yellow locoweed and elliptical-leaved penstemon – both are abundant here. The climb ends at a junction atop a cliff. Although this vantage point is called Prairie View, Barrier Lake is the centrepiece. Walk south a short distance for the best vista. When you have had your fill, retrace the route to the trailhead.

IT'S ALL McCONNELL'S FAULT

In this part of the Rockies, the McConnell Thrust is responsible for the mountain front – the dramatic wall of front range peaks – where ancient limestone has been thrust up and over not-quite-so ancient sandstones and shales of the foothills. This thrust fault runs for almost 400 km, from the Highwood River to near the Athabasca River. Just as you can't miss the effect of the McConnell Thrust, you also can't miss the fault itself. On this hike, you stand atop the leading

edge of the thrust, with the foothills and prairies falling away to the northeast, and the front ranges stacking up to the southwest.

If you bashed your way to the base of McConnell Ridge from the northeast, you could literally put a fingertip on the trace line of the fault – the contact surface between rock formations that are 445 million years difference in age. Your feet would be in the foothills geological province, your head and shoulders in the front ranges. The McConnell Thrust commemorates Richard George McConnell, surveyor and geologist of the Canadian wilds between 1880 and 1914, and later Canada's Deputy Minster of Mines. He travelled in this area with George Dawson between 1883-86, and made the first description of the fault that was named for him more than 60 years later.

117. Chester Lake

Chester Lake

TRAIL THUMBNAIL

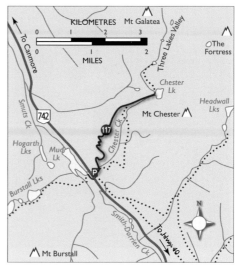

Trailhead
From the west end of Main Street in downtown Canmore, follow signs for the Nordic Centre and the Smith Dorrien-Spray Trail (Route 742). Follow this road 44 km south to the Chester Day Use area turn-off. Turn east (left). The trailhead is at the northeast corner of the parking area.

Rating: moderate, 4.0 km

Special consideration: Seasonal closure, May 1-June 29. You share the first 1.6 km with cyclists.

Best lighting: afternoon

Short and sweet – and perhaps, crowded – sums up the outing to Chester Lake. The trail to this beautiful tarn is justifiably popular. The meadows near the lake are flush with wildflowers, and the afternoon light seems to animate the slabby cliffs of Mt. Chester. Don't let the crowdedness of this hike fool you; grizzly bears like these meadows, too.

The trail begins as a gravelled path through a spruce-fir forest. Look and listen for gray jays and hermit thrushes. The path soon reverts to an old logging road. You cross Chester Creek after about 150 m. By keeping left at all the upcoming forks and junctions, you won't end up on a winter ski trail or on an abandoned skidder track. Labrador tea, fireweed, paintbrush, wild strawberry, buffaloberry, and arnica grow in the forest understory. The road makes a series of wide switchbacks with the grade at times moderately steep. Views back include the environs of Burstall Pass, Mt. Smith Dorrien (3151 m), and up French Creek to Mt. Robertson (3177 m) and Mt. Sir Douglas (3411 m).

Beyond the bike lock-up, the trail narrows and becomes rooted. It levels and then descends to a frost

meadow whose earth hummocks are topped with yellow mountain heather. The east edge of this clearing features a fantastic larch tree snag – chewed on by porcupines, and riddled with woodpecker holes. After a short forested section, you emerge into a second meadow; this one larger, with fine views ahead to Mt. Chester (3054 m). HMS *Chester* was a British battle cruiser, severely damaged in the Battle of Jutland in 1916 but back at sea a few months later.

Where the trail re-enters the forest, you might notice that the character of the tread is different. The trail here has been capped with gravel, delivered in barrel buckets slung under a helicopter, and placed over soil blanket. The blanket prevented the gravel from quickly being punched down into the muck. It's an expensive fix for a muddy trail, but the only worthwhile method on a route this popular. Further on you'll see where trees have been transplanted into trail braids to encourage you to keep on track.

The last meadow bisected by the trail is the largest of the three. Although the lake is close by, the wildflower displays here may slow your pace. Western anemone, yellow paintbrush, Sitka valerian, fleabanes, and – in early summer – superb displays of glacier lilies, colour the meadow. Just before the lake, you pass an outhouse that appears to be on stilts. The explanations: This is a popular skiing destination; if you elevate the outhouse, you don't have to shovel the door as much. Also, if you keep the waste barrel (which is flown out when full) above the ground, you don't have to dig a hole for it.

The trail forks at the lakeshore. The right-hand path crosses the outlet to a grove of spruce, larch, and subalpine fir – a good place to take in the view. Across the lake, a seasonal stream tumbles from a slot canyon. The songbirds I have seen and heard here did not surprise me – hermit thrush, pine siskin, Tennessee warbler, boreal chickadee, yellow-rumped

141

Glacier lily

118. Black Prince Cirque

Warspite Lake

warbler, robin, white-winged crossbill, and dipper – but the behaviour of two of the species amazed me. While I waited for the light, I watched two pairs of dippers come and go. They fed at the outlet of the lake, diving underwater and hauling out onto rocks. Two robins joined them, hopped into the stream and foraged underwater. They, too, hauled out on rocks, mid-stream. The robins did everything to emulate the dippers but sing their songs and bob their tails. I have also seen yellow-rumped warblers here, foraging on foot for bugs at creekside.

TRAIL THUMBNAIL

Trailhead

1. Follow Highway 40 (Kananaskis Trail), 49.5 km south from Highway 1 to the Kananaskis Lakes Trail junction. Turn west (right). Follow this road 2.2 km to the Spray Lakes Trail junction (Route 742). Turn north (right) and follow this road 8.3 km to the Black Prince Day Use. Turn left.
2. From the west end of Main Street in downtown Canmore, follow signs for the Nordic Centre and the Smith Dorrien-Spray Lakes Trail (Route 742). Follow this road 56.2 km south to the Black Prince Day Use Area turnoff. Turn right. See map, p. 144.

Rating: moderate, 4.5 km loop

Special consideration: To read or download the K-Country brochure for this hike, visit the *Walks and Easy Hikes* page at mountainvision.ca and follow the links.

Best lighting: morning

DIP, DIP, DIPPER

The dipper is the only aquatic songbird in North America, and is a marvel of adaptation. It is a year-round resident of the mountains, protected from the chill of glacial water and winter by thick, soot-coloured down that is impregnated with oil. The dipper feeds on insects, snails, and fish fry in turbulent streams. It has flaps that cover its nostrils during dives – allowing it to remain submerged for more than a minute – and an extra set of transparent eyelids that allow it to see underwater. Its call is a metallic, staccato trill, made on the wing. Dippers also have a fine repertoire of songs – warbler-like, buzzy, and whistling. K-Country is dipper country. The Christmas bird counts here consistently yield North American highs for the species.

From the parking area the trail descends to Smith-Dorrien Creek. Look for yarrow and star-flowered Solomon's seal. Horace Smith-Dorrien was a British general in World War I. Why was his name applied here? The Alberta-British Columbia Boundary Commission of 1913-25 faced an enormous job. While

Bracted honeysuckle

Limestone boulder garden

delineating the boundary between the two provinces, the surveyors trooped up and down the slopes of hundreds of mountains, packing their survey gear and cameras. The enterprise seemed not to exhaust them physically, but when it came to naming features – many of which they were the first ones to closely inspect – their imaginations kept to a single theme.

Rather than appending names that described an aspect of the landscape, in some locations the surveyors – led by A.O. Wheeler – named groups of mountains after Italian, French, and British politicians, military commanders, and warships – particularly those vessels involved in the 1916 Battle of Jutland. Of the 44 named mountains in Peter Lougheed Provincial Park, Wheeler named 38. So prominent was his naval vessel motif in this area, locals formerly knew the peaks as the "Battleship Mountains".

Across the creek, the trail turns downstream for a short distance before looping back to the west. For the next 800 m, you climb through an upper subalpine forest along an old logging road, with fine views back across the valley to Kent Ridge. HMS *Kent* was a British naval destroyer…. You can probably guess the rest. I have seen moose droppings on the trail, here, and many of the trailside willows have been browsed. This slope was logged in 1972.

At the top of the climb, the trail descends a short distance to the loop split. Keep straight ahead and

A.O. Wheeler

soon cross Warspite Creek on a bridge. The trail turns sharply southeast (left) to approach Warspite Lake, passing through several rock gardens. These shattered limestone boulders are debris from a rockslide off the north ridge of Mt. Warspite. The lake now initially drains underground beneath the boulders.

The limestone rock jumble is a wonderful flower garden. You may see the blooms of dwarf dogwood, windflower, yellow columbine, moss campion, paintbrush, arnica, valerian, rock jasmine, evergreen violet, glacier lily, and calypso orchid. Flowering shrubs include bearberry, grouseberry, crowberry, sticky currant, red elderberry, buffaloberry, and bracted honeysuckle. The yellow blooms of this last plant yield twin, purple-black berries; attractive to look at but repulsive to taste. Pikas and least chipmunks frequent the boulders.

Warspite Lake sits in the opening of a deep cirque backed by Mt. Black Prince (2932 m). This is a great place to while away some time. The lake is known to "green up" each summer as algae proliferate. Birders can look and listen for yellow-rumped warblers, common yellowthroats, killdeers, and northern waterthrush. The waterfall to the southwest, Warspite Cascades, drains the Black Prince Lakes, concealed in a pocket cirque high above. Scan the avalanche slopes and cliffs for grizzly bears and mountain goats.

THE BLACK PRINCE

In distant history, the "Black Prince" was Edward, Prince of Wales, born in 1330. He died in 1376, one year before his father, King Edward III, and thus became the first Prince of Wales not to accede to the throne. Edward was reportedly named the "Black Prince" for two reasons: he is said to have worn black armour, and he was brutal in his military campaigns. However, he was not known as the Black Prince while he was alive.

In more recent history, there have been five ships named *Black Prince* in the British Navy. The features named in Kananaskis Country commemorate HMS *Black Prince*, an armoured cruiser, disabled and sunk in the Battle of Jutland, May 31, 1916, with the loss of all 857 hands. The features named Warspite commemorate the battleship, HMS *Warspite*, one of the few British vessels to survive the Battle of Jutland and continue on to serve during World War II.

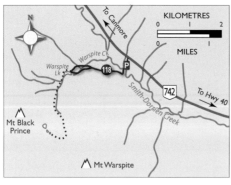

Rawson Lake

To begin the return, walk south (left) a short distance along the lakeshore. The trail soon cuts away to the east, traversing more rock gardens. Almost every tree that grows on and around these rocks is an Engelmann spruce. A possible explanation? The roots of spruce trees do not tap downward as much as those of pine and fir. There's not much soil here, so deeper-rooted tree species can't make a go of it. This rockslide is evidently quite ancient, as the boulders now resemble heaps, shattered by thousands of years of frost and weathering. Look for solution grooves called *rillenkarren* on some of the rocks. Limestone dissolves in water. The trickles from snowmelt, flowing in the same place year after year, have eroded these grooves. About 1 km after you leave the lake, you rejoin the outbound trail. Turn southeast (right) to return to the trailhead.

119. Rawson Lake

TRAIL THUMBNAIL

Trailhead

From Highway 1, follow Kananaskis Trail (Highway 40), 49.5 km south to the Kananaskis Lakes Trail junction. Turn south (right) and follow the Kananaskis Lakes Trail, 12.5 km to the Upper Kananaskis Lake Day Use Area. The trailhead is at the south end of the most southerly parking area.

Rating: moderate, 3.9 km

Best lighting: anytime

Nearby trails: 128 129 130 131

Two lakes bookend this outing; one a massive reservoir, scarred by human manipulation; the other a jade gem nestled in a deep limestone pocket. Between them you climb through a tract of forest that defines the subalpine life zone. You probably won't be hiking alone. I once counted more than a hundred people bound uphill as I was coming down. Most had dogs with them.

The trail starts as a broad path, heading slightly downhill. You soon enter an ancient forest of Engelmann spruce and subalpine fir. I have seen a snowshoe hare and least chipmunks here. Look and listen for bird species that love the deep woods: dark-eyed junco, hermit thrush, varied thrush, Swainson's thrush, ruby-crowned kinglet, golden-crowned kinglet, gray jay, and the ubiquitous robin. The trail parallels the lakeshore, offering fine views of Mt. Indefatigable (2670 m) to the north. At km 1.1 you cross Sarrail Creek just below Sarrail Creek Falls. The 10 m drop of the cataract creates quite a racket and a fine mist that coats everything. Not such a bad thing on a hot day.

Just beyond the falls, turn south (left) from the lakeshore to begin the climb to Rawson Lake. For the next kilometre you switchback through dense subalpine forest on a north-facing slope. Savour the dank smell of decay punctuated by the sweet aroma of resin from the subalpine fir trees. Woodpeckers love this forest. Look for Engelmann spruce trees whose bark is reddish-purple, where woodpeckers have stripped away the brown outer scales in quest of grubs.

The trail levels for the last 400 m to the lake and draws alongside the outlet stream. Split log boardwalks span wet areas. Snow sometimes lingers here until mid-July – which makes this a great place for white globeflower, alpine buttercup, and evergreen violet – wildflower species that thrive in the chill of receding snowbanks. Step carefully. Look for trout in the outlet stream.

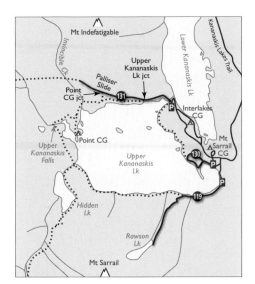

Engelmann spruce

Subalpine fir

The maintained trail continues a short distance along the lake's east shore. Mt. Sarrail (3174 m) rises more than 1000 m above, creating a tremendous backdrop. General Sarrail was a commander of the French Third Army in World War I. Donald Rawson was a pioneering limnologist who studied many lakes in western and northern Canada in the mid-1900s, including the Kananaskis Lakes.

WILD MEETS TAME

It's a poignant image, the unfettered outflow of Sarrail Creek running across the rubble- and stump-strewn shoreline of Upper Kananaskis Lake. Before people intervened, the two Kananaskis Lakes were the epitome of a watery wilderness. The Upper Lake emptied into the Lower Lake along a 1 km stretch of river that included twin waterfalls. In 1858 John Palliser rhapsodized over this scene on "the wild and beautiful Kananaskis River". The Lower Lake emptied through another cascade into the Kananaskis River.

The lakes are now reservoirs, their levels controlled from Calgary; the waterfalls are submerged; the shorelines are barren. Six of the seven former islands in the Upper Lake are now submerged – only the tip of Hawke Island pokes above high water. The natural regimes of the lakes have also been grossly altered by fish-stocking. It is thought that the Upper Lake was originally fish-less. Five species now inhabit the lake; seven species inhabit the Lower Lake. Many specimens are hybrids of introduced species. The rationale for the continued stocking of the reservoir system is that the fluctuating water levels make difficult the establishment of the food web needed to support fish populations. Translation: Fish don't survive so more have to be added each year to support any kind of recreational fishery.

120. Elbow Lake

TRAIL THUMBNAIL

Trailhead
From Highway 1, follow Kananaskis Trail (Highway 40), 61.7 km south to Elbow Pass Day Use Area; 12.2 km south of the Kananaskis Lakes Trail junction. This section of Highway 40 is closed between December 1 and June 15. See map, p. 146.

Rating: moderate, 4.0 km loop

Special considerations: You share the trail with cyclists and equestrians. If you would like to camp at Elbow Lake, you will need a permit from the Peter Lougheed Provincial Park information centre.

Best lighting: anytime

Nearby trails: 121 122 133

This outing makes a quick ascent into the cleft between Elpoca Mountain and Mt. Rae to reach Elbow Pass and its namesake lake. It's a wonderful place but don't come seeking solitude – the routes of hikers, backpackers, campers, anglers, equestrians, and cyclists all converge here.

145

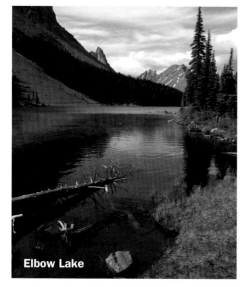

Elbow Lake

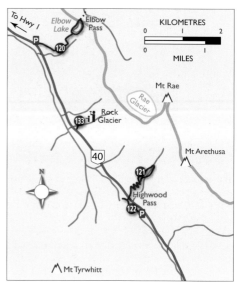

The road-width trail climbs steeply around the base of Mt. Elpoca, bisecting a few rockslides. Look and listen for hoary marmots and pikas. The blooms of wildflowers that prefer dry, rocky settings colour the slopes. Among these are numerous common dandelions, whose seeds have been transported here in horse dung. You may also see sky pilot and scorpionweed.

The trail hooks northeast and crosses an avalanche slope from Mt. Rae. In most years, you will find snow here well into July. Notice how the smaller

trees have been bent over as a result of being buried in avalanche deposit. The trail switchbacks north and then east, crossing the true height of Elbow Pass (2088 m) before descending to the west shore of Elbow Lake and a junction. Take the trail to the east (right), toward the campground to make a counterclockwise circuit of the lake.

The main trail through the campground is covered in crushed rock, but you may still end up taking a wrong turn that leads to the biffy. Keep close to the lakeshore and you should stay on route. Beyond the

A RAE OF LIGHT

It is often the case in K-Country that the name doesn't fit the peak (battleships, battleships, battleships), but Mt. Rae (3225 m) is an exception. Located on the east side of Highwood Pass, Mt. Rae ranks 71st in height among named peaks in Alberta, and, on a clear day, is the highest peak visible from Calgary. The mountain commemorates John Rae, a Scottish explorer of the mid-19th century. Appointed as the Hudson Bay Company doctor at Moose Factory in 1836, Rae became known for his phenomenal abilities to travel in winter. The Inuit called him *Aglooka* – "He who takes long strides." Shunning the cumbersome approach typical of European explorers of the day (wool trench coat, frozen boots, and canned food), he learned to live off the land and to travel as First Peoples did. On foot, he covered 36,000 km during his career. In the winter of 1844-45, Rae snow-shoed from Hudson Bay to southern Ontario and back in two months – a distance of 1930 km.

Rae made the first of his four Arctic expeditions in 1846, and later took part in searches for the Third (lost) Franklin Expedition. It was Rae who brought back to England the unwelcome (but true) news that

at least some of Franklin's men had resorted to cannibalism. For this, he was vilified. James Hector of the Palliser Expedition, however, thought highly of Rae, and named the peak for him. Rae Glacier, in the westerly of the two cirques on the peak's north slope, is, until it soon disappears, the easternmost glacier in Alberta. First studied in 1881, the tiny glacier had lost 76 percent of its mass by 1991, when it measured 0.22 km².

White mountain avens

121. Ptarmigan Cirque

Ptarmigan Cirque

campground, where you drop into willows, don't take the right-hand trail that appears to be better travelled. It leads to Rae Glacier. Instead, veer northeast (left) to keep close to the lakeshore, where you will enjoy fine views of Elbow Lake and its backdrop peaks – Elpoca Mountain (3029 m) and Tombstone Mountain South (3000 m). "Elpoca" refers to the mountain's position between the Elbow River and Pocaterra Creek. George Pocaterra homesteaded along the Highwood River, just south of here, in the early 1900s.

After a short section through willows you soon round the north end of Elbow Lake, whose outlet you cross on a log bridge. This trickle is often cited as the source of the Elbow River. It's certainly one of the sources; but the stream that comes from the two cirques on Mt. Rae (3225 m), to the south, is probably the most distant source from the river's mouth. Look south for fine views of that setting. The Elbow River was named for a prominent bend in its course, about 8 km south of Calgary. The name soon migrated upstream to the various features nearby.

Complete the circuit of Elbow Lake by turning south (left) to follow the lake's west shore. The trail crosses a scree slope whose base is literally carpeted with white mountain avens. Just before you rejoin the outbound trail, you enter an ancient pocket of spruce-fir forest. I call this the "Thrush Grove" – I have twice heard all three Rockies' thrush species here: Swainson's thrush, hermit thrush, and varied thrush. You may also hear white-crowned sparrows and yellow-rumped warblers. From the junction on the lake's south shore, retrace the first part of the outing to the trailhead.

Yellow-rumped warbler

TRAIL THUMBNAIL

Trailhead
From Highway 1, follow Kananaskis Trail (Highway 40), 66.9 km south to Highwood Pass (17.4 km south of the Kananaskis Lakes Trail junction). The parking area is just across the pass on the west side of the road. This section of Highway 40 is closed between December 1 and June 15.

Rating: harder, 4.4 km loop

Special consideration: Use caution crossing Highway 40. Be bear aware on this outing. To read or download the K-Country brochure for this hike, visit the *Walks and Easy Hikes* page at mountainvision.ca, and follow the links.

Best lighting: afternoon

Nearby trails: 120 122 133

The valley that leads to Ptarmigan Cirque is a miniature version of hundreds of other recently deglaciated valleys in the Rockies. Plants and animals cling tenaciously to life; the hallmark of ice is everywhere. The bedrock reveals the fossilized remains of lifeforms that lived in ancient seas. Although the trail is popular – often crowded – grizzly bears frequent the area. The trail may be closed from time to time to prevent encounters. If it is closed, please hike elsewhere.

Walk north from the parking area on a wide, gravelled path through the Highwood Meadows. Look for bighorn sheep nearby. You reach the Ptarmigan Cirque junction in 400 m. Turn northeast (right), and ascend to the west shoulder of Highway

Tree islands

40. Look and listen for traffic (and sheep!); cross the road when it is safe to do so, and pick up the trail on the other side.

The climb begins through an upper subalpine, spruce-fir forest. Yellow hedysarum, blue penstemon, wild strawberry, grouseberry, daisy fleabane, western anemone, paintbrush, common fireweed, alpine springbeauty, bracted lousewort, yellow mountain heather, arnica, glacier lily, low larkspur, and stickseed all grow at trailside. The trail switchbacks steeply in a pocket of subalpine fir as it heads southeast toward the drainage from the cirque. You have fine views down to Highwood Pass. Listen for hermit thrushes.

ROCK SANDWICH

The southwest ridge of Mt. Arethusa (2912 m) is a classic signature of front range geology. The Rundle Group of formations that comprises the mountain was tipped toward the vertical during mountain-building, 85 million-years-ago, when great sheets of rock were being driven north-east-ward. The rock fractured along thrust faults, the sheet behind each fracture being driven northeast, up and over rocks ahead, creating what are now called dip-slope mountains. Alternating resistant (limestone and dolomite) and recessive (shale) layers create what appears to be a multi-layered sandwich, dropped on end. The mountain was not named for the nymph of Greek mythology, but for an ill-fated British battle cruiser, sunk in the 1916 Battle of Jutland, just two days after the craft was put to sea.

The trail soon angles back to the northwest. The first larches appear at trailside just before the loop trail junction. Trail signs encourage you to keep straight ahead so that your hike will match the numbered interpretive stops, but feel free to be unfettered in your choice of route. Keeping straight ahead, the trail soon breaks through treeline into a heath meadow. Look for Columbian ground squirrels. Listen for white-crowned sparrows. You've done most of the climbing now; the trail ahead sidehills and undulates on its approach to the limestone benches at the apex of the loop. Complex lichen colonies cover the screes.

As at other locations in the Rockies, snowcover, wind, and temperature sculpt the vegetation in this valley, dictating what can grow, and where. Gullies offer shelter from the drying effects of wind, promoting growth; depressions collect cold air, stunting growth. Taller, supple plants – able to withstand moving snow – grow on avalanche paths, offering browse for large mammals. Mat-like plants hug the ground in the open, a survival strategy to thwart the full blast of the wind. Many of the wildflowers have fuzzy stems and leaves – natural insulation to buffet the cold and to reduce moisture loss. Some of the trees flag the wind, others are wind-trained – a few branches curl around the trunk from the windward side to the leeward side. Except for the wet meadow in the base of the valley, much of the landscape is virtually desert. Water is frozen for much of the year; the poor, rocky soils drain rapidly. Wind and harsh sunlight quickly evaporate much of what water is available. One area of permafrost – permanently frozen soil – has been found in these meadows.

The outbound leg of the loop ends where the trail swings southeast (right) at a low headwall. The rock here is limestone of the fossil-rich Mt. Head Formation. If you examine the boulders nearby, you may see bumps – the fossilized remains of horn corals that date to 350 million-years-ago. Looking downvalley, you can see Mt. Tyrwhitt (2876 m) on the west side of Highwood Pass. Reginald Tyrwhitt was a British naval commander in World War I.

When the valley is clear of snow, you can follow a rough track northeast from the apex of the loop for 700 m to a second headwall at the mouth of the cirque. But please keep to the trail. The route ascends beside a stream that bisects a meadow. The blooms of moss campion, sawwort, and alpine forget-me-not brighten the rocks. True to the name of the trail, I have seen a ptarmigan hen with four chicks here. Seeps on the second headwall feature travertine deposits. Travertine is thin limestone, deposited by algae as a byproduct of photosynthesis. From the top of the headwall, the view north reveals the upper part of the cirque on the slopes of Mt. Rae (3225 m) (see p. 146). The valley contains a rock glacier. Travel beyond this point is on a sketchy trail exposed to rockfall – not recommended.

122. Highwood Meadows

Trailhead

As for Ptarmigan Cirque (outing 121). See map, p. 146.

Rating: easy, 500 m

Best lighting: anytime

Nearby trails: 120 121 133

Highwood Pass (2206 m) is the highest pass crossed by a paved road in Canada. Walk north from the parking area on a wide, gravelled path through the Highwood Meadows. Look for bighorn sheep nearby. The chemistry of bedrock influences the plants that grow on the resulting soils. In many places in the Rockies, the bedrock is mostly limestone, which creates alkaline, calcium-rich soils that limit the growth of many plants. The bedrock in Highwood Pass is shale, coal, and sandstone, which foster a relative abundance of plant species. Permafrost in the meadows churns the soil and creates sinkholes. When, over a period of centuries, a series of sinkholes connects, a new stream is created.

The Canadian Rockies contain relatively few rock arches – natural features eroded from ridge crests. So it is unusual that from Highwood Pass you can, weather and lighting permitting, see two arches. To the southeast, look for the handle-shaped arch on Storm Mountain (3095 m), south of Highwood Pass. To the southwest, look for a much more delicate arch on the east ridge of Mount Tyrwhitt (2876 m).

One of the creatures that lives in the Highwood Meadows is the rock crawler, a slender, wingless insect. The name "ice crawler" might be more appropriate, for these bugs of the genus *Grylloblatta* live in caves, under rocks, or on snow and ice, thriving at temperatures that cause most lifeforms to shut down. Only 10 species are known. They are thought to be related to cockroaches, mantids, and locusts. Rock crawlers eat other insects that become torpid on the snow. Because of where and how they live, rock crawlers probably survived glaciations that killed-off many contemporaries. So cold-adapted is this insect, if you were to place one in the palm of your hand (please don't), it would die from the effects of your body heat.

Leaving the loop trail's high point, you rock-hop the stream and descend the south flank of the valley. The trail is atop the crest of a ridge of rocks – a combination of glacial moraine and rockslide debris from Mt. Arethusa. Pikas and hoary marmots inhabit the boulderfields nearby. Hop the stream again at treeline. A sidetrail leads south (left) to a bench and a viewpoint that overlooks a cascade. The rock exposed is sandy dolomite of the Kananaskis Formation. This waterfall marks the true mouth of the hanging valley that contains Ptarmigan Cirque. It was near here that, during the Late Wisconsin Glaciation, the Ptarmigan Cirque glacier merged with the main valley glacier that once filled Highwood Pass. This point is known as the "break in slope". The slope beneath – as you know from the approach – is steeper than the slope above.

After a short descent through forest, you meet the approach trail at the loop junction. Turn southwest (left) to return to the trailhead. If you have the time, detour north (right) at the Highwood Meadows trail junction, 400 m from the parking area. Interpretive signs along this short trail describe the tough life of plants and animals in the upper subalpine life zone.

SNOW-BIRD, ROCK-BIRD

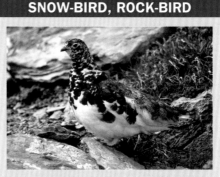

The white-tailed ptarmigan (TAR-mih-gan) is a ground-dwelling grouse-like bird of the high country. Its feathers change colour from mottled brown, gray, and black in summer; to white in winter. The tail is always white. Males have a reddish-orange comb over each eye during mating season. In winter, feathers grow on all surfaces of the feet, and the toes grow longer, creating natural, insulated snowshoes that decrease the bird's penetration into snow. Ptarmigan are well-camouflaged but unwary, advertising their presence with clucking and soft cooing. The clutch of up to ten chicks typically dwindles drastically through predation. Ptarmigan are non-migratory, foraging for berries, buds, flowers, and bugs. They gather into small flocks in winter. Skiers in the high country occasionally encounter snowbanks with many sets of blinking, black eyes – ptarmigan bedded down. When alarmed, these birds make explosive bursts of flight.

123. Heart Creek Canyon

Heart Creek Canyon

between Mt. McGillivray and Heart Mountain, Heart Creek Canyon is a classic front range limestone slot, whose cliffs are favourites with the sport climbing crowd. The rocks are part of the Rundle Group of formations. The trail crosses Heart Creek seven more times before ending at a cliff. On the way, look for the "weeping wall", where spring water is building a travertine drape on the wall to the south. The canyon offers its trees protection from Chinook winds in winter. The warm winds can kill trees by thawing them and starting sap flow when no water is available from the ground. At trail's end the creek does indeed tumble over the step, but the waterfall is tucked up around a corner, just out of view.

Heart Mountain (2135 m) is named for a syncline fold in the rocks at its summit. Mt. McGillivray (2451 m) commemorates Duncan McGillivray, a fur trade colleague of David Thompson. On November 30, 1800, Thompson, McGillivray, and another man ascended a mountain just across the Bow Valley – one of the earlier mountaineering ascents recorded in the Rockies.

TRAIL THUMBNAIL

Trailhead
Follow Highway 1 to the Lac des Arcs exit, 14.4 km east of Canmore; 91.6 km west of Calgary. Turn south into the Heart Creek Day Use Area. See map, p. 138.

Rating: moderate, 2.0 km

Best lighting: morning

Special consideration: To read or download the K-Country brochure for this hike, visit the *Walks and Easy Hikes* page at mountainvision.ca, and follow the links.

Nearby trail: 124

The first 500 m through damp montane forest follows a powerline right of way with Highway 1 just to your left. There are some great wildflower displays here to compensate – paintbrush and northern blue columbine, an uncommon find.

Cross Heart Creek on a bridge and turn south (right) at the junction just beyond. Sandwiched

124. Bow Valley Provincial Park

Mt. Yamnuska and Middle Lake

The six trails in Bow Valley Provincial Park explore a landscape at the interface of the foothills and the front ranges. Glacial landforms – moraines, eskers, kames, drumlins and kettle ponds – are central to this landscape. Many of these features were created at the wane of the Late Wisconsin Glaciation, 12,000 years ago. Early season hikers will be treated to exceptional wildflower displays, particularly on

TRAIL THUMBNAIL

Trailhead
Follow Highway 1, 27.4 km east of Canmore; 78.6 km west of Calgary, to Highway 1X. Turn north and follow the road 1 km. To reach the Flowing Water trail, turn east (right) into Willow Rock Campground. For the other trails, turn west (left) into Bow Valley Provincial Park.

Ratings: All six trails are easy. You can connect the Moraine, Middle Lake, Many Springs, and Bow River trails to make a harder outing of up to 10.6 km.
- Flowing Water: 3 km loop
- Montane: 1.5 km loop
- Middle Lake, 2.5 km loop
- Moraine, 1.5 km
- Many Springs: 1.6 km loop
- Bow River: 2 km

Special considerations: Pick up a detailed trail map from the park information centre, or visit the *Walks and Easy Hikes* page at mountainvision.ca, and follow the links.

Nearby trails: 115 123

the Flowing Water and Montane loops. Birders will enjoy the Middle Lake and Many Springs loops.

Everything that grows and lives here has to deal with Chinook winds that blow often, reducing the snow cover and creating a relatively arid chunk of montane habitat. In the shelter of the glacial landforms, and in the wetlands that they have helped to create, small pockets of damper habitat endure, boosting the area's biodiversity.

Views north from many of these outings feature the cliffs of Yamnuska (yam-NUSS-kah) (2240 m), at the base of which lies the McConnell Thrust Fault. If you were to hike to the bottom of the cliff, you would be able to literally put a fingertip on the trace line of the fault – the contact surface between rock formations that are 445 million years difference in age. Your feet would be in the sandstones and shales of foothills geological province, your head and shoulders in limestone of the front ranges. *Yamnuska* is a Stoney word that means "flat faced mountain".

125. Barrier Lake

Barrier Lake

TRAIL THUMBNAIL

Trailhead
Follow Highway 40 (Kananaskis Trail), 10.9 km south from Highway 1 to the Barrier Lake Day Use Area. Don't take the first right-hand turn but carry on to road's end in about 600 m.

Rating: moderate, 700 m

Best lighting: morning

Nearby trail: 116

This short outing switchbacks up onto a rocky knoll on the south shore of Barrier Lake, providing a fine view of that reservoir and the surrounding limestone peaks. It's a great trail for early season wildflowers, and also for birding. Species that dwell here include Swainson's thrush, hermit thrush, redbreasted nuthatch, and yellow-rumped warbler. The forest is shaped by the near constant wind. We normally think of kruppelholz trees as occurring near treeline and being coniferous. Here you will see low elevation species – lodgepole pine, trembling aspen, and even cottonwood poplar – blasted by the wind into misshapen forms. Deer and bighorn sheep frequent the area. Check yourself for wood ticks after early season hiking.

126. Mine Scar

Trailhead
Follow Highway 40 (Kananaskis Trail), 22.8 km south from Highway 1 to the Kananaskis Village junction. Turn west (right) onto Mt. Allan Drive. Cross the Kananaskis River and turn southwest (left) onto Centennial Drive. In 250 m, turn northwest (right) onto Ribbon Creek Road. Follow this 500 m to the Ribbon Creek parking area at road's end. The trailhead is at the northeast (closest) corner of the parking area.

Rating: harder, 2.2 km

Special consideration: The trail is closed each year from April 1 to June 21, inclusive, to protect bighorn sheep lambing habitat.

Best lighting: anytime

Nearby trail: 127

This outing climbs 254 m onto the south ridge of Mt. Allan to provide a great view of the middle reach of the Kananaskis Valley. You need to tag a few junctions in the early going to stay on track. In 2011, these were all clearly marked with the ubiquitous, metal K-Country trail-map signs. The initial routing is north for 400 m on the road-width, Hidden Lake trail. At the first junction, turn west (left). Follow this trail, still road-width, for 700 m to another junction. Keep straight ahead. The tread narrows and the grade steepens. Lodgepole pines dominate the forest. Arnica is common in the understory.

You will note that a wider track switchbacks across the trail in places. This is an old mining road, now used for cross-country skiing. Follow the marked hiking trail. Eventually, you hook up with the road, where the trail angles southwest. At the Mine Scar viewpoint, the trail forks. Walk south (left) a short distance onto a grassy slope. Between 1947 and 1952, this area was the site of coal mining – both a strip mine and an underground operation. A town called Kovach developed on the north bank of Ribbon Creek; at one time it numbered 200 residents. You can see some debris from the mining operations, downslope. From the Mine Scar, retrace your route to the trailhead.

Mine Scar

127. Eau Claire

Trailhead
From Highway 1, follow the Kananaskis Trail (Highway 40) 34.6 km south to the Eau Claire Campground turnoff. The trailhead is between sites 48 and 49.

Rating: easy, 1.5 km loop

Best lighting: anytime

Special consideration: To read or download the K-Country brochure for this hike, visit the *Walks and Easy Hikes* page at mountainvision.ca, and follow the links.

Nearby trail: 126

The Eau Claire (owe-CLAIR) (French for "clear water") trail loops through a pocket of wet spruce forest, providing contrasting views: the tranquillity at riverside along the Kananaskis River, and the stark walls of limestone that flank the valley. After a stint on the riverbank, the trail veers east to loop around an abandoned river channel. From several places, in the view north you can see the overturned fold in Mt. Kidd, near where terminates the Lewis Thrust – one of the larger thrust sheets on Earth.

The Eau Claire and Bow River Lumber Company began operations just south of here in 1884. Logging took place each year in winter, with log drives to Calgary on the Kananaskis and Bow rivers the following spring. You can see many stumps where the Eau Claire loggers high-graded prime floodplain spruce for the Calgary sawmill. You will also see charred forest, evidence of a 1936 forest fire. The lichen-draped trees that remain are favoured by golden-crowned kinglets,

Swainson's thrushes, and varied thrushes. Near trail's end you pass through a stand of trembling aspen whose bark is bronze-coloured. Baneberry, horsetails, willow, and cow parsnip abound. This is a great pocket of bear habitat. Keep your head up. The Eau Claire Campground dates to 1977, however archaeological evidence shows that campers have been coming here for at least 5000 years.

m) have weathered, through differential erosion, to create triangular-shaped formations known as flatirons. The dead trees in view on the lower slopes are lodgepole pines, killed by mountain pine beetles.

129. Marl Lake

Marl Lake

128. Rockwall

Flatirons in the Opal Range

TRAIL THUMBNAIL

Trailhead
From Highway 1, follow the Kananaskis Trail (Highway 40) 49.5 km south to the junction with the Kananaskis Lakes Trail. Turn west (right). Follow this road 5.8 km to the Elkwood parking area. Campers in Elkwood can pick up the trail at the back of any of the loops in the campground, and head south.

Rating: moderate, 3.6 km loop (shorter from the campground)

Special considerations: You share part of the trail with cyclists.

Best lighting: morning at Marl Lake

Nearby trails: 119 128 130 131

TRAIL THUMBNAIL

Trailhead
From Highway 1, follow the Kananaskis Trail (Highway 40) 49.5 km south to the junction with the Kananaskis Lakes Trail. Turn west (right). Follow this road 3.6 km to the Peter Lougheed Provincial Park information centre. You can begin from porch, accessed from within the building, or from the trailhead to the north (left).

Rating: easy 400 m, paved loop. Wheelchair ♿ accessible with assistance.

Best lighting: anytime

Nearby trails: 119 129 130 131

The forest opening adjacent to the information centre is a fen (see p. 16), the remnant of an ancient lake created by a glacier river channel. In recent years, grizzly bears have been foraging in the meadow – when we visited in 2011, park staff had installed an electric fence to deter them. The trail loops through a damp pine and spruce forest to the crest of the rockwall – a cliff that overlooks another wetland. In the view east, the Opal Range rises dramatically. The upturned rocks of Mt. Wintour (2700

The trail begins as a paved bike path. Follow directions for Marl Lake at all junctions near the campground. The tread reverts to natural surface. Interpretive panels explain the creation and transformation of the valley bottom wetlands, as well as the life cycle of the lodgepole pine forest. The variety of habitats makes this a great outing for birders. The early summer displays of calypso orchids are, in my experience, without equal in the Rockies. At Marl Lake, you have tremendous views to the south and southwest, respectively, of the peaks near Highwood Pass and above Upper Kananaskis Lake. Marl is a form of calcium sediment, dissolved from the limestone of the surrounding peaks and deposited in the lake.

153

130. Canadian Mount Everest Expedition Trail

TRAIL THUMBNAIL

Trailhead
From Highway 1, follow Kananaskis Trail (Highway 40), 49.5 km south to the Kananaskis Lakes Trail junction. Turn south (right) and follow the Kananaskis Lakes Trail, 12.5 km to the Upper Kananaskis Lake Day Use Area. The trailhead is at the north edge of the parking area. See map, p. 145.

Rating: moderate, 2.4 km loop

Best lighting: anytime

Nearby trails: 119 128 129 131

Named to commemorate the 1982 expedition to Mt. Everest, which put two Canadian climbers on that summit, this trail loops through a damp subalpine forest of Engelmann spruce and subalpine fir. Although trees interfere with the views from the modest highpoint, the vistas are far-reaching. They include the Kananaskis Lakes and their backdrops – the peaks of the Opal Range, and Mangin Glacier – the most southerly named glacier in Alberta.

131. Palliser Slide

Palliser Slide and
Upper Kananaskis Lake

Begin by crossing the earth-filled Interlakes dam between Upper Kananaskis Lake and Lower Kananaskis Lake. Calgary Power built the dam in 1955. Cliff swallows nest on the spillway gate, and

TRAIL THUMBNAIL

Trailhead
From Highway 1, follow Kananaskis Trail (Highway 40), 49.5 km south to the Kananaskis Lakes Trail junction. Turn south (right) and follow the Kananaskis Lakes Trail, 12.5 km to road's end at the North Interlakes Day Use Area. The trailhead is at the north end of the parking area. See map, p. 145.

Rating: easy, 2.2 km

Best lighting: anytime

Nearby trail: 119 128 129 130

anglers inevitably dot the bouldery shore of Upper Kananaskis Lake. Across the spillway, the trail (formerly a fire road) curves west through subalpine forest along the north shore of the lake. Keep right at junctions.

At km 2.2 you break out of the trees into the debris of the Palliser Slide, the largest measured rockslide in Peter Lougheed Provincial Park. The jumble consists not of Palliser Formation limestone, but mostly of limestone and dolomite of the Rundle Group of formations, which were deposited in ancient seas approximately 350 million-years-ago. The name, "Palliser", comes from the site's connection with the Palliser Expedition. John Palliser's party clambered over the rockslide in 1858.

It is true in the Rockies that what went up during mountain building must, eventually, come down. This is mostly accomplished through the chip-chipping of erosion but, occasionally, calamitous events such as rockslides tear the mountains down. The rock of Mt. Indefatigable is layered and dips steeply to the southwest – at angles as great as 50°. When the ice of the Late Wisconsin Glaciation flowed through this valley, it widened it, cutting into the lower valley walls, removing some of the support for the rocks above. Enter gravity. With such a steep dip, it was only a matter of time before rock layers broke free along their beds and slid to the valley floor. The process was expedited by the freezing and thawing of water that had percolated into fissures between the beds, pushing them apart and providing lubricant. The volume that let go here is estimated at 90 million m³.

Travel beyond the slide leads to the two Kananaskis passes or a circuit of Upper Kananaskis Lake. Casual walkers should turn back here.

132. West Wind Pass

West Wind Pass

for the pinkish-purple blooms of inflated oxotrope. The trail cuts over a few limestone benches to deliver you to the meadowed highpoint, the 2085 m saddle between the Windtower (2695 m), to the east, and the cliff known as the Rimwall, to the west. Bighorn sheep frequent the area. A few ragged kruppelholz spruce and fir trees cling to life in the rocky saddle. The view northeast includes the Wind Valley, with the Bow Valley near Lac des Arcs in the distance.

TRAIL THUMBNAIL

Trailhead
From the west end of Main Street in downtown Canmore, follow signs for the Nordic Centre and the Smith Dorrien-Spray Lakes Trail (Route 742). Follow this road 22.1 km south to the Spurling Creek parking area. Park on the west side of the road, north of the creek. Cross the road with caution to the trailhead.

Rating: harder, 2.1 km

Special considerations: Recommended to experienced hikers only. The trail may be subject to seasonal wildlife closures. Avoid this outing after recent snowfall.

Whereas most trails in this book have been "built", the trail to West Wind Pass is more of an "organic" route; beaten by people following animal trails. The outing follows the more northerly (left-hand) of the two trails that are across the road from the parking area. (If you take the right-hand trail, you will soon reach a dead-end at a spring.) After 150 m on the left-hand trail, you jog north (left) into the forest and switchback up to parallel a dry stream course. Views ahead include the destination pass; views back take in the Spray Lakes Reservoir.

Where the trail crosses water-worn slabs do not wander upslope, follow cairns. If you lose the way, backtrack. It is often the case that you will find the correct route by descending slightly during the ascent. Look and listen for hermit thrushes. Cinquefoil, scorpionweed, columbine, and paintbrush are among the wildflowers you may see. As you near the pass, ancient Engelmann spruce trees lean over the trail. In the limestone rubble underfoot, look

133. Rock Glacier

Rock Glacier

TRAIL THUMBNAIL

Trailhead
From Highway 1, follow Kananaskis Trail (Highway 40), 64.4 km south toward Highwood Pass (14.9 km south of the Kananaskis Lakes Trail junction). The parking area is on the east side of the road. This section of Highway 40 is closed annually between December 1 and June 15. See map, p. 146.

Rating: easy, 50 m

Best lighting: afternoon

Nearby trails: (120) (121) (122)

A rock glacier is a rock landform that contains just enough ice to enable the entire mass to creep downhill. Rock glaciers are lobe-like, just like ice glaciers, and in the Rockies may advance as much as 1 m per year. The shattered slopes of Mt. Rae (3225 m) (see p. 146) here provide no end of material for rock glacier formation. Bighorn sheep frequent the area. Look and listen for pikas and hoary marmots. Wildflower blooms include alpine forget-me-not, dwarf yellow columbine, and alpine daisies.

Tree Guide

If you consider yourself a budding botanist, you can develop a quick expertise in the Rockies with regard to those single-stemmed, vascular plants that typically attain heights of at least 10 m – meaning trees. Although there may be literally mountainsides of trees in any given view, only 15 coniferous (cone-bearing) species and 6 broad-leaved, deciduous species grow in the Rockies. Of the conifers, seven species are uncommon. That's right; you can count the common coniferous tree species on two hands, and the broad-leafed trees on one hand. If you can identify trees you are well on your way to sorting out the life zones. Let's journey up a mountainside, meeting the trees as we go.

Balsam poplar and Black cottonwood poplar

Where: montane, near water; occasionally lower subalpine
Height: 25-40 m
Bark: Gray, deeply furrowed
Leaves: triangular-shaped, glossy green

Trembling aspen

Where: montane – grasslands, river gravels, avalanche paths
Height: 15-25 m
Bark: White, smooth
Leaves: heart-shaped, toothed, light green

White birch

Where: montane, shaded woods near water
Height: 15-20 m
Bark: white with pinkish tones, peeling
Leaves: small, toothed, light green

Western redcedar

Where: montane, rainforest, west slope
Height: 30-40 m
Bark: gray, vertical strips
Needles: scaly, fan-like

Douglas-fir

Where: montane
Height: 30-40 m
Bark: brown, deeply furrowed
Needles: short, flat
More details: p. 22, p. 29

White spruce

Where: montane
Height: 20-30 m
Bark: brown, scaly
Needles: short, spiky

Lodgepole pine

Where: montane, lower subalpine
Height: 15-20 m
Bark: brown, gray, orange tones, raised scales
Needles: long, in pairs

Limber pine

Where: montane, cliff edges, river terraces
Height: 5-10 m
Bark: gray, smooth
Needles: long, in bunches of 5
More details: p. 24

Engelmann spruce

Where: montane, subalpine
Height: 20-30 m
Bark: brown, reddish-purple, scaly
Needles: short, spiky
More details: p. 36, p. 40, p. 145

Subalpine fir

Where: subalpine
Height: 25-35 m
Bark: gray, smooth, blistered
Needles: short, flat
More details: p. 36, p. 40, p. 145

Whitebark pine

Where: cliff edges, any elevation
Height: 5-10 m
Bark: gray, smooth
Needles: long, in bunches of 5
More details: p. 38

Lyall's larch

Where: upper subalpine
Height: 5-10 m
Bark: knobby, covered in dark down
Needles: bright green, soft
More details: p. 13, p. 47

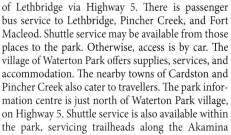

Upper Waterton Lake

Waterton Lakes National Park

Established in 1895 as Canada's fourth national park, Waterton Lakes includes 505 km² of the front ranges in the extreme south-western corner of Alberta. The park's theme is "where the mountains meet the prairie". Many viewpoints along the park's 200 km of trails reveal remarkable vistas of the front ranges rising from the plains.

Waterton Lakes National Park is 264 km south of Calgary via highways 22 and 6; and 130 km southwest of Lethbridge via Highway 5. There is passenger bus service to Lethbridge, Pincher Creek, and Fort Macleod. Shuttle service may be available from those places to the park. Otherwise, access is by car. The village of Waterton Park offers supplies, services, and accommodation. The nearby towns of Cardston and Pincher Creek also cater to travellers. The park information centre is just north of Waterton Park village, on Highway 5. Shuttle service is also available within the park, servicing trailheads along the Akamina

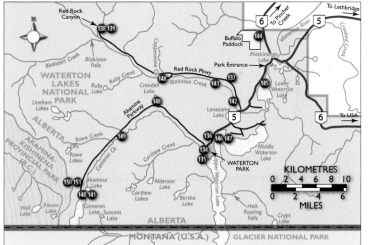

Parkway and Red Rock Parkway. Visit the *Walks and Easy Hikes* page at mountainvision.ca for a link. You can easily spend a few days walking and hiking at and near Waterton Park village without having to start a vehicle. Bike rentals are available.

Access to the Wall Lake and Forum Falls outings in neighbouring Akamina-Kishenina Provincial Park, B.C, is the same as for Waterton. Although you may find a park ranger at the cabin at Forum junction, the park has no developed facilities.

157

134. Cameron Falls and Waterton Park Village

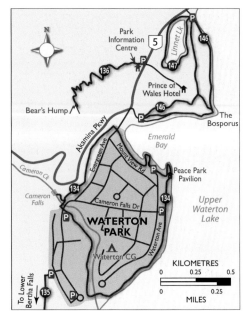

Cameron Falls

TRAIL THUMBNAIL

Trailhead

In Waterton Park village at Cameron Falls. Follow Cameron Falls Drive west to the parking area at the bridge over Cameron Creek.

Rating: easy, 3.2 km loop. Wheelchair ♿ accessible with assistance.

Special consideration: Use caution crossing roads.

Best lighting: anytime. Cameron Falls are lit best in the morning.

Nearby trails: 135 136 146 147

T his circuit of Waterton Park village is an ideal introduction to Waterton Lakes National Park. Cameron Falls makes a logical starting point for this outing, most of which is on paved or brick sidewalks.

Cameron Falls drops 10 m over an outcrop of Waterton Formation limestone. Not long ago, guide-book authors (ahem) would tell you that the rock exposed here was "the oldest visible in the Canadian Rockies". Oooops! Various geological de-thronings of "oldest rocks" have recently taken place, with the result that this 1.5 billion year old limestone, though venerable, can only be lauded in this fashion: It is the oldest sedimentary rock known in Alberta. You can follow a short trail from the north side of the bridge

to the rim of the canyon above the falls. Mule deer frequent this spot.

Cameron Creek is responsible for the alluvial fan that is now home to the village of Waterton Park. From time to time, the creek "blows out" – in one year it exhibited a thousand-fold increase in volume of flow between November and the following July. In 1964, runoff from Cameron Creek and other tributaries raised the level of Upper Waterton Lake 2.8 m above its previous record high. The most recent flash-flood was in June 1995. Cross the road and follow the path southeast along Cameron Creek toward Upper Waterton Lake. You will see shoring in the creek, installed to mitigate the flash-floods.

If the day is typical, it will be windy as you circle the campground. The park's average daily wind speed is 32.5 km per hour. Wind gusts of over 100 km per hour are common. Chinook winds (see p. 24), which can raise the temperature 40°C in a few hours, contribute to the warmest winters in the province of Alberta. The winds also bear wetter fruit; the park has the greatest annual precipitation in the province.

Siksika (Blackfoot) First Peoples know the Waterton Lakes by several names, one of which means "big water". With a maximum depth of 157 m, Upper Waterton Lake is the deepest lake in the Canadian Rockies. It is 11.1 km long, has an area of 941 ha, and is by far the largest of Waterton's 80 lakes and ponds. It holds approximately 645,200,000 m^3 of water. The southern reach of the lake extends 4.5 km into Glacier National Park, U.S.A. Waterton Lakes National Park is home to 17 native species of fish, and 8 introduced species. The largest catch on record was a 23.2 kg lake trout caught in Upper Waterton Lake in July 1920.

Cameron Creek

Upper Waterton Lake

DEER

The two species of deer in the Rockies are similar in size and appearance. The mule deer (photo, known to some people as the blacktail deer) has larger, mule-like ears, and a narrow, white tail with a black tip. The tail of the white-tailed deer is wider and is completely white underneath, and is held erect when the deer flees. Both species have white rump patches. Their coats are reddish-brown in early summer, changing to gray in winter. The coats of the young are spotted. Adult males (bucks) stand about 1 m tall at the shoulder.

About that head gear... When referring to members of the deer family, the bony protrusions are properly called antlers. It is sheep, goats, and bison that grow horns. Antlers grow each year and fall off; horns are permanent. Although white-tailed deer are more common in North America, in the Rockies, and especially in Waterton, you are more likely to see mule deer.

Because their hooves are small, deer have difficulty travelling in snow deeper than 25 cm. Deer proliferate in Waterton because of the wind, which keeps snow cover at a minimum along the mountain front. They share a problem with most mammals in the Rockies – when conditions are the toughest, food is the most hard to come by.

Please keep at least 30 m away if you see deer, and remember, where there are deer there may be cougars.

Turn north (left) at the lakeshore, and follow the sidewalk around the campground, toward town. You can make a sidetrip to the Waterton Heritage Centre on Waterton Avenue. Exhibits in this building describe the human and natural history of the park. There's also a great bookstore. At the north edge of town, you reach the International Peace Park Pavilion, constructed in 1982 on the 50th anniversary of Waterton-Glacier International Peace Park. Established as an expression of goodwill between Canada and the United States, the peace park was the first of its kind in the world.

Swing northwest along the shore of Emerald Bay. *The International* departs from the marina, touring Upper Waterton Lake. The vessel's maiden

SEA DUCK, MOUNTAIN DUCK

Cameron Creek is summer home to harlequin ducks. The plumage of the drake (male) of the species makes it among the more colourful ducks – slate blue, with rust highlights, and white streaks. Harlequin ducks winter on the west coast, moving inland in April and May to breed on fast-flowing streams and rivers in the mountains, away from human intrusion. After mating, the male soon heads for the surf, leaving the female to tend the nest of five to seven eggs and to raise the fledglings. Most harlequins mate for life. The pairs rendezvous at precise locations at each end of their migration. Although the western population of harlequins numbers about 200,000, the species is in decline. The eastern population numbers less than 2000, and is considered endangered. Park staff appreciate reports of harlequin duck sightings.

voyage was in 1927, the year that the Prince of Wales Hotel opened. The wreck of a paddle wheel steam ship, *Gertrude*, rests on the bottom of Emerald Bay. Brought to Waterton in 1907 to tow log booms, the vessel was later moored at the dock and used as a tea-room, before being scuttled in 1918. Today, the novelty of a shipwreck in inland waters attracts divers from throughout western Canada.

At the west end of Emerald Bay, turn south (left) on Evergreen Avenue to return to the Cameron Falls parking area, or turn north (right) to access the Prince of Wales and Linnet Lake trails.

Lower Bertha Falls

135. Lower Bertha Falls

TRAIL THUMBNAIL

Trailhead

 Bertha Lake trailhead parking area, at the south end of Evergreen Avenue, 500 m south of Cameron Falls. Easily reached on foot from any point in Waterton Park village.

Rating: moderate, 2.9 km

Best lighting: anytime

Nearby trails: 134 136 146 147

The Lower Bertha Falls outing explores a classic montane forest along the west shore of Upper Waterton Lake. The destination is a raucous waterfall – a cool, shady destination on a hot day. The trailside wildflower displays of early summer can be superb. The botanical bounty begins right at the trailhead, where thimbleberry, cow parsnip, and white geranium bloom in profusion.

Nothing is constant in nature. Avalanches, blowdowns, beetle infestations, and fires all affect forests. A large blowdown took place along this trail in June 1964, when winds reached more than 160 km per hour. Mountain pine beetles killed half of Waterton's lodgepole pine trees between 1976 and 1983. The beetles moved on and the forests recovered, but the bugs came back. Goodbye, pine forest, again. These processes help to sustain biodiversity by creating a

mosaic of habitats. In the clearings on the forest floor, deer family members find food sources in the new growth. The older trees that surround the clearings provide habitat and cover for other species.

At km 1.7 you reach a junction. Go straight ahead for 40 m to a viewpoint that provides a wonderful panorama of Upper Waterton Lake and the mountains along its east shore. You can see Mt. Cleveland (3194 m), the highest mountain in Glacier National Park, U.S.A. Once upon a time, limber pine, an uncommon tree in the Rockies, grew on this viewpoint. Mountain pine beetles killed the trees but their skeletal forms remain. Backtrack to the main trail. Descend southwest for 50 m to a junction. Lower Bertha Falls is straight ahead. The trail to the south (left) carries on along the lakeshore.

You climb gradually for the remaining distance to Lower Bertha Falls. Note how the route traverses shaded and sun-exposed habitats. On the rocky outcrops, look for Douglas-fir trees and sun-loving wildflowers.

Your destination is a bridge over Bertha Creek, where Lower Bertha Falls cascades across a tilted, resistant outcrop of the 1.5-billion-year-old Altyn Formation. At the base of the falls, another resistant rock lip captures the stream, producing a right-angle turn – a feature that geologists call structural control. This area is in the path of a prominent storm track. The winds bring plant seeds from the interior of B.C., and the high annual precipitation and shade along lower Bertha Creek favours their growth. The trail beyond the falls climbs steeply for 2.8 km to Bertha Lake. Bertha Ekelund was an early Waterton resident, reportedly jailed for issuing counterfeit "prescriptions" for alcohol during Prohibition. She was, no doubt, a folk hero.

Mt. Cleveland

136. Bear's Hump

View from the Bear's Hump

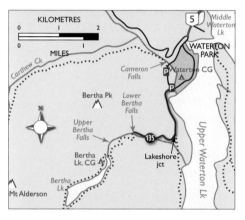

Piikani (Peigan) First Peoples knew Mt. Crandell, just north of today's Waterton Park village, as Bear Mountain. The Bear's Hump is a limestone bluff on the south ridge of the peak. The trail that gets you there climbs at an average grade of about 16 percent. The last half of the outing is like a giant's staircase. Your reward for completing this unrelenting climb is a panorama that includes the Waterton Lakes, Waterton Park village, and the contact between mountain and prairie for which the park is famous. The Bear's Hump is one of Waterton's windier places. Take a sweater, windbreaker, toque, and mitts with you.

The trail ascends a shaded slope cloaked in a damp montane forest. The shrub, thimbleberry, grows profusely here. The aspen groves are alive with songs of warblers in late spring and early summer. Just before you reach the top of the climb, look for

MEET THE BEETLES

As of 2012, with the recent infestation in decline, the mountain pine beetle had killed 73,248 km² or 33 percent of the forest in B.C. Moving east into the mountain national parks, the beetle first took hold in the lodgepole pine forests of the Kicking Horse Valley in Yoho. The female beetle bores tunnels into the sapwood, into which she deposits eggs. When the eggs hatch, the larvae chew galleries around the tree, stopping the flow of sap and nutrients. The tree will try to expel the intruders, exuding sap through the beetle holes. The larvae that survive the treatment take wing the following spring, seeking other host trees in which to repeat the cycle. The needles of an afflicted tree turn red in the first year after infestation, then gray in the second year. The sapwood of a killed tree will show a blue-stain fungus (photo). The mountain pine beetle can affect any pine species (it was first catalogued in Ponderosa pine), and has also become viable in spruce trees.

The rapid spread of the mountain pine beetle through B.C. and into Alberta is a result of fire suppression and a warming climate. Forest fires kill beetles

and their larvae; as do winters with sustained temperatures of -40°C early in the season. Unless winters get colder nation-wide, the mountain pine beetle is poised to sweep east across the continent. Parks Canada is using prescribed burns to remove patches of beetle habitat. As the standing dead pines topple, their nutrients are added to the soil. Although the initial effect appears destructive, biodiversity will increase as the homogenous pine stands are broken.

TRAIL THUMBNAIL

Trailhead
Parking area at the Waterton Lakes National Park Information Centre, 1 km north of Waterton Park village on Highway 5. See map, p. 158.

Rating: harder, 1.2 km

Special considerations: Caution! Fall risk! The summit area is unfenced. Keep well back from cliff edges, especially when it is windy. Avoid this outing when the trail is snow- or ice-covered and when lightning is forecast or evident.

Best lighting: anytime

Nearby trails: 134 135 146 147

Bear's Hump

limestone rocks and slabs that exhibit *rillenkarren* – grooves and fissures eroded by meltwater.

From the Bear's Hump, Upper Waterton Lake is the centrepiece in the view. The lake has an area of 941 hectares, is 11.1 km long, 750 m wide, and extends 4.5 km into Montana. It holds an estimated 645,200,000 m^3 of water. With a maximum depth of 157 m, it is the deepest lake in the Canadian Rockies, and is also probably the biggest tarn in the range. An ice-age glacier created the U-shaped valley that contains the lake, scooping out the bedrock and undercutting the adjacent mountainsides. Middle Waterton Lake and Lower Waterton Lake were

formed in a different manner. They are massive kettle ponds, created by the melting of massive detached blocks of ice when that same ice-age glacier receded.

Streams and rivers carry boulders, silt, and rubble away from the mountains, depositing them where the angle of the stream bed lessens. This creates a landform called an alluvial fan. Waterton Park village is built on the fan formed where Cameron Creek descends from its hanging valley into the Waterton Valley. Geologists speculate that much of the material in alluvial fans in the Rockies was deposited during a tremendous meltwater surge between 8000 years ago and 5000 years ago, when the vestiges of ice-age glaciers finally melted. Material is still being deposited on the Waterton fan, although diversions of Cameron Creek (designed to prevent flooding) have interfered with the natural process.

Looking north from the Bear's Hump, you can see where the front ranges of the Rockies end abruptly on the prairie. The streamlined contours of the Bear's Hump indicate that it was completely covered by glacial ice during the Late Wisconsin Glaciation. Before that ice age, the Bear's Hump was probably connected

THE BIG DADDY

The Lewis Thrust Sheet is the foundation block of the southern Canadian Rockies and is among the larger thrust sheets on Earth. It extends from Steamboat Mountain in Montana, to near Mt. Kidd in the Kananaskis Valley. Whereas mountains elsewhere in the Rockies can be described as resulting from many major and minor thrust faults, the mountains of the Waterton area exist primarily because of this one fault alone. (There is some secondary faulting in the layers of the Lewis Thrust at its leading edge.) The Lewis Thrust Sheet was up to 30 km thick, 110 km wide, and 315 km long. It slid 140 km. The fault was named for Meriwether Lewis of the Lewis and Clark Expedition.

Why the Lewis Thrust Sheet held together so well during mountain building is a mystery. The almost horizontal inclination of the fault was probably a significant factor. The integrity of the rocks has created an unusual front range landscape. Missing here are the steeply tilted, sawtooth and overthrust

mountains that occur in parallel ranges in Banff and Jasper. Waterton's peaks are irregular in shape and arrangement, and the rock layers are mostly horizontal. Although these mountains are oriented along the southeast-northwest axis of the Rockies, the network of valleys is haphazard. The average elevation of summits is lower than farther north in the Rockies. The highest peak is Mt. Blakiston (2910 m).

to Vimy Peak on the opposite side of the valley. The ancient Waterton Glacier eroded The Bosporus, the narrow strait that links Upper Waterton Lake and Middle Waterton Lake, through this ridge.

Glaciers removed that natural rock dam, but in 1919, a proposal was made to build a concrete dam at The Bosporus to impound Upper Waterton Lake for irrigation. A dam would have greatly altered the ecology and the appeal of the national park. James B. Harkin, Commissioner of Dominion Parks, dismissed the proposal. Dams have since been constructed downstream on the Waterton River and on other tributaries of the South Saskatchewan River.

Bellevue Prairie

137. Bellevue Prairie

On the Bellevue Prairie you explore the place where mountains and prairie meet. Although Waterton's peaks are not high by Rockies' standards, the abrupt manner in which they rise close-at-hand from the rolling prairie makes this a unique setting among the Walks and Easy Hikes.

In common with the other Rocky Mountain parks, Waterton includes the montane, subalpine, and alpine life zones. The north-eastern part of the park – reached on this outing – incorporates three other life zones – prairie, aspen parkland, and foothills transition. As a

TRAIL THUMBNAIL

Trailhead
Follow the Red Rock Parkway for 3.0 km from Highway 5, to where the road makes a prominent turn to the west (left). Park in the pull-off on the east (right). See map, p. 164.

Rating: easy, 2.0 km

Best lighting: morning

Special consideration: The Red Rock Parkway is closed to vehicles from November 1 to mid-May.

Nearby trails: 142 143

A PRAIRIE GARDEN

Wildflowers abound on Bellevue Prairie, including several species uncommon in the Rockies, found here in prolific numbers. You won't stumble across the three-spot mariposa lily on many other outings in this book, but if you time it right on Bellevue Prairie you can drink your fill. Two other showy, delicate, grassland species that you may see are pasque flower (so named because it often blooms soon after Easter), and prairie smoke. And what about those sunflower-type blooms? Most belong to two species: brown-eyed Susan, and arrowhead balsam root. The former is taller (up to 50 cm), with solitary blooms that have a brown or reddish-purple centre. The latter is generally shorter, blooming in clumps, and with large (20 cm long) arrow-shaped leaves that are pale green, and fuzzy on the underside.

Brown-eyed Susan

Mariposa lily · Pasque flower · Prairie smoke · Balsam root

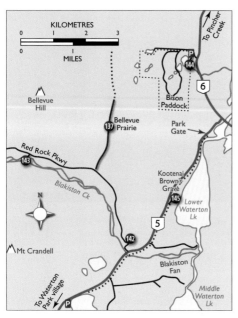

Red Rock Canyon

138. Red Rock Canyon

TRAIL THUMBNAIL

Trailhead
Follow the Red Rock Parkway to road's end, 14.3 km from Highway 5.

Rating: easy, 700 m loop. Wheelchair ♿ accessible with assistance.
🪑

Special considerations: Caution! Fall risk! Stay within the fencing along the canyon edge. The Red Rock Parkway is closed to vehicles from November 1 to mid-May.

Best lighting: anytime

Nearby trail: 139

result, the park boasts 1270 plant species, including 870 vascular species – 55 percent of the total in Alberta. Of these, 113 species are rare in Alberta, 43 species are rare in Canada, and 34 species are unknown in Alberta outside the park. The rarest plant in the park – a minuscule fern called the Waterton moonwort – grows nowhere else on Earth. Botanists have identified 45 vegetation communities in Waterton – four of these are considered at extreme risk because of cattle grazing nearby and the spread of invasive weeds.

Although this description implies a tension in the landscape, to walk on Bellevue Prairie between late May and mid-July, when the prairie is awash with wildflowers, is one of the greatest joys in the Rockies.

To botanists, it's a fescue prairie; to glaciologists, Bellevue Prairie is an eskerine complex. An esker is a sinuous ridge of gravel that was deposited by meltwater flowing beneath a glacier. You will see where many eskers snake their way across this prairie. Their windward sides are devoid of trees, but in the shade and shelter of these low ridges, out of reach of the near constant wind, soils remain moist and stunted aspens and limber pines grow.

The Buffalo Trail – an ancient travel route between B.C. and the plains – crossed Bellevue Prairie. Many artifacts have been found in the area, including rock structures associated with ritual sites, buffalo jumps, campsites, and the ruts left by sleds called travois.

Bellevue is French for "beautiful view". Bellevue Hill (2112 m) was named for the view from its summit, but the view toward it from the prairie also merits the name. It is possible to traverse Bellevue Prairie to Indian Springs near the Bison Paddock, but most walkers turn back at the obvious high point about 2 km from the trailhead.

The paved trail at Red Rock Canyon makes a circuit of a water-worn slot in an exposure of 1.5-billion-year-old mudstone. The canyon is 23 m deep. Its steep walls indicate rapid erosion during the wane of the Late Wisconsin Glaciation, 12,000 years ago. Swirling rocks, trapped in eddies, created potholes. Other geologic features of the canyon include ripple rock, which records wave action along a prehistoric shoreline. On the east side of the canyon, the trail crosses a honeycomb of mud cracks. These cracks opened where mud dried on an ancient tidal flat. The cracks were later filled with a different type of sediment. The formation was subsequently turned to rock by the pressure of other sediments that accumulated rapidly above.

At trailside you may see examples of a fossil formation known as a stromatolite. These miniature,

Mud cracks

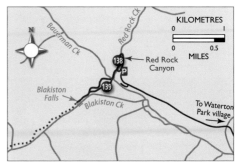

reef-like accumulations were created 1.5-billion-years-ago, from calcium carbonate produced by algae. Similar algae grow today, creating reefs in warm, shallow seas elsewhere in the world.

The last item of geological interest is an intrusion of igneous (once molten) rock near the mouth of the canyon. Nearly all the rock in the Rockies is sedimentary. However, blobs of molten rock sometimes oozed into cracks within the hardened sedimentary layers. This gray, igneous rock is diabase of the Purcell Lava Formation. You may see phenocrysts in this rock – star-shaped crystals of feldspar.

A travel route called The Buffalo Trail, used by First Peoples for thousands of years, crossed South Kootenay Pass and followed Blakiston Creek past the mouth of Red Rock Canyon. Seasonal hunting camps have been found near the canyon, dating to 8000 years ago. If you see bighorn sheep at the parking area, please do not feed them.

ARGILLITE

The rock in Red Rock Canyon is argillite (ARE-jill-ite) – something of an inter-grade between shale (which is created from clay) and slate, which is shale that has been made brittle by heat and pressure. Iron-rich argillite sediments were deposited on ancient tidal mud flats. Where the mud flats were exposed to air, the iron oxidized and turned red. (It rusted.) The green and white rocks in the canyon are also argillite, but contain iron that did not oxidize. These rocks are part of the Grinnell Formation, named for George Bird Grinnell, who championed the establishment of Glacier National Park, U.S.A., in 1910.

139. Blakiston Falls

Trailhead and Special considerations
As for Red Rock Canyon (outing 138).

Rating: moderate, 1 km

Best lighting: anytime

Nearby trail: 138

Cross the bridge over Red Rock Creek at the lower end of Red Rock Canyon. At the junction immediately beyond, turn west (left) onto the Blakiston Creek trail. You descend to cross Bauerman Creek and enter a damp pocket of lower subalpine forest. The trail soon breaks out of the dampness onto dry slopes overlooking Blakiston Creek. There are two fenced viewpoints, one below the falls, and one at the brink. Buchanan Peak (2409 m) is the backdrop. Look for dippers in the creek, and for blobs of dark, igneous rock. Thomas Blakiston was the meteorologist with the Palliser Expedition. In 1858 he became the first European to walk through this valley.

140. Cameron Lake

Cameron Lake

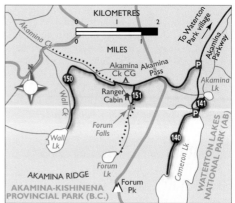

TRAIL THUMBNAIL

TRAIL THUMBNAIL

Trailhead
Follow the Akamina Parkway, 15.7 km southwest from its junction with Highway 5 to road's end at the Cameron Lake parking area.

Rating: easy, 1.6 km

Special consideration: The avalanche slopes at the far end of the lake are prime grizzly bear habitat. Do not go past the end-of-trail barrier.

Best lighting: morning and late afternoon

Nearby trails: 141 149 150 151

The Cameron Lake trail visits the extreme southwest corner of Alberta – a place where three parks, two provinces, and two countries meet. The trail follows the west shore of the lake through an ancient subalpine forest to end at a barrier and platform.

Although glaciers have long been absent from Waterton's mountains, their legacy is evident at Cameron Lake. The lake is situated in a bowl-shaped valley known as a cirque. A glacier that flowed from the north flank of Mt. Custer eroded this cirque. When the glacier receded, it deposited a moraine that dammed the lake. Although some of the snow on the north face of Mt. Custer may endure the summer, the glacier is gone.

The forest around Cameron Lake is a true snow forest. The most common tree species are Engelmann spruce and subalpine fir, both coniferous. The subalpine fir is spire-like to help shed the heavy snow

load. There are other ways to differentiate these tree species. Fir needles are flat, whereas spruce needles are spiky and square, and will roll between your fingers. (If the needles are in bundles of two, the tree is a lodgepole pine. If they are in bundles of five, the tree is the less common whitebark pine, or limber pine.)

Tree bark and cones also help with identification. Engelmann spruce bark is reddish-brown and scaly. The bark of the subalpine fir is silvery-gray and smooth, with resin blisters. Spruce cones hang downward; fir cones sit upright. New fir cones are often purple in colour. As you investigate, please be gentle with tree branches and needles, and avoid trampling the surrounding vegetation.

While you are focussed on trees, look and listen for bird species that love the deep woods:

NO BOUNDARIES

The screeching of a jay greets you from tree branches above a picnic table at Cameron Lake. But wait a minute; that jay is blue and black! Yes, it's a Steller's jay, the provincial bird of B.C. What's it doing here, in Alberta? It likes the habitat – ancient upper subalpine forest. Boundaries on maps mean nothing to species; they go and grow where they belong. Speaking of boundaries, you may have been wondering, where do the Canadian Rockies end? Geologically speaking, the southern end of the Canadian Rockies is at Marias Pass in southern Glacier National Park, U.S.A.

Swainson's thrush, varied thrush, robin, dark-eyed junco, Steller's jay, gray jay, three-toed woodpecker, black-capped chickadee, and mountain chickadee. Common loons nest on the lakeshore. For a link to a birding checklist for Waterton, visit the *Walks and Easy Hikes* page at mountainvision.ca

The undergrowth at trailside features arnica, queen's cup, cow parsnip, foamflower, dwarf dogwood, purple geranium, glacier lily, false hellebore, evergreen violet, white globeflower, and pearly everlasting – all species that like it cool and wet. Keep an eye out for the blooms of red monkey flowers, a relatively common plant in Waterton but not often found elsewhere in the Rockies.

The ridgecrest above the west shore of Cameron Lake separates Waterton Lakes National Park in the province of Alberta, from Akamina-Kishinena Provincial Park in B.C. The boundary between Canada and the U.S.A. follows a more arbitrary line. The 49th parallel cuts across the southern end of Cameron Lake. Mt. Custer (2707 m), centrepiece in the view, is entirely within Glacier National Park, U.S.A. The mountain was not named for the famous general, but for Henry Custer, a topographer with the U.S. Boundary Survey of the 1860s. The Herbst Glacier lies just over the mountain's east (left-hand) ridge. It is, by a few seconds of arc and until it melts away completely, the northernmost glacier in the continental U.S.A. As of 2005 it was considered defunct, covering an area of just 0.053 km², having decreased 70 percent in area in the previous 40 years.

141. Akamina Lake

Trailhead
As for Cameron Lake (outing 140), on the east side of the parking area.

Rating: easy, 500 m

Best lighting: anytime

Nearby trails: 140 149 150 151

Akamina Lake is a peaceful body of water, a short walk from the hubbub of the Cameron Lake parking area. The trail winds through damp subalpine forest to a platform on the lakeshore – a tranquil spot. You may see moose, waterfowl, and fish. Horsetails, ferns, arnica, white globeflower, and foamflower are some of the common plant species. *Akamina* (ah-kah-MEE-nah) is a Ktunaxa (toon-AWK-ah) word that means either "high bench land", "watershed", "mountain pass", or "valley".

142. Blakiston Fan

TRAIL THUMBNAIL

Trailhead
Follow the Red Rock Parkway for 500 m from Highway 5. See map, p. 164.

Rating: easy, 100 m

Special consideration: The Red Rock Parkway is closed to vehicles from November 1 to mid-May.

Best lighting: afternoon

Nearby trails: 137 143 145

The Blakiston Fan is a colossal landform (something like 8 km² in area) created during the last 12,000 years by material carried by Blakiston Creek and deposited into the Waterton Valley. The fan has, in effect, created two lakes (Middle Waterton and Lower Waterton) out of what was formerly one. The Blakiston Fan contains grasslands and patches of aspen forest, and is important habitat for many mammals, especially in winter. This short walk leads to a viewpoint that overlooks the fan. If you would like to explore the Blakiston Fan directly, consider visiting the Marquis Hole or Hay Barn picnic areas, reached from Highway 5.

143. First Peoples

TRAIL THUMBNAIL

Trailhead
Follow the Red Rock Parkway 5.2 km from Highway 5. Park on the south (left). See map, p. 164.

Rating: easy, 50 m

Special consideration: The Red Rock Parkway is closed to vehicles from November 1 to mid-May.

Best lighting: afternoon

Nearby trails: 137 142 148

Blakiston Valley

Bison

This short path leads to a gazebo with a fine view of the Blakiston Valley. Before the park was created, First Peoples travelled through this valley for at least 8000 years.

144. Bison Paddock Viewpoint

TRAIL THUMBNAIL

Trailhead
Follow Highway 6 for 2 km north from its junction with Highway 5 to the Bison Paddock Road. Turn west (left) and then south (left) into the parking area. See map, p. 164.

Rating: easy, 300 m. Wheelchair ♿ accessible with assistance.

Special consideration: This trail is outside the Bison Paddock. Bison can be dangerous. Remain in your vehicle if you drive within the paddock.

Best lighting: morning

In the view west from the Bison Paddock Viewpoint, a rolling fescue prairie, dotted with kettle lakes, ends abruptly at the base of Bellevue Hill and the front ranges of the Rockies. The grasses and wildflowers of this mini-prairie represent the natural vegetation of the northern interior plains.

As many as 60 million bison lived on the interior plains in 1790. When horses and rifles were introduced onto the bison's range, the animal was subjected to a senseless slaughter by both whites and First Peoples. Settlers burned the prairie and put it under plough. Diseases imported with domestic cattle took a heavy toll. By 1890, the population of the plains bison was 1090.

The return of the plains bison from the brink of extinction can be attributed to Walking Coyote, who captured wild bison in southern Alberta in 1874 and sold some of them to two ranchers in Montana. In 1907, the Canadian government purchased 716 bison from the captive Montana herd. Descendants of these animals now live at Elk Island National Park and here. The Waterton Lakes bison paddock, established in 1952 with one bull and five cows, usually holds 12-15 bison.

The bison paddock area features many glacial landforms. The lakes are kettle ponds. The sinuous, moraine ridges are eskers, deposited in streams that flowed beneath glacial ice. Oval-shaped mounds are drumlins – perhaps created when a glacier advanced over existing moraines. Kames are conical-shaped piles of rubble deposited at a glacier's edge by meltwater flowing from the glacier's surface. This viewpoint is on a kame.

There are many archaeological sites in this vicinity. The Buffalo Trail from South Kootenay Pass crossed the area. First Peoples used a nearby cliff as a bison jump.

After walking the viewpoint trail, you may choose to drive through the Bison Paddock where, with luck, you will obtain a close view of these impressive animals.

Fescue prairie

145. Kootenai Brown's Grave

Kootenai Brown's Grave

TRAIL THUMBNAIL

Trailhead
East side of Highway 5; 3 km south of its junction with Highway 6; 5.4 km north of Waterton Park village. See map, p. 164.

Rating: easy, 500 m

Special consideration: In 2010, Parks Canada completed a bike path along the east side of Highway 5, between the Linnet Lake picnic area and the park gate. Cyclists may use this path to access the trailhead, although as of 2011 there was no bike lock-up.

Best lighting: anytime

Nearby trail: 142

John Kootenai Brown epitomized the "wild west" of the 1800s. Brown's pre-Waterton life read like an encyclopaedia of adventure. He had served with the British Army in India, made and lost a fortune in the Cariboo gold fields, served as a police constable at Cranbrook, ran whiskey, was a pony express rider, trapped furs, and was accused and acquitted of murdering a business partner. Brown first saw the Waterton Lakes in 1865. He returned three years later to settle near the mouth of Blakiston Creek, the first of five locations where he lived in what is now Waterton.

Brown's idyllic life of guiding and trapping was disrupted in the 1890s. He had witnessed the demise of the plains bison, and now increasing numbers of visitors were threatening other wildlife. Local ranchers pressured the federal government to set aside a reserve in the area in 1895 – the Kootenay Lakes Forest Park Reserve. (The Waterton Lakes had been originally known as the Kootenay Lakes.)

At age 71, Brown became the park's first employee and guardian; a position he held for three years. The park area was then increased thirty-fold, requiring a younger man in the patrol saddle. Brown died in 1916. He was buried where this trail ends on the shore of Lower Waterton Lake, between the graves of his two wives, Olivia and Isabella.

146. Prince of Wales

TRAIL THUMBNAIL

Trailheads

1. East side of Highway 5, 400 m north of the park information centre.
2. Emerald Bay picnic area, east side of Highway 5, 300 m south of the park information centre. You can easily walk to the trailhead from the village. See map, p. 158.

Rating: moderate, 2.0 km loop

Best lighting: anytime

Nearby trails: 134 135 136 147

The Prince of Wales Hotel was the brainchild of Louis Hill, president of the Great Northern Railway. With Glacier National Park established as a tourist draw in the U.S.A., Hill sought to expand his business with side trips into Canada. Construction of the hotel began in 1926. During the work, chinook winds that gusted to 144 km per hour pushed the hotel 20 cm off its foundation. Nonetheless, the hotel opened the following summer, and soon became part of Waterton's trademark view.

The hotel sits atop a glacial deposit known as a kame – a conical pile of boulders and sediment, laid down by meltwater streams at the edge of a retreating glacier. This kame is especially high because it accumulated on a bench of bedrock.

The trail loops around the base of the kame, crossing a pebbled beach to The Bosporus – the narrows that separate Upper Waterton Lake and Middle Waterton Lake. Archaeologists have inventoried an 8000-year-old native fishing camp here. The stunted and gnarled shapes of the trees are evidence of Waterton's windiness. After following the lakeshore north to the Linnet Lake trailhead, the Prince of Wales Trail climbs back over the kame and descends to the picnic area at Emerald Bay.

147. Linnet Lake

TRAIL THUMBNAIL

Trailhead

Picnic area on the east side of Highway 5, 400 m north of the park information centre. You can easily walk to the trailhead from the village. See map, p. 158.

Rating: easy, 1 km paved loop. Wheelchair ♿ accessible

Best lighting: anytime

Nearby trails: 134 135 136 146

Parks Canada paved the Linnet Lake trail in 1985 to commemorate the national parks centennial. The lake is a kettle pond. The surrounding forest features Douglas-fir, balsam poplar, white birch, lodgepole pine, and the shrub, saskatoon. The linnet (Carduelis cannabina) is a type of finch found in Europe. The pine siskin, a common resident of Waterton, was commonly referred to as a linnet. The mini-culverts nearby on Highway 5 help to direct long-toed salamanders to safe crossing places.

148. Crandell Lake

Crandell Lake is situated on a rocky bench that separates the valleys of Cameron Creek and Blakiston Creek. During the Late Wisconsin Glaciation, glacial ice flowed from the south over this bench, scooping out the hollow that now contains the lake. Both approaches ascend onto the bench, following the route of a wagon road constructed in 1902 to allow access to the Discovery Oil Well on Cameron Creek. E.H. Crandell was a Calgary businessman who helped finance the well. There is a sandy beach on the lake's north shore. The trails feature great wildflower displays. The forest is a delight when the leaves of aspen and birch trees have changed in late summer and early autumn.

TRAIL THUMBNAIL

Trailheads

1. North side of the Akamina Parkway, 6.7 km from Highway 5.
2. Follow the Red Rock Parkway, 8.2 km from its junction with Highway 5. Turn south (left) onto the Crandell Lake/Canyon Church Camp Road (1.2 km west of Crandell Campground), and follow this 400 m to the parking area. Campers can walk here from the rear of the campground.

Ratings
- From Akamina Parkway: easy, 1.6 km
- From Red Rock Parkway: moderate, 2.4 km

Special considerations: You share the trail with cyclists and equestrians. You require a permit to camp at the backcountry campground. The Red Rock Parkway is closed to vehicles from Nov. 1 to mid-May.

Best lighting: anytime

Nearby trails: 137 148 149

149. Oil City

TRAIL THUMBNAIL

Trailhead

From the junction with Highway 5, follow the Akamina Parkway 9.2 km to a parking area on the south side of the road.

Rating: easy, 250 m loop

Best lighting: anytime

Nearby trails: 140 141 148 150 151

Following the drilling of the Discovery Well on Cameron Creek in 1901, surveyor A.P. Patrick plotted a town nearby that he called Oil City. The post office opened in 1905 but, due to problems with the well, the town of 450 lots never amounted to much. All that remains today is the foundation laid for a 10-room hotel that was never completed. You may also visit the First Oil Well in Western Canada National Historic Site, 1.3 km east on the Akamina Parkway.

150. Wall Lake

Wall Lake

TRAIL THUMBNAIL

Trailhead
Follow the Akamina Parkway, 14.3 km from Highway 5 to the Akamina Pass parking area on the east side of the road. The trailhead is across the road. See map, p. 166.

Rating: harder, 5.2 km

Special considerations: Use caution crossing the road. You share the trail with cyclists and equestrians. If you would like to camp at Akamina Creek, you will need a camping permit from B.C. Parks. See p. 177.

Nearby trails: (140) (141) (149) (151)

Long a favourite haunt of backcountry skiers, Wall Lake became a popular summer destination with the establishment of Akamina-Kishinena Provincial Park in 1995. In a good year, the bear grass blooms at trailside are stunning.

Waterton's Cameron Lake region is the snowfall capital of southern Alberta. The forest at the trailhead is wet in character, more like what you would expect in British Columbia, which is but a 20 minute walk away. As testimony to the wetness, thimbleberry, queen's cup, false hellebore, cow parsnip,

western meadowrue, water hemlock, birch-leaved spirea, and bear grass provide much of the ground cover at the trailhead.

The trail to Akamina Pass was cut as an exploratory tote road following the discovery of oil on Cameron Creek in 1901. In 1927, there was a proposal to extend the recently-constructed Akamina Parkway over Akamina Pass, to allow a "triangle tour" from Waterton to the Flathead Valley, returning through Glacier National Park, Montana. The B.C. section of the road was never built, but the tote road into Akamina-Kishinena Provincial Park remains. In places, you'll see sections of corduroy – logs laid across the width of the tread. *Corduroy* is a French expression that means "road of the king". To keep the king's carriage out of the muck of feudal France, the peasants would lay logs across the tread. A bumpy ride resulted, but at least the king got to his palace without sullying his boots and gown. Hike on – regal wonders await.

You climb steadily through an old pine forest, crossing a small stream in 400 m. Note the red rock in the streambed. It's 1.5 billion-year-old argillite of the Grinnell Formation. You catch glimpses of Cameron Lake through the trees. White rein orchids, hooded ladies'-tresses, meadow parsnip, dwarf false asphodel, groundsel, horsetails, and fleabane line a wet section of trail on the final approach to the forested pass.

There's not much to look at on the pass but a typical mass of signs that welcomes you to B.C. and the entry to Akamina-Kishinena Provincial Park. I have seen moose in the woods just north of the trail. You descend gradually from the pass to the Forum Lake junction in 700 m. To hike to Forum Falls (see p. 172), turn south (left).

It is only 200 m from the Forum Lake junction to Akamina Creek Campground, and another 50 m to the three bridges that span the outflow from Forum Lake. Across the creek, turn southwest (left) for Wall Lake.

The trail to the lake initially makes a gradual descent through an old forest of lodgepole pine,

A COUPLET FULL OF DEFINITIONS

The name of Akamina-Kishinena Provincial Park incorporates two Ktunaxa (toon-AWK-ah) (Kutenai) words, the precise meanings of which elude toponymers. *Akamina* might mean "high bench land", "mountain pass", "valley", or "watershed". All of these are appropriate for the features so named by the British Boundary Commission. Some people pronounce the name, ah-kah-MY-nah, but most say ah-kah-MEE-nah. The meanings given for *Kishinena* (kish-ih-NEE-nah) that I like best are "balsam" and "white fir". Akamina-Kishinena: It's an exotic sounding couplet that has a down-to-earth meaning – rocks and trees.

Engelmann spruce, and subalpine fir. Arnica, queen's cup, and foamflower are among the wildflowers. After about 1.9 km, the trail swings south to enter the Wall Creek valley, where it begins a gradual ascent. The trail runs along the base of avalanche slopes off the spur that separates Forum Lake from Wall Lake. Huge spruce grow here – some are more than 1 m in diameter at the base and 45 m tall. These avalanche slopes – with their glacier lilies, bear grass, cow parsnip, and berry bushes – are deluxe bear habitat. Fireweed, ragwort, wild onion, and bracted honeysuckle grow on the trail margins.

151. Forum Falls

Trailhead
As for Wall Lake (outing 150). See map, p. 166.

Rating: moderate, 2.8 km

Best lighting: anytime

Nearby trails: 140 141 149 150

The first 2.2 km of this outing follows the Wall Lake trail (see outing 150). At the Forum Lake junction, turn south (left). The park ranger cabin is 175 m along the trail. Branch left just beyond. This is the end of the bike trail. Just 50 m into the trees you come to a junction. Forum Falls is a short distance to the west (right). It's a pleasant (sometimes slippery) sidetrip to the base of the small cascade. Dippers nest here and frequent the stream. White globeflowers bloom in early summer.

At Wall Lake, Akamina Ridge rises some 750 m from the south shore, shutting out the sky. An ancient forest with a lush understory rings the north shore. Look for red monkey flowers at trailside. Cutthroat trout abound in the lake. If you packed a fishing rod, make sure that you also packed a B.C. Fishing Licence.

A good trail leads around the north and west shores of the lake to two bays on the southwest shore, passing the Bennett Pass junction in 400 m. The first of the bays was the former site of a backcountry campground, closed in 1997 on the advice of a bear biologist. Don't camp here. I have seen solitary sandpipers and redhead ducks near shore. The trail ends 150 m later on a scree fan above the second bay. Here, a perennial snow patch – the product of innumerable avalanches – melts into the lake. Please keep off the snow. It has been the site of mishaps and close calls over the years. You may see gray-crowned rosy finches feeding on torpid insects on the snow. A visit to the far shore of the lake will add about 1.2 km to your round-trip.

BEAR GRASS

Bear grass, the floral emblem of Waterton Lakes National Park, also grows abundantly along the Wall Lake trail. Growing from a stem that is 50 cm to 120 cm tall, bear grass blooms from mid-June to August. Some bear grass plants exhibit a peculiar crook in the upper stem, turning them into Dr. Seuss-like creations. It is thought these bends occur when the flower head matures during wet periods. Individual bear grass plants bloom sporadically, averaging one to three times in every ten years. Adjacent plants often bloom together, so the local "intensity" of the displays varies greatly from year to year.

Bighorn sheep, deer, and elk eat bear grass flowers. Mountain goats eat the mature leaves, and bears eat the younger leaves in spring. First Peoples wove the leaves into baskets and items of clothing. Although the leaves appear grass-like, the plant is a member of the lily family. Bear grass does not grow north of Crowsnest Pass in the Rockies.

Wildflower Guide

Here are thumbnail images of 109 plants that bloom in the Rockies, and one that doesn't bloom (horsetail.) Most of these are wildflowers, some are shrubs, one is a sedge, and one (surprise) is a horsetail. Most are common to abundant; a few are gems not seen often. With the exceptions of ox-eye daisy, butter and eggs, and goatsbeard, all are native to the Canadian Rockies. The page numbers indicate where a plant is described in detail or where you will find a larger image. To find the best places to see wildflowers, look under "wildflower hot spots" in the index or use the wildflower icons in the trail thumbnails. Please remember: Pick only with your eyes.

Common fireweed (p. 128)	Mountain fireweed	Arctic raspberry	Pink mountain heather (p. 92)	Pink paintbrush
Nodding onion	Bearberry (p. 122)	Pink wintergreen (p. 78)	Prickly wild rose	Twinflower
Red monkey flower	Western meadowrue	Hybrid columbine	Red paintbrush (p. 125)	Mountain sorrel
Western wood lily (p. 94)	Western columbine	Roseroot	False azalea	Brown-eyed Susan (p. 163)
Alpine hawksbeard	Rocky mountain goldenrod	Rocky mountain groundsel	Yellow lady's slipper	Yellow mountain avens
Goatsbeard	Alpine buttercup	Arnica (p. 128)	Stonecrop	Yellow-flowered false dandelion

Double bladder pod	Golden fleabane	Bracted honeysuckle (p. 143)	Alpine cinquefoil	Butter and eggs
Evergreen violet	Glacier lily	Mountain meadow cinquefoil	Northern dandelion	Yellow columbine
Yellow draba	Yellow mountain saxifrage	Yellow mountain heather (p. 92)	Yellow hedysarum	Early locoweed (p. 70)
Yellow paintbrush	One-sided winter-green (p. 78)	False hellebore	Bracted lousewort	Bracted orchid
Horsetail	Prairie crocus (p. 163)	Stickseed	Alpine forget-me-not	Alpine harebell
Alpine speedwell	Butterwort	Blue clematis (p. 39)	Harebell	Jacob's ladder
Aster	Fleabane	Four-parted gentian	Western wake robin	Alpine lousewort
Calypso orchid (p. 114)	Creeping beardtongue	Elephant-head	Inflated oxotrope	Mackenzie's hedysarum

Moss campion
(p. 102)

Northern blue
columbine

Purple saxifrage

Scorpionweed

Bear Grass
(p. 172)

Coltsfoot

Cow parsnip

Daisy fleabane

Dwarf dogwood
(Bunchberry, p. 109)

False Solomon's seal

Foam flower

Fringed
grass-of-Parnassus

Tall white bog orchid

Labrador tea
(p. 110)

Mountain marsh
marigold

Northern green
rein-orchid

Ox-eye daisy

Pearly everlasting

Queen's cup
(p. 112)

Red and white
baneberry

Red elderberry

Red osier dogwood

Spotted saxifrage

Twisted stalk

Rock jasmine

Silver rockcress

Sitka valerian

Spotted orchid

Western anemone

Western anemone
seedpod (p. 53)

White camas

White geranium

White globeflower

White mountain
avens (p. 147)

White mountain
heather (p. 92)

White rhododendron

Wild strawberry

Woolly everlasting

Western Canada
violet

Cotton grass

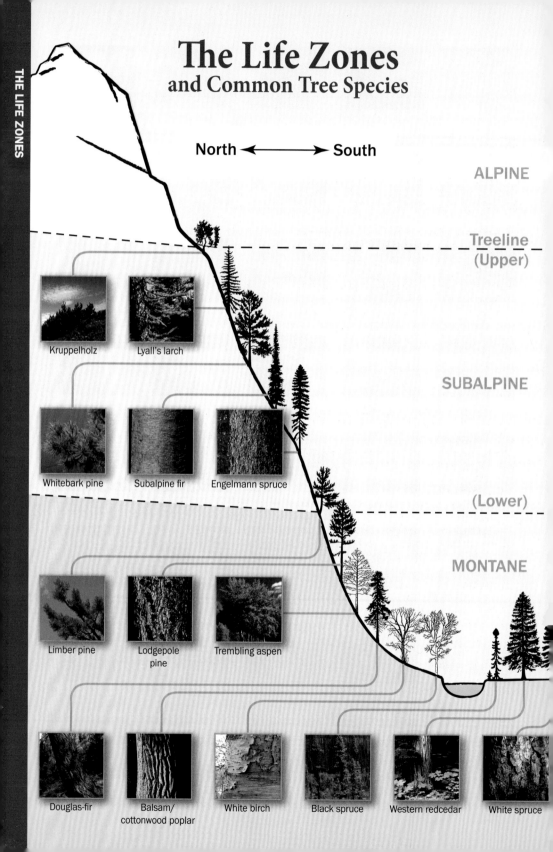

The Life Zones
and Common Tree Species

North ← → South

ALPINE

Treeline
(Upper)

Kruppelholz

Lyall's larch

SUBALPINE

Whitebark pine

Subalpine fir

Engelmann spruce

(Lower)

MONTANE

Limber pine

Lodgepole
pine

Trembling aspen

Douglas-fir

Balsam/
cottonwood poplar

White birch

Black spruce

Western redcedar

White spruce

Nuts and Bolts

Park Regulations

Please abide by the following rules when you visit the mountain national parks. Please note that some of these are enforceable laws which, if broken, can result in criminal charges.

- Drivers of vehicles stopping in national parks must pay the appropriate fee at a park gate or at a park information centre. Call 800-748-7275 for details.
- Firearms are not permitted unless securely locked or dismantled.
- Hunting and trapping of wildlife is not permitted.

- Anglers must obtain a national park fishing permit or a provincial fishing licence, and be aware of relevant regulations.
- It is illegal to disturb, remove or deface any natural, cultural or historic object or artifact.
- It is illegal to approach, feed, entice or harass wildlife.
- It is illegal to enter a closed area.
- Mountain biking is permitted only on certain trails. Check at a park information centre.
- There are restrictions on taking dogs on trails in most parks. Check at a park information centre.

Contacts

To contact the Minister responsible for national parks, call Reference Canada, 800-622-6232, or email: Minister@ec.gc.ca

- 💻 To find web pages for any national park, visit: www.pc.gc.ca and navigate to the appropriate link.
- ✉ To contact the Superintendent of any national park, use this formula, changing the park name as required: Banff.Superintendent@pc.gc.ca
- ☎ For assistance contacting Alberta provincial parks while in Alberta, call 310-0000.
- ☎ For assistance contacting BC provincial parks while in BC, call 800-663-7867.

Banff National Park
Box 900, Banff, AB, T1L 1K2
- ✉ banff.vrc@pc.gc.ca
- ☎ 403-762-1550
- ✉ lakelouise.vrc@pc.gc.ca
- ☎ 403-522-3833
- ☎ Road report: 403-762-1450
- ☎ Trail conditions: 403-760-1305
- ☎ Weather: 403-762-2088 (24 hr. recording)
- ☎ Highway conditions: 403-762-1450
- ☎ Emergency: 911 (ask for Banff park dispatch)

Parks Canada frontcountry campgrounds:
- ☎ 877-737-3783
- 💻 www.pccamping.ca

Jasper National Park
Box 10, Jasper, AB, T0E 1E0
- ✉ pnj.jnp@pc.gc.ca
- ☎ 780-852-6176
- ☎ Columbia Icefield Centre: 780-852-6288
- ☎ Weather: 780-852-3185 (24 hr. recording)
- ☎ Highway conditions: 780-852-3311
- ☎ Emergency: 911

Yoho National Park
Box 99, Field, BC, V0A 1G0
- ✉ yoho.info@pc.gc.ca
- ☎ 250-343-6783
- ☎ Emergency: 911

Kootenay National Park
Box 220, Radium Hot Springs, BC, V0A 1M0
- ✉ kootenay.info@pc.gc.ca
- ☎ 250-347-9505
- ☎ Emergency: 911

Waterton Lakes National Park
Box 200, Waterton Park, AB, T0K 2M0
- ✉ waterton.info@pc.gc.ca
- ☎ 403-859-5133
- ☎ Emergency: 911

Please note: The @pc.gc.ca email suffix may be changing to @canada.ca

Kananaskis Country
Suite 201, 800 Railway Ave.
Canmore, AB, T1W 1P1
☎ 403-678-5500

Peter Lougheed Provincial Park
✉ PLH.InfoCenter@gov.ab.ca
☎ 403-678-0760
☎ Emergency: 911

Barrier Lake Visitor Centre (Kananaskis Country)
✉ BarrierVisitor.InfoCentre@gov.ab.ca
☎ 403-678-0760

Mt. Robson Provincial Park
Box 579, Valemount, BC, V0E 2Z0
☎ Information Centre: 250-566-4325
☎ Emergency: 911

Akamina-Kishinena Provincial Park
Box 118, Wasa, BC, V0B 2S0
☎ 250-422-3212
☎ Emergency: 911 (from Waterton)

Tourism Contacts

At the park information centres at Canmore, Banff, Lake Louise, Columbia Icefield, Jasper, Mt. Robson, Field, Golden, Radium, K-Country, and Waterton Park, you will find publications that provide detailed descriptions of where to dine and where to shop in the Rockies. Use the following websites and phone numbers to help find accommodation and information about local businesses and services.

Banff Lake Louise Tourism
🖥 www.banfflakelouise.com
☎ 403-762-8421

Field
🖥 www.field.ca

Jasper Tourism and Commerce
🖥 www.jaspercanadianrockies.com
✉ info@jaspercanadianrockies.com
☎ 780-852-3858, 800-473-8155

Radium
🖥 www.radiumhotsprings.com
✉ info@radiumhotsprings.com
☎ 250-347-9331, 888-347-9331

Tourism BC
🖥 www.hellobc.com
☎ 800-435-5622

Tourism Canmore Kananaskis
🖥 www.tourismcanmore.com
✉ info@tourismcanmore.com
☎ 866-CANMORE, 403-678-1295

Tourism Golden
🖥 www.tourismgolden.com
✉ info@tourismgolden.com
☎ 250-439-1111, 800-622-4653

Travel Alberta
🖥 www1.travelalberta.com
✉ travelinfo@TravelAlberta.com
☎ 800-252-3782

Recommended Reading

Mountain Equipment Co-op's website is the best reference for information on hiking equipment, tips, and how-to:
🖥 www.mec.ca

Gadd, Ben. *Handbook of the Canadian Rockies*. Jasper: Corax Press, 2008.

--------------- *Canadian Rockies Geology Road Tours*. Jasper: Corax Press, 2009.

Kershaw, Linda, Andy MacKinnon and Jim Pojar. *Plants of the Rocky Mountains*. Edmonton: Lone Pine Publishing, 1998.

Pole, Graeme. *Canadian Rockies Explorer*. Hazelton: Mountain Vision Publishing, 2010.

--------------- *Classic Hikes in the Canadian Rockies*. Hazelton: Mountain Vision Publishing, 2011.

Sibley, David. *Field Guide to the Birds of Western North America*. New York: Knopf, 2003.

Glossary

Alluvial fan (ah-LOO-vee-ull) A fan-shaped landform created from rubble that drops from flowing water, where a steep mountain stream enters a valley.

Alpine lifezone The vegetation zone above treeline, characterized by rocky soils, low-lying wildflowers, lichens, and mosses.

Anticline An arch-shaped fold in rock, produced by compressive forces during mountain building

Avalanche An accumulation of snow that releases and sweeps the mountainside below.

Cirque glacier An accumulation of ice that erodes rearwards and downwards into bedrock, creating a bowl-shaped pocket called a cirque (SURK).

Delta A fan-shaped landform created from sediments that drop out of the flow where a stream enters a lake.

Dolomite Limestone rock in which the calcium has been replaced by magnesium.

Glacial erratic A rock or boulder that has been transported from its place of origin by glacial ice.

Glacial landforms Landforms created from glacial rubble. Includes: moraines , drumlins , eskers , kames , and kettle ponds.

Glacier A mass of ice formed from consolidated snow, and able to move slowly downhill under its own weight.

Hanging valley A tributary valley which was not as deeply eroded by glacial ice as the adjacent major valley.

Kettle pond A lake that formed in a hollow created by a slump in the underlying glacial rubble.

Kruppelholz Gnarled and stunted forms of Engelmann spruce, subalpine fir, whitebark pine, lodgepole pine, and Lyall's larch. Found at treeline, on cliff edges, and near glaciers.

Late Wisconsin Glaciation An ice age that lasted from 31,000 to about 14,000 years ago. Ice sheets were a kilometre thick in the Rockies.

Lateral moraine A crested ridge of glacial rubble pushed up alongside a glacier.

Limestone Sedimentary rock created from deposits of lime, or from the skeletal remains of primitive marine life.

Montane lifezone The vegetation zone in the major valley bottoms and on lower mountainsides.

Moraine (more-RAIN) Rock eroded and deposited by a glacier.

Quartzite A quartz-rich sandstone in which the quartz particles have liquefied and then reconsolidated, binding the rock together.

Rock flour Minute particles of glacial sediment suspended in lake water. These particles reflect the blue and green wavelengths of light, giving the lakes their colours.

Sedimentary formation A layer of rock that represents an episode in the deposition of sediments on the floor of an ancient sea. Sedimentary formations are named after areas or mountains where they are prominent.

Sedimentary rock Rock comprised of sediments eroded from other rocks, precipitated chemically, or created from the skeletal remains of marine life. Common types include limestone, dolomite, sandstone, quartzite, shale, slate, conglomerate, gritstone, mudstone, siltstone, and tillite.

Subalpine lifezone The vegetation zone between the montane and alpine. Found on mountainsides and in valley bottoms at higher elevations.

Succession A natural process of change in a vegetation community.

Syncline A U-shaped fold in rock, produced by compressive forces during mountain building.

Tarn A lake that forms in a hollow that was scoured from the bedrock by glacial ice.

Terminal moraine A horseshoe-shaped ridge of rubble pushed up by a glacier and marking the maximum extent of a glacial advance.

Thrust fault A line along which a mass of rock has slid upwards and over adjacent rock.

Thrust sheet A mass of rock that slid upwards and northeastwards along a thrust fault.

Tundra A treeless area at high elevation or near glaciers.

U-shaped valley A valley that has been eroded or enlarged by glacial ice. Also called a trough.

Hike names are in bold. Entries with bold page numbers include an explanation or a photo.

The Photographs

With the exceptions noted below, colour photography is © Graeme Pole/Mountain Vision. Other photographers are credited where known.

8 pika © Marnie Pole; gray jay and Clark's nutcracker © Michael Shuster; 20 © Dwayne Lepitzki; 27 Glenbow Museum, NA 1363-5; 28 lower © Alex P. Taylor; 35 Glenbow Museum, NA 1753-28; 43 W.M. Notman, Glenbow Museum, NA 293-3; 51 J.N. Collie, Whyte Museum, V14/AC-OP/772; 61 James Monroe Thorington, collection of Graeme Pole; 78 Mary Schäffer, Whyte Museum, V439 PS-20; 84 Jasper-Yellowhead Museum Archives, 997.07.314.31; 102 Charles Horetzky, Glenbow Museum, NA 1408-19; 106 left © Marnie Pole; 106 right George Kinney, collection of Graeme Pole; 119 collection of Graeme Pole; 122 John McGregor, Alexander Turnbull Library, Wellington, NZ, PA1-q-261-17-4; 124 Smyth Brothers, Glenbow Museum, NA 782-9; 127 lower Glenbow Museum, NA 699-1; 129 lower © Alex. P. Taylor; 132 © Marnie Pole; 140 right, collection of Graeme Pole; 143 lower, collection of Graeme Pole; 159 lower © Michael Shuster; 168 upper right © Marnie Pole; 184 © Marnie Pole; back cover, bighorn sheep © Marnie Pole

---

Graeme Pole

Graeme Pole has written thirteen books that describe the human history and the natural history of western Canada. He lives with his family near Hazelton in northwestern BC, where he serves as a paramedic.

🖥 www.mountainvision.ca
✉ Graeme@mountainvision.ca

Look for these **Canadian Rockies Companion Guides:**

Canadian Rockies Explorer

Classic Hikes in the Canadian Rockies